BUYING FOR THE HOME

In memory of Judy Attfield

Buying for the Home

Shopping for the Domestic from the Seventeenth Century to the Present

Edited by

DAVID HUSSEY AND MARGARET PONSONBY
University of Wolverhampton, UK

ASHGATE

Published by
Ashgate Publishing Limited
Gower House
Croft Road
Aldershot
Hampshire GU11 3HR
England

Ashgate Publishing Company
Suite 420
101 Cherry Street
Burlington, VT 05401-4405
USA

www.ashgate.com

British Library Cataloguing in Publication Data
Buying for the home : shopping for the domestic from the seventeenth century to the present. – (The history of retailing and consumption)
1. Home economics – History 2. England – Social life and customs 3. United States – Social life and customs
I. Hussey, D. P. (David P.) II. Ponsonby, Margaret, 1952–
640.9

Library of Congress Cataloging-in-Publication Data
Buying for the home : shopping for the domestic from the seventeenth century to the present / edited by David Hussey and Margaret Ponsonby.
p. cm.—(The history of retailing and consumption)
Includes bibliographical references and index.
ISBN 978-0-7546-5807-8 (alk. paper)
1. Home economics—History. 2. England—Social life and customs. 3. United States—Social life and customs. I. Hussey, D. P. (David P.) II. Ponsonby, Margaret, 1952–

TX15.B985 2008
640—dc22

2007044794

ISBN 978-0-7546-5807-8

Mixed Sources
Product group from well-managed forests and other controlled sources
www.fsc.org Cert no. SA-COC-1565
© 1996 Forest Stewardship Council
FSC

Printed and bound in Great Britain by
MPG Books Ltd, Bodmin, Cornwall.

Contents

Part Three Fashioning the Domestic: Making and Re-Making the Home through Consumption

Part Four Consumption for the Home as Cultural Practice

The History of Retailing and Consumption General Editor's Preface

It is increasingly recognised that retail systems and changes in the patterns of consumption play crucial roles in the development and societal structure of economies. Such recognition has led to renewed interest in the changing nature of retail distribution and the rise of consumer society from a wide range of academic disciplines. The aim of this multidisciplinary series is to provide a forum of publications that explore the history of retailing and consumption.

Gareth Shaw, University of Exeter, UK

List of Figure and Tables

Figure

Tables

List of Illustrations

Notes on the Contributors

Dr Claire Walsh is Associate Lecturer in the Humanities Department at the Open University. She has published on shop design, retailing and advertising in the early modern period, including 'The newness of the department store: a view from the eighteenth century', in Geoffrey Crossick and Serge Jaumain (eds), *Cathedrals of Consumption: The European Department Store 1850–1939* (Ashgate, 1999) and 'Social Meaning and Social Space in the Shopping Galleries of Early-Modern London,' in John Benson and Laura Ugolini (eds), *A Nation of Shopkeepers: A History of Retailing in Britain 1550–2000* (I.B. Tauris, 2003). She is currently completing a book on the practices, social relations and sites of shopping in early modern London.

Dr Karin Dannehl is a Research Fellow at the University of Wolverhampton. She is currently working on the *Dictionary of Traded Goods and Commodities, 1550–1820* (with Dr Nancy Cox) the first edition of which was published by British History Online in 2007. Her doctoral research, 'A Life Cycle Study of Eighteenth-Century Metal Cooking Vessels: A Reflexive Approach' (unpublished PhD thesis, Wolverhampton, 2005), focuses on metal hollowware, investigating eighteenth-century material culture through a mundane object of use, and approaching its analysis via a life cycle model. Her book, *Perceptions of Early-Modern Retailing*, with Dr Cox, was published by Ashgate in 2007.

Dr David Hussey is Senior Lecturer in History at the University of Wolverhampton. He has published widely on commerce and society in the seventeenth and eighteenth centuries, including *Coastal and River Trade in Pre-Industrial England* (Exeter University Press, 2000) and is currently working on masculinity and consumption. His research and teaching interests encompass consumption, sexuality and crime in the long eighteenth century.

Dr Sonia Ashmore is currently a Research Fellow at the Victoria & Albert Museum, London, studying the museum's nineteenth century collections of Indian textiles as part of a broader ESRC funded project, 'Fashioning Diaspora Space', jointly with Royal Holloway University of London. Her main research interests are in nineteenth-century cultural exchange. Recent publications include contributions to C. Breward and D. Gilbert (eds), *Fashion's World Cities* (Oxford: Berg, 2006); C. Breward, D. Gilbert and J. Lister (eds), *Sixties Fashion* (London: V&A, 2006 and Tokyo: Blues Interactions 2006) and to the V&A's 'Sixties Fashion' exhibition website.

Dr Yasuko Suga is Associate Professor at Tsuda College. Her publications include '"Purgatory of Taste" or Projector of Industrial Britain? The British Institute of Industrial Art', *Journal of Design History*, 16/2 (2003) and 'Designing the Morality of Consumption: "Chamber of Horrors" at the Museum of Ornamental Art, 1852–53', *Design Issues*, 20/4 (2004). Her current research concentrates upon the production and consumption of Japanese domestic goods for export. Her book, *The Politics of Beauty and Utility: British Society and Design*, was published in Japanese in 2005.

Dr Clive Edwards is Reader in Design History at Loughborough University. He has published widely on furniture history and technology, interiors and textiles and has a particular interest in retailing and the subsequent consumption of domestic furnishings. His work has appeared in such academic journals as *Journal of Design History*, *Furniture History*, *Textile History* and *History of Technology*. His most recent major publications include the *Encyclopaedia of Furniture Making Materials, Trades and Techniques* (Ashgate, 2000) and *Turning Houses into Homes* (Ashgate, 2005).

Dr Margaret Ponsonby is Senior Lecturer in Cultural Studies/History at the University of Wolverhampton. Her research focuses on the acquisition and use of furniture and furnishings in the home, 1750–1850. Her article, 'Ideals, Reality and Meaning: Homemaking in England in the First Half of the Nineteenth Century', *Journal of Design History*, 16/3 (2003), deals with the methodology of using inventories qualitatively. Her book, *Stories from Home: English Domestic Interiors, 1750–1850* was published by Ashgate in 2007.

Dr Shirley Teresa Wajda, a graduate of Boston University and The University of Pennsylvania, teaches American material culture studies and social and cultural history at Kent State University, OH, USA. Her publications include studies of children's collecting habits in the nineteenth-century United States, the rise of portrait photography as a consumer spectacle, the contemporary American second-hand goods market, and the vexed meaning of Martha Stewart.

Dr Irene Cieraad is a social anthropologist based at the Department of Interior Architecture, Faculty of Architecture of Delft University of Technology. She has published widely on the home, interior decoration, household technology and consumption and was the editor of *At Home: an Anthropology of Domestic Space* (Syracuse University Press, 1999). Her recent publications include '"Out of my kitchen!" Architecture, Gender and Domestic Efficiency', *The Journal of Architecture* (Autumn, 2002); 'Milk bottles and Model Homes: Strategies of the Dutch Association for Correct Living (1946–1968)', *The Journal of Architecture* (Winter, 2004); and 'A Nation Under Re-Construction Never Sleeps: The Rise and Fall of the Dutch Wall Bed', *Journal of Design History* (2005).

Dr Lisa Taylor is Senior Lecturer in Film and Media Studies at Leeds Metropolitan University. She is co-author (with Andrew Willis) of *Media Studies: Texts, Institutions and Audiences* (Blackwell, 1999) and has published on film and media theory. More recently her publications have been about class, taste and lifestyle television.

Dr Judy Attfield was Leverhulme Research Fellow at the Winchester School of Art, University of Southampton. Her research interests focused upon the social meaning of everyday things, identity, oral history and modernity in contemporary material culture. She published widely in these areas, editing (with Pat Kirkham) *A View from the Interior: Feminism, Women and Design* (Women's Press, London 1989). Her book, *Wild Things: The Material Culture of Everyday Life* appeared in 2000 (Berg), and the compilation *Bringing Modernity Home: Writings on Popular Design and Material Culture* was published by Manchester University Press in 2007.

Preface

Buying for the Home: Shopping for the Domestic from the Seventeenth Century to the Present Day is a collection of essays that explore connections: connections between homemakers and retailers; between individual customers and manufacturers; and between the taste and outlooks of real householders and the published advice of 'tastemakers' and 'legislators' in books and magazines. While encompassing a broad time span and a number of geographical locations (UK, USA, Holland and Japan) the central theme throughout is the homemaker and the process by which they acquire the elements that are assembled into a home. By focusing on this process the contributors seek to expand and advance the knowledge of homes past and present and to illuminate the methods through which such knowledge is transmitted. In so doing, we hope that *Buying for the Home* will encourage the scrutiny of the many subtle and nuanced meanings that are attached to the wider constructions of 'home'.

The ambitious nature of the collection springs from ongoing research in many scholarly fields. The work presented here was first delivered at a colloquium on the subject of retailing and the home held at the University of Wolverhampton in 2005 under the aegis of the Centre for the History of Retail and Distribution (CHORD).[1] While most of the essays here were presented at the colloquium, a few were derived from other CHORD events. A further two papers were commissioned specially to balance the chronological distribution of the volume as well as to add a contribution on American homemaking.[2] The rich seam of material that the editors were able to draw on is testimony to the variety of scholarship that CHORD has generated and we see this volume as adding to the many conferences, seminars, colloquia and publications that have resulted from CHORD-sponsored collaborative work.[3]

As with all edited collections, the list of acknowledgements is too extensive to compress into a short preface. The editors would like to formally thank the numerous people who have aided this project from gestation to publication. Our special thanks go to Thomas Gray and the staff at Ashgate for their support. However, most importantly, we wish to acknowledge the excellent work and patience of the contributors to this collection during the long process of editing.

1 CHORD was founded by Prof. John Benson and is now run by Dr Laura Ugolini.

2 Shirley T. Wajda's work was brought to our attention by Dr Lesley Whitworth. Shirley and the editors would like to thank Lesley for her interest in and support for the project.

3 See, for example, John Benson and Laura Ugolini (eds), *A Nation of Shopkeepers: Five Centuries of British Retailing* (New York: I.B. Taurus, 2003); John Benson and Laura Ugolini (eds), *The Culture of Selling: Perspectives on Consumption and Society since 1700* (Aldershot: Ashgate, 2006).

Introduction

Between the Shop and the Home

David Hussey and Margaret Ponsonby

Buying for the Home: Shopping for the Domestic from the Seventeenth Century to the Present Day is a book about the experiences of shopping and the tensions and polarities that exist between the retail and domestic environments. As recent work has emphasized, the workplace, the shop and the home form key arenas in which identities and practices are formed, shaped and negotiated. Yet conceptualizing these spaces as discrete entities remains problematic. Academic enquiry still tends to address the sites of retailing, consumption and use in a separate manner and where attempts have been made to provide linkage or common ground they have tended to be rooted in discussions of contemporary cultural practice.[1] This collection seeks to collapse these distinctions by analysing the ways in which the agencies and discourses of the retail environment mesh with the processes of physical and imaginative re-creation that constitute the domestic space. We argue that the nexus that exists between domestic and retail spaces, often viewed as a corollary of purely mundane cultural practice, needs to be critically reappraised if we are to understand how middle-class and plebeian homes were culturally apprehended in both past and current experience.

The main aim of this collection is to tease out the negotiations and interactions that mediate this key arena. Much of the recent scholarly work on the history and impact of shopping has tended to emphasize narratives of retail change, the development of the institutions and spaces of shopping, and the shifting fortunes of business performance in the retail sector.[2] We are also acutely aware that whilst the home has been constructed in contradistinction to other forms and centres of cultural action, very little academic work has sought to combine this central site of commodity use and consumption with the fullness of the retail experience and, moreover, locate this within a broadly defined yet historically sensitive context. With this in mind, the chapters presented here seek to examine how the strategies of retailers were both arbitrated by and negotiated through the actions and desires of the homemaker as

1 Daniel Miller (ed.), *Material Cultures: Why Some Things Matter* (London: UCL Press, 1998).

2 John Benson and Gareth Shaw (eds), *The Retailing Industry* (New York: I.B. Taurus, 1998); John Benson and Laura Ugolini (eds), *A Nation of Shopkeepers: Five Centuries of British Retailing* (I.B. Taurus, 2003); G. Crossick and S. Jaumain (eds), *Cathedrals of Consumption: The European Department Store* (Aldershot: Ashgate, 1999); John Benson and Laura Ugolini (eds), *The Culture of Selling: Perspectives on Consumption and Society since 1700* (Aldershot: Ashgate, 2006).

consumer. In particular, this approach emphasizes how contemporary interest in the layered existence of domestic life focuses attention upon the home and the 'private life of households' as the 'single most important site for material culture'.[3]

In order to address these concerns *Buying for the Home* draws upon a wide selection of interdisciplinary work from established scholars and new researchers. Bridging the disciplines of cultural, social and economic history, social anthropology, ethnography and cultural studies, the book encompasses analyses of retail space, consumption and consumption practices, the material culture of the home, the construction of self, and lifestyle shopping. It also seeks to broaden traditional Anglo- and Euro-centric perspectives to include important trans-national studies. The reader is here directed to the work on Japanese, American and Dutch cultural histories. Whilst the book does not aim to be a comprehensive survey of domestic or retailing practice, it has been our intention to provide a chronological perspective that combines historical analyses of the seventeenth, eighteenth and nineteenth centuries with cultural and ethnographic discourses of twentieth and early twenty-first century practice.

Within the general aims and purpose of the book lie discrete themes and approaches that intersect across the individual chapters. This dovetailing results from homemakers having somewhat similar concerns even if they have evolved over time. Each contributor has also placed their emphasis differently, resulting in some chapters being slightly more weighted towards the retailer while others focus attention on the consumer. Therefore, chapters deal with the tension between fashion and homemaking (Hussey, Ashmore, Suga, Edwards and Ponsonby, Wajda, Taylor, Attfield), and with attitudes to comfort (Edwards and Ponsonby, Wajda). The economic management of the home by consumers and the resulting compromises or imaginative solutions by homemakers can also be seen to have important longitudinal resonances (Walsh, Dannehl, Edwards and Ponsonby, Wajda, Cieraad, Attfield), as too can mediation of advice, whether it be early modern conduct manuals and prescriptive literature (Walsh), historic advertising (Dannehl, Ashmore) or recent media in the form of magazines and television (Taylor, Attfield). The methods by which homemakers invest meaning in the home through physically reshaping purchased goods allow another dimension of appropriation to be examined (Edwards and Ponsonby, Wajda, Cieraad, Taylor, Attfield). The dual nature of the home as both public and private space is analysed with particular reference to the interaction between homemakers and servants or tradespeople (Walsh, Dannehl, Cieraad). The creation of the home has also been used in self-creation and to project identity (Hussey, Taylor, Attfield). Despite the broad sweep of history that this collection encompasses, there are themes that occur and reoccur repeatedly. All essays touch on matters of class, gender, taste and the everyday and, similarly, all deal with the symbolic meaning of acquiring goods for the process of homemaking. The collection of essays can therefore be used to trace themes and attitudes to homemaking across time and to some extent across geographical boundaries.

3 D. Miller (ed.), *Home Possessions: Material Culture behind Closed Doors* (Oxford and New York: Berg, 2001), p. 5.

Organization of the Book

The collection of essays are organized around four key themes – retail arenas and the everyday; identity and lifestyle; fashioning domestic space; and cultural practice. The ten case studies cover a range of cultural encounters and locations from the late seventeenth century to the present. The titles applied to the sections indicate the approach taken in the book, to make connections between the simple act of shopping and the cultural meaning that the objects and the means of acquisition had for homemakers. While the separate chapters are positioned within a particular section, the reader will find that some essays could easily be described by the title of another section. Crossovers are an inevitable and indeed happy occurrence in a collection of this kind. To aid interpretation, the editors have placed the chapters according to the modalities of consumption and the approach adopted by individual authors. This has produced a broadly chronological structure. The book should not, however, be seen as guided by a rigidly temporal overview and we are keen, as editors, to stress the synergies and linkages that exist between specialists and scholars across the disciplines.

A stronger influence on methodology is the sources that are available for each period and the approaches taken by historians, contemporary cultural studies practitioners and anthropologists in analysing their sources. The authors of the essays in this collection have endeavoured to extend the parameters of their particular discipline to uncover meaning that will lead to greater understanding of consumption practices for the home. Historians here are using techniques borrowed from cultural studies and anthropology to 'read between the lines' of the often fragmentary documentary evidence of inventories, wills, advice literature and diaries. Others have tried to uncover the latent or virtual actor, the 'hidden consumer' that is obscured and collapsed within the formalities of business accounts and the semiology of advertisements. Conversely, cultural studies and anthropology are represented here by scholars who have used historical evidence in addition to contemporary ethnographic evidence to situate and contextualize the evolution of aspects of contemporary consumption practice.

Retail Arenas and the 'Everyday'

The notion of the 'everyday' has in recent years received much attention and has become a useful means of retrieving the cultural importance of 'ordinary' activities and behaviour.[4] Such issues have found important resonances in Daniel Roche's work upon the 'historicity of what constitutes the texture of ordinary life'.[5] Roche's concern with 'the history of the relation between a society and its goods from the standpoint of our analysis of mediations involved' intersects with current

---

4 See, for example, B. Highmore, *Everyday Life and Cultural Theory* (London: Routledge, 2002).

5 D. Roche, *A History of Everyday Things* (Cambridge: Cambridge University Press, 2000), p. 1.

interest in pre- and early-industrial modes of shopping.[6] This has emphasized that the retail experience was not wholly characterized by basic, exchange-driven economies of scale. The eighteenth-century shop or even the market stall was far from being a 'dark and unappealing' antediluvian space, wherein goods merely sold themselves by nature of their condition and availability. Instead a succession of scholarly work has reinterpreted the pejoratively viewed 'small shop' as a sophisticated locus of subtle negotiation between skilled cultural agents: proprietors employed advanced strategies of display, advertising, credit and product placement to encourage sales and an equally informed, knowledgeable and selective customer-base navigated the variety of outlets and opportunities on offer.[7] This cultural choreography of selling was felt most strongly in the everyday act of shopping for the household. Here, as Walsh argues, shopping was an intense, onerous and highly regularized activity demanding market awareness and no little physical endurance. It involved a highly developed affinity, an 'art', for recognizing the main variables of seasonality, price, condition and supply and as such was too vital for the functioning and status of the household to be devolved to mere servants. Lack of surveillance and the opportunity for petty malfeasance meant that the most menial of shopping tasks remained core activities for the mistresses of middling and genteel households. Mundane shopping and food provisioning thus constituted 'the most skilled form of shopping in this period'. It reflected the integrity, probity and management skills of the mistress: a factor endlessly emphasized by the weight of contemporary conduct literature. It follows then that the 'new and expressive goods' stressed by many historians as key diagnostic commodities in gauging the extent and penetration of consumer markets, were not perhaps the most central concern for female shoppers of the middling sorts.

In contrast, Hussey stresses that eighteenth- and nineteenth-century men, like their female counterparts, were acquisitive and sagacious shoppers. Masculine forms of middling sort and elite consumption were, however, not constrained to the high-order, expressive or gender-specific goods that have traditionally occupied historical scholarship. Using diary testimony, Hussey argues that male articulation with the consumer market was far less shallow than has hitherto been appreciated. Whilst politeness and manliness undoubtedly provided the prescriptive tropes to male shopping, male consumers engaged in retail activity in a vigorous manner. Interestingly, Hussey questions the prevailing notion that mundane food shopping remained the preserve of female competence or at least surveillance. To be sure in the patriarchal, established households of the bourgeoisie and lesser elite, domestic household management and shopping was deferred to women, but the 'iron law' of separate spheres suggested by Davidoff and Hall, did not always translate smoothly

---

6 Roche, *History of Everyday Things*, p. 8.

7 See, for example, N.C. Cox, *The Complete Tradesman: A Study of Retailing, 1550–1820* (Aldershot: Ashgate, 2000); C. Edwards, *Turning Houses into Homes: A History of the Retailing and Consumption of Domestic Furnishings* (Aldershot: Ashgate, 2005) and M. Berg, *Luxury and Pleasure in Eighteenth-Century Britain* (Oxford: Oxford University Press, 2005), esp. pp. 247–78.

to practice.[8] Both single men (bachelors and widowers alike) and even established family men – entered into domestic shopping with enthusiasm.

The concern with the negotiations implicit in supplying middling households with basic provisions also finds important resonances in Dannehl's examination of domestic utensils and their use in the eighteenth century home. Whilst Walsh locates the tensions between home and retail firmly in the negotiated liminality that existed between the retailer, the servant and the superordinate female mistress of the household, Dannehl directs her attention to the cockpit of domestic life, the kitchen. Following the work of McKendrick,[9] Dannehl unpicks the marketing strategies employed by contemporary manufacturers and dealers to introduce novel domestic metalware tools and utensils and thereby culinary procedures into the kitchens of the middling sort. From the perspective of the retailers, the 'virtual' space extended by advertising and marketing strategies encouraged and sustained the dialogue between simple commercial agency and end-use. However, domestic routine and the quotidian practice of supplying, storing and processing food was the main driver that shaped and defined the parameters of shopping.

Shopping for identities?

The issues of identity, choice and lifestyle and their nuanced interrelation with the world of goods and the explicit branding of commodities have become an important subject for much recent work on shopping. Central to this is the question of identity. Primarily, both contemporary and historic identities have been seen as imbued with an essential fluidity. Commentators like Veblen have seen identity expressed through conspicuous consumption and the extension of fashion systems.[10] Bourdieu, in contrast, has read personal and group distinction through modes of acquisition and display, themselves freighted by perceptions of taste and cultural capital.[11] For Shields 'Lifestyle Shopping' becomes an end it itself, a consumerist 'way of life' to borrow Stephen Miles' phrase.[12] Here 'new modes of subjectivity (at the level of the

8 L. Davidoff and C. Hall, *Family Fortunes: Men and Women of the English Middle Class, 1780–1850* (London: Hutchinson, 1987); See also J. Tosh, *A Man's Place: Masculinity and the Middle Class Home in Victorian England* (New Haven and London: Yale University Press, 1999).

9 N. McKendrick, 'George Packwood and the Commercialisation of Shaving: The Art of Eighteenth-Century Advertising or "The Way to Get Money and be Happy"', in N. McKendrick, J. Brewer and J.H. Plumb, *The Birth of a Consumer Society: The Commercialization of Eighteenth-Century England* (London: Europa, 1982), pp. 146–94.

10 See T. Veblen, *The Theory of the Leisure Class* (Harmondsworth: Penguin, 1994) and discussions in P. Corrigan, *The Sociology of Consumption: an Introduction* (London, Sage, 1998), pp. 24–6 and J. Storey, *Cultural Consumption and Everyday Life* (London: Arnold, 1999), pp. 36–9.

11 P. Bourdieu, *Distinction: a Social Critique of the Judgement of Taste* (trans. R. Nice, London: Routledge, 1986) and T. Edwards, *Contradictions of Consumption: Concepts, Practices and Politics in Consumer Society* (Buckingham: Open University Press, 2000), pp. 130–2.

12 S. Miles, *Consumerism as a Way of Life* (London: Sage, 1998).

person), interpersonal relationships (at the level of the group) and models of social totality are being experimented with, "browsed through" and "tried on" in much the same way that one might shop for clothes'.[13]

The extended metaphor of identity as a performative act of shopping is reflected in Ashmore's examination of Liberty and Co. and Suga's analysis of the rise and decline of Japanese leather paper. Both chapters emphasize the institutional role of manufacturers and retailers in selling identity and 'lifestyle'. To Ashmore, Liberty's unorthodox approach to department store selling and its abiding focus on the aesthetic emphasized how retail pressure, strategic marketing and domestic desire, itself fuelled in part by the extension of the Liberty 'brand', collided in the form of a distinctive Liberty 'lifestyle'. Merchandizing was key to Liberty's success and the fusion of shopping with an imagined and reified domestic space was pioneered through the promotion of aspirational material goods. Consumers of Liberty's carefully selected goods were thus recreating, personalizing and appropriating the Liberty 'brand' in many ways pre-empting later associations with explicit forms of branding and 'authenticity'.[14] Suga's examination of Japanese leather paper describes the microhistory of a single product that impacted differentially upon European and Japanese consumer markets. To British consumers, leather paper was cheap, washable and practical, but above all, it conveyed 'authenticity', a flavour of genuinely handcrafted Orientalism, which could be applied to modish interiors to impart an essence of the exotic. The success of Japanese leather paper was fostered by the pervasive lifestyle marketing of all things eastern championed in part by Liberty. In contrast, leather paper secured a substantial market amongst the emerging Japanese middle class by appealing directly to local constructions of western uniformity, design and modernity.

Fashioning the Domestic: Making and Re-Making the Home through Consumption

Aspects that might be considered on the margins of consumption practice are increasingly receiving attention. Central to the essays in this section is the unfixed meaning for objects and how they are constantly reshaped by consumers both through the original act of consumption and incorporation into individual lifestyle (see above) but also through refashioning during the object's life. The discipline of anthropology has perhaps led the way in examining how people in modern day western societies make meaning out of industrial mass-produced objects.[15] Likewise, the way that

13 R. Shields, 'Spaces for the Subject of Consumption' in R. Shields (ed.), *Lifestyle Shopping: The Subject of Consumption* (London: Routledge, 1992), p. 15.

14 See D. Boyle, *Authenticity: Brands, Fakes, Spin and the Lust for Real Life* (London: Harper, 2004) and C. Lury, *Brands: The Logos of the Global Economy* (London: Routledge, 2004).

15 Miller, *Home Possessions*; A. Appadurai (ed.), *The Social Meaning of Things: Commodities in a Cultural Perspective* (Cambridge: Cambridge University Press, 1988); Mary Douglas and Baron Isherwood, *The World of Goods: Towards an Anthropology of Consumption* (London and New York: Routledge, 1996).

people have subverted such commodities to make expressive individualized and customized goods have been studied.[16] Second-hand goods lend themselves to a sophisticated recycling process. However, most of this work has focused on contemporary society, and clothing has been the most examined of commodities since it is the most obvious means of expressing taste and opposition to acceptable forms of behaviour. Edwards and Ponsonby use material culture studies as a means of extending the interest in second-hand goods to the earlier period of the eighteenth and nineteenth centuries. The focus of this essay is specifically on furniture to show how this type of object in its second-hand state, lent itself to particular consumption practices that were specific to the type of good and to the period.

Wajda explores the transition from 'traditional' forms of homemaking to modern methods that were dependent on commercially available goods, and the resultant tensions in how homemaking was perceived. Looking first at mid-nineteenth-century methods of setting up home in preparation for marriage, Wajda establishes that this was essentially a private process, known as 'going housekeeping', and was an opportunity for the bride to demonstrate her skills as a homemaker since many items were fashioned by her and her immediate family. By the later nineteenth century, the process was becoming more commercialized. Retailers were keen to supply all the requisites for a home on marriage, and department stores in particular offered a wedding list service. Was the introduction of bridal showers in the early twentieth century yet another instance of commercialization of homemaking, dependant on mass-produced homogenized goods? Wajda argues that the process was more complex. She delves into the nature of gifting on marriage, in particular the neglected area of female gifts through bridal showers.[17]

Consumption for the Home as Cultural Practice

The final section is concerned with the fashioning of the domestic space, architecturally, horticulturally, and through amateur maintenance and construction. Cieraad, a cultural anthropologist, explores the intricate relation between the public world of retail and the private world of domestic consumption, as mirrored in the evolution of domestic architecture.[18] She charts how retailing and more particularly door-to-door delivery influenced not only the exterior characteristics of Dutch domestic architecture, but also the internal structuring and ritual zoning of domestic space. As this chapter argues, ethnographic research illuminates these problems in individual households and the ways in which domestic shopping and storing protocols have been radically affected.

---

16 See, for example, D. Hebdige, *Subculture: The Meaning of Style* (London: Methuen, 1979); N. Gregson and L. Crewe, *Second-Hand Cultures* (Oxford: Berg, 2003).

17 An extensive literature exists on gifting, particularly coming out of anthropology. However, there is less published on the practice in advanced societies and gifts exchanged between women is a neglected area.

18 Matrix, *Making Space: Women and the Man-made Environment* (London: Pluto, 1985).

The area immediately surrounding the home, the garden, is often ignored in books on homes and homemaking. The garden occupies a curious liminal position in homemaking, looking outward to the public world of the street and inward to the private domain of the home. It is open to view but in Britain at least, it occupies a position that invites individual tastes and concerns to be indulged. This contested aspect of the garden means that it is particularly open to judgement, on whether it is tidy or untidy, traditional or stylish. The garden has become another aspect of life that shopping encompasses, and with increasingly fashionable solutions on offer. In recent years, there has been an increase in lifestyle programming on British primetime television. At the same time, garden centres have increased in number and size and are a key British leisure site. The garden therefore lends itself to analysis of lifestyle, in particular the position taken by Chaney who suggests that consumer lifestyles have taken over from more traditional 'ways of life'.[19] However, Taylor steers a somewhat different course by using ethnography to examine the attitudes of individual gardeners in West Yorkshire. Using local knowledge 'from below', as cultural studies has emphasized, this chapter explores the relationship between garden lifestyle programmes and ordinary viewers, how they interact with and consume lifestyle texts,[20] and how they subsequently consume their own domestic garden.

The boundaries of acceptable consumption, i.e. fashionable, stylish and in good taste, and for Design History, Modern, is explored through the ultimate in mediation of the home, DIY. Attfield presents DIY as unexplored wild territory, so far overlooked in terms of visual culture.[21] Situating amateur domestic décor and furnishing practice in the discourse of aesthetics and the history of domestic consumption suggests an alternative to the usual frame of reference, which would otherwise relegate it to poor taste or kitsch.[22] Attfield repositions DIY domestic interior décor as an aspect of domestic design consumption, of amateur craft practice and of the history of popular taste that challenges the production/consumption binary opposition and the exclusive adherence to aesthetically acceptable 'good design' styles usually assigned to design history topics.

The strengths of edited collections lie in their diversity. To an extent that is also their weakness. The eclectic range of subjects and issues, approaches and perspectives and even conflicts and divergences brought together in *Buying for the Home* suggests fertile areas of linkage and future development. Our main aim, as editors, has been to promote interdisciplinary study and to suggest bridges between disciplines that have too often viewed themselves if not in opposition then somewhat in isolation. We hope that *Buying for the Home* will encourage scholars to consider the fractured space that

---

19 David Chaney, 'From Ways of Life to Lifestyle: Rethinking Culture as Ideology and Sensibility', in James Lull (ed.), *Culture in the Communication Age* (London: Routledge, 2001) pp. 75–88.

20 See also David Gauntlett and Annette Hill, *TV Living: Television, Culture and Everyday Life* (London: Routledge, 1999).

21 See also Judy Attfield, *Wild Things: The Material Culture of Everyday Life* (London and New York: Berg, 2000).

22 A more nuanced reading of kitsch is explored through the special edition on the subject, edited by Judy Attfield, of *Home Cultures*, 3/3 (November 2006).

existed between the world of goods and the middle- and working-class home. We hope also that in so doing we can interrogate in a more subtle and nuanced way how middle-class and plebeian homemakers view, imagine and ultimately occupy their domestic spaces in early-modern, modern and post-modern society.

PART ONE
Retail Arenas and the 'Everyday'

Chapter One

Shopping at First Hand? Mistresses, Servants and Shopping for the Household in Early-Modern England

Claire Walsh

Household Management and Household Shopping

The non-reflexive, everyday activity of shopping for the household in the eighteenth century has left minimal traces, so clues to this every day practice have had to be gleaned from a range of sources: letters, diaries, account books, cookery books and, drawn on in particular here, servants' guides and household advice manuals.[1] While the moralizing, prescriptive sections of the household advice manuals have often been studied by historians, the practical advice on housewifery, often combined in the very same volumes, has been much less explored yet provides valuable guidance on the nature of household shopping.

Although men did go shopping in the early-modern period, and did make purchases for the home, the key managerial tasks of household buying fell to the mistress or housekeeper.[2] It was the mistress of the house who took charge of decision making about what was needed, when and where it should be bought and for how much.

Shopping for the household was burdensome. Unlike shopping for consumer durables, it had to take place regularly, it involved shopping for the same items over and over again, required continuous haggling over small sums, alertness to cheating, careful monitoring of fluctuating prices and careful account keeping. When shopping for the household a range of interlocking decisions had to be made about levels of supply and the types of goods on offer: about how much would be needed and for how long; how long produce might last; whether tainted (rotting) produce would do and could it be rectified; what could be bought in bulk; what could be stored or preserved; and what should be bought as the finished article and what should be made or finished in the home. Household shopping demanded a constant interaction of ideas between the retail site and the home as shoppers balanced the price of what was on sale with how much was needed by the household, the produce available

1 For a range of different kinds of shopping in the eighteenth century see Claire Walsh, 'Shopping in Early-Modern London, c. 1660–1800', PhD thesis, European University Institute, Florence, 2001 and chs 4 and 5 for household shopping in particular.

2 See Amanda Vickery, *The Gentleman's Daughter: Women's Lives in Georgian England* (New Haven and London: Yale University Press, 1997).

with how it could be cooked and stored. Immediate and long-term needs had to be balanced against financial constraints and budget flow. Household shopping involved co-ordinating the acquisition of goods from different areas, whether from home production, local or distant suppliers, pedlars, markets or shopkeepers, and as well as purchasing new it involved shopping for second hand, repairing, reconditioning and reworking objects. What was bought and how goods were maintained in the house had reverberations for the mistress's status as a housewife.[3] Household shopping was onerous, yet it demanded high levels of skill, and it was crucial to the efficient running of the home. Much household provisioning would have been regular and burdensome, yet to label this kind of purchasing as subsistence shopping is to mask the managerial skills involved and the complexity of the practice of shopping.

The Nature of Foodstuffs and the Art of Shopping

One of the elements that made household shopping so complex and difficult in the early-modern period was the very different nature of foodstuffs in the period from today. In the early-modern period no chemical fertilizers, preservatives or pesticides existed and breeding for disease resistance was less developed, with the result that produce was rarely, if ever, perfect, and was certainly never of a consistent nature nor even standardized. There were no brand names to act as markers of quality assurance, and while there were regulations against the adulteration of produce, there were no agreed or legislated standards for consumer goods or foodstuffs. There were no refrigerators.

Consumers' focus today centres most often on uniformity in size and quality in produce and a desire for unblemished surfaces. In the early-modern period most produce would have been, in modern opinion, blemished or damaged in some way, and the idea of freshness would have operated on a very different scale. Meat might be clammy and musty smelling with green spots but still worth buying (and eating). There would not have been the same expectations of regularity or standardization in appearance or taste. Early-modern housewives were not shopping for standardized quality, but the best quality that they could lay their hands on at a given time. Shopping for food did not mean choosing what you wanted, but was a matter of deciding if you had made the best pick of a variable, or simply bad, or sometimes rotten, bunch.

Because there was very little uniformity, shoppers had to be acutely aware of the variety of conditions and circumstances surrounding what they were buying. Most household manuals, cookery books and guides to frugality contained a section instructing the reader how to judge the freshness of foodstuffs on sale. Advice for how to test for freshness was offered for each type of meat, fowl, fish and dairy product. While this advice to ascertain freshness could also have been used to assess food stored at home, the manuals make it clear that its first application was at the point of purchase, using such terms as 'chusing', 'trying' and 'buying'.

3 Vickery, *The Gentleman's Daughter*, p. 190.

The early-modern housewife faced a daunting variety within the field of basic foodstuffs. *The Female Instructor* (1704) listed under the subject of poultry: 'turkies and Turkey Pouts, wild geese, brand geese, and tame geese; chickens and the younger sort of other Fowl; Heath cock and Hen, Snipe and Woodcock, Heath and Pheasant Pouts; Wild Duck, and Tame Duck etc.'.[4] Each type had to be treated individually: it was useless to advise on how to buy poultry in general, as each type of fowl would taint (go off) differently, cook differently, be priced differently and taste differently. Identification was important to avoid paying too much or being deceived as to what the shopper was buying.[5] Finally, the household shopper needed to decide not just whether to have tame duck, but whether they wanted *this particular* tame duck in front of them, given its age, size, price, freshness, the way it had been fed and where it had come from. Shopping for the early-modern household was complex because the range of knowledge shoppers needed about different types of foodstuffs was vast, and the decisions they made had to be much more finely honed than they are today.

Given the lack of refrigeration, the ability to judge how long produce might keep and to manage meals in a way that used up produce efficiently without waste was crucial. *The Accomplish'd Housewife* (1745) made this explicit in its list of signs of tainting:

> To Know Whether Lamb be Good or Bad.
> If you propose to purchase a Fore-Quarter of Lamb, cast your Eye on the Vein in the Neck; if it be turning yellowish, tho' the Meat may possibly smell well enough at that Time, yet it is about tainting; and if the Weather be warm, it will not keep sweet till the next Day: ... As for the Hind-Quarter, smell under the Kidney of the Loin, and feel whether the Joint of the Huckle be limber or stiff; and if you meet with a faint or ill Scent in one Place, and a more than usual Limberness in the other, then it is not for your turn ... [6]

The health implications of choosing foodstuffs too far gone was well recognized, yet with little perfect produce to chose from, fine judgements still had to be made.[7]

In all likelihood mistresses would have gained knowledge about the extensive varieties and types of foodstuffs as girls as they grew up within the family home and as they were trained for housekeeping, rather than depending on the formal descriptions in the manuals, and this learning process must have been continuous throughout their lives as suppliers, supplies and fashions changed. It seems likely that the tests for freshness and identification in the manuals were based on well-known practices and common usage as they are repeated consistently across the different manuals and down the centuries. The surviving texts merely point to the formal analysis of some aspects of the intricate world of habitual knowledge needed for food buying and preparation.

---

4 *The Accomplish'd Female Instructor: or, a Very Useful Companion for Ladies, Gentlewomen, and Others* (London, 1704), pp. 115–17.

5 *The Accomplish'd Housewife; or the Gentlewoman's Companion* (London, 1745), p. 161.

6 *The Accomplish'd Housewife*, p. 153.

7 *The Accomplish'd Female Instructor*, p. 115.

In the main, advice for choosing and buying food in the manuals excluded discussion with the retailer and concentrated on the shopper's need to establish knowledge independently using sensory skills – her touch, sight, hearing, smell and taste in order to make her own, uninfluenced, judgements, and not to be distracted or misled by the seller's sales patter. *The Female Instructor* advised under 'Poultry': 'A true Pullet has a smooth Breast and Leggs, and if pinched on the breast, is very tender: If with Egg the Breast will feel soft, and the Vent will be open, if not hard and close; if stale, a loose Vent; if new a close and hard one ...'.[8]

These checks for freshness required some sensitivity to texture, sensation and appearance: 'If Ram-mutton, the Fat feels spungy, the Flesh close grained and tough, not rising again, when dented by your Finger: ...'.[9] And handling the food might not be tentative; the buyer was expected to pull, squeeze, pinch and poke: Of ewe-mutton: 'If you squeeze it hard, some Drops of Water will stand up like Sweat.'[10] Of pork: 'If it be young, the Lean will break in pinching between your Fingers, and if you nip the Skin with your Nails, it will make a Dent.'[11] Any inspection had to be thorough and an understanding of animal carcasses and the different rates at which parts would taint was important: 'As for the Freshness or Staleness, try the Legs, and Hands, or Springs, at the Bone that comes out in the middle of the fleshy Part, by putting in your Finger, and smelling to it; for there it first taints.'[12]

The degrading or adulteration of produce was common too, such as adding rye to wheat bread, or brick dust to tea; and the manuals are full of tests for these too. Whatever the test, however, the housewife had always to deploy her own judgement in deciding whether to buy or not, based on her own needs and finances and what was available. According to *The Accomplish'd Housewife*, if shoulder of veal showed greenish spots or clamminess it would not keep until the next day, but the customer had the 'Rule to chuse or refuse it' depending on their needs. They might buy it if it was 'for present spending, and your Price be accordingly'.[13]

One of the skills that would have aided the shopper was mental mathematics, to check on price per weight calculations, and also to make decisions in balancing cheapness versus quality. The small amounts spent mattered to the weekly budget, yet the final price would not necessarily have been evident at the start of negotiations with the retailer.[14] Keeping abreast of pricing and knowing a good price when it was offered was no easy matter. Few of the manuals offered price guides for perishables because of the difficulties in covering prices comprehensibly, the numerous

8 *The Accomplish'd Female Instructor*, pp. 115–16.

9 Hannah Glasse, *The Art of Cookery Made Plain and Easy* (London, 1747), p. 318.

10 Glasse, *The Art of Cookery*, p. 318.

11 Glasse, *The Art of Cookery*, p. 319.

12 *The Accomplish'd Housewife*, p. 157.

13 *The Accomplish'd Housewife*, pp. 153–4. See also *The Experienced Market Man and Woman* (Edinburgh, 1699), p. 2.

14 The question of buying in bulk was also an issue for households and would have added to the complexities of the calculations. Trusler advised that for buying butter 'the best way for a family is to buy a half firkin which weighs 28 of the best Yorkshire butter'. Rev Dr Trusler, *The Way to be Rich and Respectable; Addressed to Men of Small Fortune* (London, 1796), p. 33.

permutations of produce type, seasonal variations and the different pricing demanded of different types of retail outlets. *The Way to be Rich and Respectable* (1796) made an attempt to assess prices of poultry:

> A fat goose, weight about 10 lb. on Michaelmas-day, is worth 5s [. At] other times about 3s 6d. A green goose in may is worth 4s. The price of ducks is from 3s a couple to 5s. Wild ducks, in frosty weather, may be bought in Fleet-market for 2s 6d. a couple; at other times they are worth 2s each.[15]

Decision making in the complex world of food purchasing was not only the responsibility but also the right of the housewife: she alone knew her circumstances and budget and was charged with supplying the home. The basis of good shopping was, above all, judgement. Crucial in the terminology of practical household shopping were terms such as: 'managing', 'regulation', 'skill' and 'judicious choice', the application of 'judgement' and 'wisdom'. *The Ladies Miscellany* (1789) understood financial household management as a skill that could be learnt, and *The Whole Duty of a Woman* (1695) described household spending as 'The Art of laying out Money Wisely'.[16]

Contemporary advice on food purchasing provides us with indications of the complexities of everyday shopping and the possible embroilments of buying something as basic as a piece of meat. Shopping for food was perhaps the most skilled form of shopping in the period, yet it is an activity which was barely remarked upon by contemporaries and which has gone un-noted by historians.

The Role of Servants

If the mistress in middling households had responsibility for deciding the type, quantity and timing of purchases for the home, then a key question which arises is the extent to which household shopping was delegated to servants rather than being carried out by the mistress. Adherents to the public/private model of domesticity have envisaged the middling housewife as engaged only in 'leisure shopping' for frivolous and fashionable goods, mostly fashion items with which to adorn herself, while the basic shopping to maintain the household was carried out by servants (or, in the assumed period of total self-sufficiency, did not take place at all).

From the letters and diaries surviving from the period it is quite clear that men and women of the middling sort made their own purchases of durable and semi-durable consumer goods (such as china, watches and fine cloth), presumably because of the personal pleasure and personal control involved in the purchase. While servants could undoubtedly have been sent to collect these goods if purchased from a distance, letters regarding proxy shopping show that buyers relied on friends and relatives to inform them, select goods and handle the negotiations rather than entrusting these

15 Trusler, *The Way to be Rich and Respectable*, p. 30.

16 *Whole Duty of a Woman: or Guide to the Female Sex from the Age of Sixteen to Sixty* (London, 1695), p. 85.

tasks to servants.[17] Here it can be assumed that issues of taste, fashion and social appropriateness were relevant in favouring friends and relatives as proxy shoppers over servants.

The question of the extent of servants' involvement becomes more problematic when considering the purchasing of mundane household items as servants were quite capable of choosing them. However, it is clear from letters and diaries that middling men and women with servants would, at times, make purchases of food and other mundane household items themselves. In 1660 Pepys' commented in his diary, 'I went out and paid Wilkinson what I did owe him, and brought a piece of beef home for dinner.'[18] And in 1663 he recorded the time when, expecting company, his wife 'rose by 5 a-clock in the morning, before day, and went to market and bought fowle and many other things for dinner'.[19] But it is equally clear that servants also did household shopping. The questions that arise then, are not so much whether it was employers or servants who did household shopping, but why employers should have taken on the burden of mundane purchasing themselves at times; why and when servants were asked to shop; and how the process of servants' shopping was managed by employers.

Household advice manuals offered guidance both to servants (on shopping for their mistresses) and to mistresses (on managing their servants' shopping). The subject also appears in books dedicated to the management of servants and this literature is revealing of some of the conventionally perceived problems of servants undertaking shopping.

The practical issue for employers of sending servants shopping was that the latter could not be supervised while they were out of the house. The uniform anxiety in the literature about servants concentrated on whether servants could be trusted to carry out the task of shopping efficiently and whether the servant would seek to defraud the employer. Once out of the home and the watchful eye of the employer or higher servants, a servant had the potential to go astray, and according to these censorial texts, they constantly did.

There was no means of ensuring that the unsupervised servant would shop as efficiently as would the employer themselves, according to the manuals, because

17 See Walsh, 'Shopping in London', ch. 1.

18 Samuel Pepys, *The Diary of Samuel Pepys*, ed. R.C. Latham and W. Mathews (London: Bell & Hyman, 1983), 1660, vol. 1 p. 26.

19 Pepys, *Diary*, 13 January 1663, vol. 4, p. 13. Other examples include Fanny Boscawen who asked her husband to bring 'half a firkin of good salt butter and a gallon of spirits' from London. Fanny Boscawen, *Admiral's Wife: Being the Life and Letters of the Hon. Mrs Edward Boscawen from 1719–1761*, ed. Cecil Aspinall-Oglander (London: Longmans, Green & Co, 1940), 28 December 1756, p. 246; Betsy Sheridan's letter to her sister, 'I went myself to Market this morning. You know Carnaby Market which is an excellent one is close to us. I have already establish'd my self as Customer to Fish monger and Poulterer so that I have only to chuze what I wish, my Butcher calls every morning, I go sometimes however to shew that I am willing to attend to these matters. I bought a very fine sallad Lettice &c. a good dish of Purple Broccola and another of Colly flower for 18d'. Betsy Sheridan, *Betsy Sheridan's Journal (1784–90)*, ed. E.W. Lefanu (Oxford: Oxford University Press, 1986), 31 October 1784.

they did not have the same interests at heart. The *Present for a Servant-Maid* of 1743 entreated servants to 'Buy for your Master and Mistress as you would for yourself.'[20] It was possible that servants would not haggle as hard as they should with retailers, and thus would pay over the odds. Servants might also not take precautions against retailers' attempts to cheat them, either through not being alert or by simply not objecting if it took place as, after all, their own money was not involved. The servant might not be as particular about the quality of produce, resulting in waste. Finally, servants outside the home had the opportunity to prolong the shopping trip or simply to fritter away time rather than returning to their household duties. The manuals railed against visits to ale houses and gaming houses, and servants who took the opportunity to visit friends or simply spent time chatting while out shopping.

On the issue of deliberate fraud, the texts reiterated the same potential deceits through to the end of the eighteenth century. A servant might have an arrangement with a particular retailer to always take their custom there, despite consistently high prices or poor produce, a tactic that was known as 'the market penny' (from the commission the servant received, either as money or 'presents').[21] The response of *The Footman's Friendly Advice*, a defence of servants, to this accusation suggests that it was common practice:

> But as to the Custom of taking so much in the Pound of some particular Traders, when we pay their Bills, it is not so much we that exact it, as they that allow it us; and I see no Reason in the World why they should not. Gentlemen take larger Quantities of Provisions, &c. than common people, their pay is generally better, and their Custom more valuable; which, therefore, lest a Trader should lose, he thinks a Gratuity to the Servant not ill bestow'd.[22]

Furthermore, servants who bought cheaply could charge their employers more than they had paid and pocket the difference. *The Conduct of Servants* (1720) chastised: 'A more plain and direct way of Purloining is when the Servant if entrusted to buy any Thing for his master's Use, charges more to him in his Bill than he paid for The things which were bought; or if when sent on a Journey, he brings in more Expence than he was at.'[23]

20 Hannah More, *Present for a Servant-Maid* (London, 1743), p. 25.

21 Thomas Seaton, *The Conduct of Servants in Great Families* (London, 1720), p. 96. Seaton continued 'that he scorn to take from any Tradesman such Presents as 'tis not possible for him to afford to give unless he charges a very extravagant Price for the goods he sells, which will be a sort of wicked exacting upon his master, that he shou'd by no means wink at'.

22 *The Footman's Friendly Advice to his Brethren of the Livery; And to all Servants in General*, (R D now a Footman), (London, 1731), pp. 30–1.

23 Seaton, *The Conduct of Servants*, p. 199. See also Andrew Moreton (possibly Daniel Defoe), *Every-Body's Business, is No-Body's Business; or Private Abuses, Publick Grievances* (London, 1725), p. 8: 'there are those that when they are sent to market for one Joint of Meat, shall take up two on their master's Account, and leave one by the Way, for some of these Maids are very charitable, and can make a shift to maintain a small Family with what they can Purloin from their Masters and Mistresses.' Hannah More sermonized in *Present for a Servant-Maid*, p. 24: 'Do not imagine, that by taking pains to find out where you can buy

While compelling servants to carry out their domestic duties efficiently might have been a general problem for employers, servants' shopping was particularly problematic. The value of sending the servant to shop was the fact that they went unaccompanied, relieving the master or mistress of the task and saving time and effort. Thus, by its very nature, servants' shopping could not be monitored, and employers' anxieties about poor shopping and fraud had little means of being allayed. The texts consist mostly of exhortations to servants to take their responsibilities to heart, making appeals to their sense of morality and invoking the fear of God: they reiterated that they should earn their employer's 'affection' and 'esteem';[24] and 'while you are in the Condition of a Servant your Time belongs to those who pay you for it; and all you waste from the employment they set you about, is a Robbery from them';[25] 'the Devil teach [es] an ungodly Servant to make bold with his Master's Money'.[26] 'Eye-service' was much decried, a term for servants who were suspected of behaving dutifully when in the sight of their mistresses but deceitfully once out of sight. *The Duty of Servants* (1685) provided a prayer for servants' repetition:

> I know, O Lord that all things are naked and bare before thee, and that though my Master's Eye cannot, yet thine does in all times, and in all places, behold me, ... O how fatal must my frauds be, since though I may decive my master, I cannot thee?[27]

The most common phrase that appears in these texts is 'fidelity to trust'. While these texts cannot tell us of the actual level of servants' abuse of power, such a phrase neatly sums up just how ineffectual employers' attempts at regulation must have been.

For the housewife with servants, then, the decision to send a servant out shopping rather than going herself had practical consequences. The servant was trusted with money, goods, time and responsibility for quality. Retailers were adept at gauging the abilities of any individual shopper, waited for their moment to exploit weakness or inexperience, to raise prices and palm off inferior goods.

Yet even trustworthy servants may well not have made good shoppers for food for the household because of the highly variable quality and freshness of produce and the complexities of testing quality and freshness for each separate item that we saw above. In addition, assessments about current and long-term needs and cupboard-life needed to be made by the shopper on the spot. As well as judging

---

cheapest, you are intitled to that Overplus you must have given in another Place; for this is no more than your Duty, and the Time it takes to search out the best Bargains, is the Property of those to whom you belong.'

24 More, *Present for a Servant Maid*, p. 51: 'to be truly a good servant and gain affection and esteem of those you live with fane to learn certain skills'. These skills were 'marketing, cooking, washing'.

25 More, *Present for a Servant Maid*, pp. 8–9, also ch. 7: their 'time is their masters'.

26 Richard Mayo, *A Present for Servants, from their Ministers, Masters, or Other Friends* (London, 1693), pp. 30–1: 'How quickly does the Devil teach an ungodly Servant to make bold with his Master's Money, in buying or selling, and to excuse it by the secrecy, or smalness of the matter till they who made nothing to trample on God's Law for a Peny, came afterwards to Pounds and higher Robberies.'

27 *The Duty of Servants* (London, 1685), p. 80.

quality, freshness and suitability, successful shopping also required experience in haggling, a firm character and the willingness to shop around. These attributes applied also to shopping for consumer durables, but when buying produce it was even more important not to rely on a single supplier.

Reliable and experienced servants could presumably have been trusted to shop well, but the turnover of servants in the eighteenth century was high. Vickery stresses that managing servants was a crucial aspect of maintaining the household:

> Rare was the employer who could boast of reliable servants capable of assuming responsibility for the smooth running of the household. Maids were unlikely to acquire the requisite expertise since they moved on so frequently. Merchant's wife Elizabeth Shackleton of Alkincoats, saw 29 maids pass through her household in a single year, 1772. Fourteen of these women were theoretically employed on a permanent basis, yet ten of them worked for less than thirty days ...[28]

The decision of whether to send a servant shopping was therefore often a matter of judging their character and experience, and with new or temporary servants an assessment of loyalty must have been difficult. In the case of unreliable servants, housewives may have limited their tasks to fetching and carrying only. How often a servant was sent shopping was perhaps especially dependent on the nature of the purchases. It is significant that Pepys recorded that his wife went to buy provisions herself when they were expecting company for dinner (quoted above), as on this occasion, presumably, quality was important. It is unclear whether she did this on a regular basis, but when she did decide to shop herself she undertook to rise at 5 a.m. to get the best and freshest produce. The decision had constantly to be weighed up as circumstances dictated. The benefits of servants' shopping were substantial – shopping took some considerable time and application and the timing and weather could be inconvenient – and this is why housewives wanted to delegate it; and yet quality and value for money might well be sacrificed.

When or whether a servant was sent shopping would also have depended on the size of the household and the number of servants employed in it. In those few households with very large numbers of servants where executive division was possible, higher servants, particularly housekeepers, may have monitored basic purchasing by lower servants, while the mistress had ultimate regulation over all expenditure.[29] *The Servant's Directory* (1760) provided pro forma accounts for

---

28 Amanda Vickery, 'Golden Age to Separate Spheres? A Review of the Categories and Chronology of English Women's History', *The Historical Journal*, 36 (1993): 409–10. Vickery discusses the management of servants at greater length in *The Gentleman's Daughter*, ch. 4, especially the difficulties of hiring and retaining servants: 'Few senior female servants stayed long enough to liberate the elite mistress from the pressing demands of day-to-day supervision. Indeed, to say that female servants constituted a supremely unreliable workforce is to offer a fatuous understatement.' 'Genteel households could not function without servants, yet as we have seen lower servants were strikingly independent and mobile' ... 'the risk of losing a good character reference seems to have worried them not a whit'. Vickery, *The Gentleman's Daughter*, p. 135 and p. 142.

29 Vickery points out that the numbers of servants found in middling households ranged from one to ten – too small a number for the executive division of servants. Such division

recording an extensive range of food and household merchandize to be used by housekeepers (or mistresses), with the idea of establishing regular, frequent account keeping and the possibility for employers' easy overview.[30]

Because trust and skill were the qualities of good shopping, the ability to shop and being given the responsibility for it marked out better or higher level servants. *The Compleat Servant-Maid* described the tasks of a hierarchy of servants, referring to shopping as a task only for 'Chamber-Maids, to Persons of Honour or Quality, or Gentlewomen either in City or Country'.[31] The author continued that for a chamber-maid 'If you would fit yourself to serve a Gentlewoman only ... You must also learn to be skilful in buying any thing in the Market if you be entrusted therewith, if there be no Butler in the house.'[32] And Hannah More listed the skills of an accomplished servant as 'marketing, cooking, washing'.[33]

The writing on servants' shopping advocated techniques to monitor servants' shopping other than the issuing of threats, although a threatening tone still tended to creep in. One way was to remind servants that any unusually high spending on their part could be open to question,[34] or remind them that their employers were up-to-date with the price of goods:

> Those among you of any Spirit, methinks, should value the Praise of a good market-woman, far beyond those scandalous and pitiful Advantages, which cannot be made without proclaiming you either Fools or Cheats; for depend upon it, you can live with very few who will not examine into the market-prices.[35]

---

existed only in very large aristocratic households. Vickery, *The Gentleman's Daughter*, pp. 134–5. The overall control of the mistress is confirmed in *The Servant's Directory*, which tackles the duties of different levels of maid, but states that it does not deal with the level of housekeeper as its advice is about the management of the house and other servants. The 'housekeeper' is assumed to be the mistress and an attached pocket-book is addressed to 'the Mistress of a Family'. Hannah Glassse, *The Servant's Directory, or House-Keeper's Companion* (London, 1760).

30 Glassse, *The Servant's Directory*. Each pro-forma printed page lists: butcher, baker, poulterer fishmonger, cheesemonger, butterman, and provides room to write in the name of the tradesman. Similar pro-forma pages follow for: oil shop, chandler, pastrycook, confectioner, fruiterer, greengrocer, milk, alehouse, washing, perfumer. Then wine merchant, brewer, coals, grocer, tallow chandler, wax chandler, brazier, glazier, tinman, lamplighter.

31 R. L'Estrange, *The Compleat Servant-Maid; or the Young Maidens Tutor* (London, 1677), pp. 62–3.

32 L'Estrange, *The Compleat Servant-Maid*, pp. 62–3.

33 More, *Present for a Servant Maid*, p. 51.

34 For example More, *Present for a Servant-Maid*, p. 23, which points out that if a servant has fashionable clothes, 'your Honesty is liable to be call'd in question: People will be apt to examine, how much you gave for such or such a thing, compare your Profit with your Purchases, and if the Calculation of the Expence amounts to a Scruple more than they can account for your receiving, will presently place it to the Score of those you live with, and say, you owe your Finery to your Fraud'.

35 More, *Present for a Servant-Maid*, p. 24.

In order to stay up-to-date with the prices of provisions, unfortunately, the mistress of the household in this period would have had to have spent a considerable amount of time shopping. This was because there were no fixed prices and no price ticketing on foodstuffs,[36] and the final price for any food item was arrived at through a process of haggling, meaning that it would vary from retailer to retailer for the same sort of produce. The housewife could not assess prices by simply browsing the shops and stalls in order to discover current reasonable prices (fluctuating considerably due to supply and demand and with each season), she had to enter into the haggling process for each and every item her household would need.

It was clear that the housewife had to be actively engaged in household shopping, though the advice manuals attempted to provide practical solutions by emphasizing the need for housewives to keep careful accounts and referring the reader to the pro forma accounts supplied in the book. Texts on the conduct of married women, while mostly geared to inculcating moral behaviour, did continuously treat the problems of servants' shopping. The notably high-brow *Matrimonial Preceptor* (1760) counselled:

> Nothing is so common as for people to be plundered by their servants. Of all things that are easy to be gone through at first, accounts of this kind are the easiest; of all others, when they are neglected, they become the most confused displeasing and impracticable. You recollect the circumstances when a thing is recent, but you forget them after the time is elapsed. You expect the expence of a few days in articles that you remember; you are astonished at the sum when you have forgot the things it concerns: but this is not all; your servants will soon perceive whether you inspect their accounts, and whether you do it regularly; they will know all the profit that may be made of your forgetfulness, and will not part with any portion of the advantage.[37]

Another method was to be careful about methods of payment: 'If you send 'em with ready money they turn Factors, and take 3d. or 4d. in the Shilling Brokeridge.'[38] However, if a retailer billed a housewife the servant might still be in league with them, and she was burdened with the problem of being dependent on one tradesman who might raise his prices or lower his quality. *The Servant's Directory* (1760) advised how accounts should be filled out, whether by the housekeeper or mistress:

> If you pay read-money, still have a Bill and Receipt at bottom, and enter it in this Book, paid. If any Disputes arise, refer to your Bills of Parcels on the File; but if you have very large Accounts of this sort to keep, first enter them in a Waste-book for that purpose,

36 This was not the case for all consumer durables, some of which were advertized with fixed prices. See Nancy Cox, *The Complete Tradesman: A Study of Retailing, 1550–1820* (Aldershot: Ashgate, 2000), pp. 35–6.

37 *The Matrimonial Preceptor: A Collection of Examples and Precepts Relating to the Married State* (London, 1760), pp. 220–1. See also Trusler, 'If every mistress keeps a weekly book in the manner she will find pointed out to her in the next page and has an eye upon her servants, should she exceed her expences one week, she may retrench them in another.' Trusler provides examples of a housekeeper's book to record prices paid by the month for bread, butter, cheese, etc. Trusler, *The Way to be Rich and Respectable*, p. 176.

38 Moreton, *Private Abuses, Publick Grievances*, p. 8.

> wich should be big enough to last the whole Year, or a Month, and lay them by very carefully; and every Night enter all the Day's Account in here, to make it more concise and commodious; and if any Disputes arise, you must refer to your Day-book, and from that to your Bills of Parcels on the Files; so that your Account must always be right, as one answers for the other. [39]

This account keeping required not only prices paid to be recorded but also the weight of the produce, so that its price per pound could be analysed, and space was provided for tradesmen to sign on receipt. This account keeping was most laborious for basic items and food stuffs that would be bought in frequently, and whose amounts and prices were small and fiddly, but it was for these very items that account keeping was most vital. As well as for food purchasing, accounts were expected to be kept for the upholsterer, linen-draper, china-shop, silversmith, apothecary, chemist, distiller, blacksmith and chimney sweep.[40] *The Footman's Friendly Advice*, a pamphlet in defence of servants, replied that 'As to defrauding our Masters in laying in Provisions, 'tis almost impossible to do it, since most Butchers now send in a Note with their Meat every Day.'[41] Whatever the case, in order to keep servants' shopping and tradespeoples' deliveries effectively managed, mistresses had to pay some considerable attention on a daily basis to the provisioning of her household. Whoever carried out the actual task of shopping, the decision making and organizing and monitoring of shopping were essential elements of household management and the responsibility for them lay with the mistress of the household. Fanny Boscawen on moving to Surrey in 1755 wrote to her husband:

> The first employ is to feed young ducks and chickens, ... Then I visit Mrs Farr (your honour's housekeeper), order dinner, and talk of household affairs. By the way, beef is 4d. a pound, and they threatened me with 4 1/2 d when first I came, and made me pay that price for one sirloin.[42]

The group of texts on servant management does not lead us any closer to knowing how great a percentage of mundane shopping was carried out in practice by mistresses rather than by servants, but it does show us that there were compelling reasons for mistresses to take on the burden of household shopping when they judged it necessary or possible. The literature on the management of servants' shopping was only intended to concern itself with those occasions when servants shopped rather than when the mistress did. However, where household advice literature or other works on cookery turned to the question of fresh produce for cooking or building up stores for the kitchen, the advice was very specifically that it should be the mistress who shopped herself ('at first hand') rather than send a servant. *The House-keeper's Pocket-Book* (1733) counselled visiting the shop rather than letting a tradesman deliver, without countenancing that a servant should be involved:

39 Glassse, *The Servant's Directory*, p. 4.

40 Glassse, *The Servant's Directory*, p. 4.

41 *The Footman's Friendly Advice*, p. 30.

42 Fanny Boscawen to her husband, Boscawen, *The Admiral's Wife*, 9 June 1755, p. 179.

> I have experinc'd in my own House-keeping, that to buy things at the first hand, is to save at least one third of the Expence: By living in the Country for the most part remote from a Market Town, I found it so; and then could always procure such things as I would, besides the trouble of sending a Man and Horse for them; and when I have been in London the Case was little mended, if I sent for spices or such things to the Chandlers Shop, by little and little.[43]

Domestic Management of 1800 did tackle the subject of servants' shopping, but advised under the chapter on 'The Cook' that: 'It is imprudent to send a cook to market. Self-interest is much more persuasive than the interest of her master. It is an honest cook indeed, that will take pains to cheapen provisions ...'.[44] *The Way to be Rich and Respectable* (1796) reinforced the financial benefits of going into the shop oneself, and it included a reckoning table to be taken out shopping for fast calculation of prices and weights:

> I must repeat here, that 15 or 20 percent may be saved in many articles, by buying them at the first hand, and paying ready money, where it conveniently can be done, besides preventing things being charged a family never had.[45]

Conclusion

By examining this range of advice literature it can be seen that the purchasing of basic household goods was considered a skilled task and that the literature on good housewifery proposed that the mistress should take charge herself. Whether in practice she did or not is another matter, because for each housewife the decision about time and personal control was dependent on the current situation or exigency, but the extensive literature on servants suggests that there could be significant practical problems attached to servants' shopping, of which every mistress would have been well aware. Indeed, deciding who should shop and when must have been one of the skilled elements of managing household shopping. The practical problems involved in delegating to others make it seem very likely that mistresses would have, to a lesser or greater degree, carried out basic household shopping themselves.

Whereas the prescriptive moralizing texts on household management sought to contain and devalue women's work in and outside the home, and to stress women's dependence on their husbands, the practice of shopping for the household enabled women to display personal control over their household budget, constant interaction with people and places outside the home on a daily basis, and decision making and the application of sound judgement and thrift. Letters and diaries point to women's consideration of their management of household shopping as a personal, and independent achievement, and not necessarily in the submissive manner suggested in the prescriptive sections of conduct literature. Fanny Boscawen wrote to her husband in 1756, 'Having just paid Mrs Whaley's book, I am extremely of the opinion which

---

43 Mrs Sarah Harrison, *The House-keeper's Pocket-Book and Compleat Family Cook* (London, 1733), pp. 2–3.

44 *Domestic Management, or The Art of Conducting a Family* (London, 1800), pp. 31–2.

45 Trusler, *The Way to be Rich and Respectable*, p. 43.

you so honourably pronounced upon me viz.: that I keep a good house. Butcher's bills 2 weeks – £7, besides a sheep and a hog.'[46] Mistresses did not necessarily allow recognition of their achievements to be circumvented by literature which dismissed their power. Pride in the purchasing of household provisions could be meaningful to mistresses of the house. Mary Hamilton wrote in her diary in 1784, 'Mrs Carter call'd, she left me a Pound of Coffee as a Present for me, as she thinks that she buys it cheaper & better than any other ...'.[47] Women could value their abilities as shoppers and their contribution to the household, even when these were ignored or reframed on the level of discourse.

Consumers required extensive knowledge about even the most mundane of goods in the period in order to make their purchase decisions, so that even the repetitious task of shopping for the table and store cupboard required authority and competence. The early-modern world of non-standardized goods was complex: shoppers faced extensive ranges and subdivisions of goods, constantly variable qualities and prices, elisions between imitation, improvement and adulteration. Levels of skill required in a period of non-standardization were as great, or, more probably, even greater, than in a later period of extensive branding. This assessment of the complexities of shopping for the household helps us revalue women's roles as shoppers in the seventeenth and eighteenth centuries: if women managed the material and nutritional make-up of the household, then their consumption was not frivolous but valuable. The skills, and ultimately the power, involved in women's work in the home, are therefore significant for our understanding of consumption.

46 Boscawen, *The Admiral's Wife*, 14 December 1756, p. 235.

47 Mary Hamilton, *Mary Hamilton afterwards Mrs John Dickenson at Court and at Home from Letters and Diaries 1756 to 1816*, ed. Elizabeth and Florence Anson (London: John Murray, 1925), diary entry 20 May 1784, p. 185.

Chapter Two

'To Families Furnishing Kitchens': Domestic Utensils and their Use in the Eighteenth-Century Home[1]

Karin Dannehl

Introduction

Eighteenth-century kitchens were important facilitators of domestic life, from the provision of food to the enjoyment of sociability and conviviality. Like all rooms, they needed the appropriate furniture and tools to function in the way they were designated to perform, but unlike most other rooms in the early-modern house, kitchens were workrooms. As such, they were quite different in their contribution to the efforts of homemaking, particularly if the definition of 'home' centres on the notion that homes were places where work was not performed. The busiest, hottest and messiest activities took place in and around the kitchen, seconded by the scullery and the washhouse. Despite the focus on functionality, and therefore stripped of most opportunities for taste and fancy, eighteenth-century kitchens were not set pieces but spaces that had to be adapted and customized.[2] Only the hearth, the source of heat, can be taken as a given at the centre of all activity.

---

1 The chapter is based on a doctoral thesis 'A Life Cycle Study of Eighteenth-Century Cooking Vessels: A Reflexive Study' (University of Wolverhampton, unpublished PhD thesis, 2005) and some of its material was further used in ch. 4 of Nancy Cox and Karin Dannehl, *Perceptions of Retailing* (Aldershot: Ashgate, 2007). The work has benefited from conversations with fellow researchers Nancy Cox and Barbara Caddick, respectively about aspects of advertising and retailing, and about the household, its management and provisioning. Our exchanges provided a stimulating and rewarding research context, a privilege for which I remain very grateful.

2 Miller's study of a 1990s north London council estate and their owners' relationship towards the fitted kitchens revealed that despite the uniform nature of the fittings which were standard and not occupant-choices, their users had found a variety of ways in which heterogeneity and customization were effected. See Daniel Miller, 'Appropriating the State on the Council Estate', in Neil Cummings (ed.), *Reading Things* (Sight Works vol. 3, London: Chance Books, 1993), pp. 93-101. He also observes, p. 111, that housewifery is commonly condemned for its 'lack of possibilities of self-actualisation' not because the activity itself does not permit it or because its actors lack the capabilities to grasp or implement such possibilities, but because investigators refuse to treat housewifery as anything other than trivial.

The period under review is one on the cusp of more dramatic change. Between the eighteenth and nineteenth centuries new fuels and new cooking technologies were developed by science and industry. They were accompanied by a notable increase in the availability of cast iron utensils and fittings, which went hand in hand with an overall trend towards greater specialization in tools and their uses. Consequently, domestic kitchens consumed not merely food and fuel, but also the services required to maintain and run them, making repairs and re-fashioning, replacing and making new additions, all of which reflected the needs of cooking throughout a kitchen's existence. Cooking itself was a much wider set of routines than merely the application of heat to more or less prepared foodstuffs. It entailed preparation work in addition to tasks not normally performed by private households today, such as brewing, cleaning, preserving and medicinal preparation. Here cooking utensils, however humbly they may rank in the hierarchy of material goods, performed important functions as tools used in the preparation of food and meals.[3]

And finally, the kitchen was also the locality where many women users, and not necessarily owners, worked many hours every day of their lives. In the course of the eighteenth century, and throughout Europe, changes such as guild restrictions and journeymen taking over the tasks of preparing and finishing, which had most likely been performed by wives and daughters, removed women from production and resulted in 'further identifying females with cleaning, cooking, maintenance and selling'.[4]

The story of the kitchen, its development through the ages, the changes in heating technology and changes in the utensils employed have been the focus of numerous studies, from a range of perspectives.[5] The aim here is not to assemble a comprehensive picture of this story, but to gain a better understanding of what

3 Histories of food leave no doubt that eating and feasting, fasting and hunger, and recipes whether these be old or new, were important in a far deeper sense than merely for the fulfilment of a physical and biological need. See for example, Carole Counihan and Penny Van Esterik (eds), *Food and Culture: a Reader* (New York and London: Routledge, 1997) for the cultural role of food, eating and the human body; Gordon G. Birch, Allan G. Cameron, and Michael Spencer, *Food science* (3rd edn, Oxford: Pergamon Press, 1986), here pp. 110ff.; and A.G. Cameron, *Food and its functions* (illustrated by A.G. Standley, 2nd edn, London: Edward Arnold, 1968) for the nutritionist's view of what cooking does do foodstuffs and their nutritional value for the human organism.

4 Deborah Simonton, *A History of European Women's Work, 1700 to the Present* (London and New York: Routledge, 1998), pp. 48–9.

5 Museums, collectors, metals specialists, practitioners and historians have turned their attention to the kitchens of the early-modern period. Little has escaped their attention. See, for example, Caroline Davidson, *A Woman's Work is Never Done: A History of Housework in the British Isles 1650–1950* (London: Chatto & Windus, 1986); Rachael Feild, *Irons in the Fire: A History of Cooking Equipment* (Marlborough: Crowood Press, 1984); Doreen Yarwood, *The British Kitchen: Housewifery since Roman times* (London: Batsford, 1981); Molly Harrison, *The Kitchen in History* (Reading: Osprey, 1972); Gertrude Jekyll, *Old English household Life: Some Account of Cottage Objects and Country Folk* (London and Sydney: Batsford, 1975, 1st edn 1925); Marjorie Filbee, *A Woman's Place: An Illustrated History of Women at Home,fFrom the Roman Villa to the Victorian Town House* (London: Ebury Press, 1980); Christina Hardyment, *Behind the Scenes: Domestic Arrangements in Historic Houses* (London: The National Trust, 1997, 1st edn 1992 with the title *Home Comfort: A History*

choices eighteenth-century homeowners faced when furnishing their kitchens. It was, after all, an essential task of anybody who had hopes of running their own, independent household and home.[6] The further aim is to add nuance to the complexity of discussions of consumption for the early-modern period, and to contribute to historians' understanding of the pre-nineteenth-century home.

For the context of buying for the home, the interest of looking more closely at this scenario lies in two areas in particular: first, kitchens were workrooms, and the objects that will be considered here were by function tools in a much more literal sense than most other objects that were used to structure space and to create 'home'. This also means that the structuring aspect of their performance was much more dynamic and achieved through activity rather than through more static display. The second area of interest lies with the buying aspect of kitchen utensils, in other words the point when these tools are not yet tools but products and displayed; a show that was in some ways entirely incongruous and removed from their destined purpose. The chapter tackles these two areas in reverse order, by looking first at the ideal presented in the promotional materials of retailers of kitchen furniture, and secondly, at the reality of the kitchen and its functions, and the processes of occupying that quintessential yet messy domestic space, the kitchen.

Sources

The challenge of researching early-modern kitchens and their contents arises mainly from the evidence. Neither ideal nor reality is readily reconstructed from the materials available, and despite the evident functionality of the objects and users' need for them, the process of buying tools for this workshop remains elusive for the eighteenth century. Document and artefact material is often patchy, incidental or simply scarce.

The problem is even more accentuated where the aim is to investigate the process of furnishing these workstations. As the primary arena of women's work, the kitchen is disadvantaged in several respects. Women's work has been less valued and consequently less recorded and researched and this pertains to the localities in which

---

of Domestic Arrangements); Una A. Robertson, *The Illustrated History of the Housewife 1650–1950* (Stroud: Sutton, 1999, 1st edn 1997).

6 The differences between domestic kitchens and the kitchens of inns and other public or semi-public institutions are not formally addressed in this chapter. It seems obvious that a big establishment with many to be catered for is not merely the larger scale model of what goes on in a smaller venue, but that size will develop its own dynamics which in turn create different types of small, repeated and synchronized movements and groupings of these activities. On the other hand, the distinction made today between professional and private is misleading within earlier contexts. The cook of the late eighteenth century, middling household was often an employee, more rarely male, most frequently female. In poorer households it was the mistress of the house who saw to the cooking, yet provided the household was not too poor to afford cooked food altogether, she would have spent such a large proportion of her time in front of the fire as be nearer to the label of cook than a full-time housewife of the twentieth century and later.

they worked. Evidence is most likely to exist for households where paid servants rather than the unpaid 'home-maker' did the work. Households where the housewife was herself the user were unlikely to be of the social standing where documents or artefacts would have been kept and preserved. Moreover, the particular type of work itself, like all manual work reliant on sequence and timing does not encourage detailed recording. The processes and the knowledge involved require practical experience and sensory knowledge, neither of which is easily translated into words and onto paper. The kitchen and the value that was created in it have consequently received less attention than their central position at the heart of the smallest economic unit, the family, would warrant.[7]

The other focus pursued here, the act of buying, starts well before the purchase of a utensil. It commences with an idea of what is needed and desirable, together with some notion as to the function of the item to be purchased, frequently with a view to incorporating it into the array of extant household furniture. These ideas need to be developed, even though it is difficult to access the mind of the eighteenth-century buyer, who may have been different from the user, and even different from the person who paid. The chapter does not rely on the sparse materials relating to individual accounts of equipping a kitchen, which though illuminating are difficult to assess in terms of their representative qualities,[8] but instead squares the prevalent cooking practices with the promotional materials to which contemporaries, men and women, mistress and servant cook, were very likely exposed.[9] Ultimately, the aim is to work around the evidential difficulties, by offering a look at buying for the kitchen via two aspects that define the process: on the one hand the promotional materials that advertise cooking utensils, especially cooking vessels,[10] and on the other, evidence gleaned from artefacts and cooking practices available to the cook and user. A reading of both may therefore assist us in narrowing the gap between what we know about retailing and cooking respectively.

---

7 Feminist geographers' contribution to the study of social environments has, amongst others, been the valuing of domestic space. Dolores Hayden with her pioneering study *The Grand Domestic Revolution: A History of Feminist Designs for American Homes, Neighborhoods, and Cities* (Cambridge, MA and London: MIT Press., 1981) elevated the home and spaces within it into the realm of serious scholarship. However, such studies tend to be of entire dwellings within Britain and the United States rather than of particular spaces.

8 Maxine Berg draws attention to the elusiveness of the eighteenth-century consumer, even for the better-documented luxury purchases, in *Luxury and Pleasure in Eighteenth-Century Britain* (Oxford: Oxford University Press, 2005), pp. 203–4.

9 The language of advertising, however exaggerated, nevertheless is also a medium where cultural influences receive a heightened profile, even to the point of distortion. On advertising as information and the idea of context of objects, one could cite the lists of goods given in advertisements, which Maxine Berg calls 'networks of goods' in Berg, *Luxury and Pleasure*, p. 273. Individual testimony in the form of diaries or letters, and data that focus on valuations and prices also provide valuable insights but they have not been included in the present effort.

10 The source base for this part of the study are surviving examples of trade cards held in collections, for example the Heal and Banks Collection of trade cards and bill heads at the British Museum, Prints and Drawings, London.

Retailers' Promotion of Cooking Utensils

Cooking utensils made of metal and other materials were produced and sold by skilled workmen, and various forms of maker-retailers left evidence of their activities in this domain. The retailers conveyed messages to their target audiences, using for their written promotions trade cards or handbills, and newspaper advertising. The section to follow will focus on two examples as well as commenting on advertising strategies more generally, to draw some conclusions about how the buying process was managed and influenced by retailers.

Illustration 2.1 reproduces a trade card from Stone & Co. (1788). Its most striking aspect is its specificity. Unlike many metal ware advertisements, it is almost exclusively concerned with the promotion of kitchen furniture. Stone & Co. call themselves 'Manufacturers of Double Block Tin and Iron Kitchen Furniture', suggesting a high degree of specialization at the level of manufacture, and imply the equally high level of expertise that could be expected to go with it. The writer of this piece of copy knew the medium, which was essentially textual, and the rules that govern it to attract the reader's attention. Apart from the essential information required by the potential customer – the goods, the location and the seller – Stone & Co. aim to convince their readers that they are the best right from the start by stressing that they combine competitiveness and superior quality. The text proceeds along a chain of information – 'greatly improved', 'most wholesome', 'cheapest' – and culminates in 'preferable to others'. In fact, the first paragraph is a single sentence, taking readers right through to the inevitable conclusion so as to give them no chance of hesitation. What follows, is an elaboration of the same theme.

Readers have already been told that Stone & Co. sell sets of kitchen furniture. They are now presented with the complete list and left in no doubt because the advertisement emphasizes that 'The following forms a complete Set.' They also offer a complete replacement. This notion of replacement, however exaggerated, would suggest an interesting move towards redundancy at a time when most people were using and recycling as a matter of course and cultural imperative rather than ecological conviction. Mending and re-tinning services, so frequently offered in metalworkers' notices may be interpreted as belonging to a particular ethos and attitude towards the idea of age and old. They contrasted with, but also complemented, the attitude to what was new and fashionable. It is helpful to think of these two labels in terms of opposites, as between soft and aggressive, embracing and confrontational, and ultimately the difference between keeping and rejecting. Readers and potential customers, who were given the information and terminology required to imagine themselves in the role of customer and subsequently to assume it, were confronted with these two opposing aspects of owning, in other words, with acquiring and getting rid. Consequently, they had to balance old versus new, and the space and importance to be accorded to it. As a final persuasion, the notion of service is contained in Stone & Co.'s promise to their potential customers: 'N.B. ... Families in the country, wishing to be served with any of the above, will have their orders punctually executed, and the Tin Ware will be sent, free of carriage ...'.[11]

---

11 Stone & Co., *The Times*, 4 January 1788.

TO FAMILIES FURNISHING KITCHENS.

STONE and Co. No. 134, Oxford-street, and No. 125, Leadenhall-street, Manufacturers of Double Block Tin and Iron Kitchen Furniture, beg leave to inform the public, that they have greatly improved their Sets of Tin Ware, which renders it the most wholesome and cheapest Furniture in use, and preferable to others offered to the public, the whole being made of Block Tin.

The following forms a complete Set, which will be replaced with new for 2 l. 2 s. per ann.

	l. s. d.		l. s. d.
Tea-kettle	o 5 o	Bread grater	o 1 o
Coffee and Chocolate pots and mill	o 6 o	Flour and pepper box	o 1 6
Set of saucepans	1 1 o	Dripping pan and batter	o 5 o
Set of stewpans	1 5 o	Slice and gravy spoon	o 3 o
Set of soup pots	1 3 o	Skimmer and ladle	o 3 o
Carp or fish-kettle	o 14 o	Set of skewers	o 2 o
Turbot ditto B.T.	o 14 o	Two tart and 12 patty-pans	o 5 6
L. Boiling pot B.T.	o 12 o	Six table, one egg-spoon	o 4 6
Dutch Oven, B.T.	o 4 6	Two scollops, and tinder-box	o 2 o
Cheese-toaster, B.T.	o 3 6		
Cullender & beer-pot	o 2 6		
Frying-pan and gridiron	o 6 6		8 8 o
Spice-box and grater	o 3 6		

N.B. The sets of Iron Furniture consist of the same number of articles, and such as are not made of iron are filled up with Block Tin. Families in the country, wishing to be served with any of the above, will have their orders punctually executed, and the Tin Ware will be sent, free of carriage. Warm and Cold Baths to sell and let.

2.1 Stone and Co. advertisement, *The Times*, 4 January 1788

The second example is the handbill or trade card of Elwell & Taylor of London, which can be dated to the 1760s (see Illustration 2.2.).[12] It displays some of the standard elements of the genre, such as the traditional shop sign, the frame surrounding the central part, with the text engraved in copperplate hand. The first thing to strike the eye is the imposing shop-sign, the 'Lock and Hinge' and the large lettering of the name 'Elwell and Taylor'. The coffee urn and the vertical jack pose as framing pillars

12 British Museum, Prints and Drawings, Heal and Banks Collection, No. 85.99. A billhead 'at the Lock and Hinge' exists dated 1766, though (John) Elwell was then not in partnership with Taylor.

to the sign. Similarly a weighty bookcase in the bottom left corner, and the grate, to the right counterbalances the heavy top. The eyes move back up again, this time to take in the coffee urn in the top left corner and the vertical jack on the right, while at the same time trying to deal with the tantalizing clutter that is sitting, standing, dangling, hanging from every convenient hook and in every cranny of the frame. The eyes of the reader perform a merry dance as they home in, and move around within the image, and the range of depicted objects leaves no space for doubt that Elwell and Taylor do what they also spell out in the text: ‘Houses Compleatly Furnish’d’.

2.2 Elwell and Taylor Trade card c. 1760s

The list of the words that appear in the text is a roll call for eighteenth-century advertising staples: 'all sorts', 'most reasonable', likewise 'best' and 'neat'. It is an exercise in ringing keywords, and in the *nota bene* alone, four key adjectives, two of them in their superlative, 'original', 'new', 'compleatest' and 'lowest', are sounded. There is no experimenting with long or unusual qualifiers; most are short, and their use is restrained. We do not find strings of adjectives. Fairly standard, too, is the range of superlatives: 'most', 'most complete', 'lowest', 'best'. Considering this, the use of 'genteel' here is atypically ambiguous. And yet, in the phrase 'fit for Genteel Rooms, Halls or Laundrys' just below the second 'Make and Sell', the reader's mind is tricked into its wholesale extension right through to the (backstage) laundry. Even if the range of adjectives is limited, each one carries with it a baggage of meaning culled from countless other advertisements.

Three sales concepts underpin this advertisement. They are expressed in the use of 'completely', 'reasonable' and 'dispatch'. Firstly, the notion of completeness is stressed throughout the text, emphasizing comprehensiveness. Completeness is coupled with quality, but it is also presented as a quality in itself. Comprehensiveness of stock is stressed in the use of 'all Sorts' (twice), an advertising staple of the time. Twice we read 'in the Compleatest Manner' with reference to the house, apparently with the intention to include all available spaces that would conceivably benefit from furnishing. Services were comprehensive in all three lines of metalworking, and further enforced by the suggestion that as triple professionals, Elwell &Taylor possessed both the expertise and the contacts that could be expected of the different areas of professionalism to substantiate their claim. Completeness hereby becomes the basis for another advertising coup, choice. The second sales concept resides in the attribute 'reasonable'. Prices in the eighteenth century were so frequently referred to as 'lowest' and 'most reasonable rates' that it is easy to overlook and dismiss these claims as commonplace. The construction 'most reasonable', however, suggests two elements of meaning. In the first instance, prices are not high, and in the second, they are governed by reason. Elwell & Taylor's prices made economic sense and were consistent with quality. A third underpinning is the assurance of 'Care & Dispatch'. Elwell and Taylor execute customers' orders and requirements 'with the Utmost Care & Dispatch'. Care and speed are part of their services, suggesting that the customer can have complete confidence in them.

Tradespeople roundly exploited the idea of completeness as being the natural way of consuming. 'Complete' was a flexible term. Ultimately, every list or inventory of a person's possessions was finite, but their number was smaller or larger dependent on the wealth and ambition of the owner. Also finite was the number of commodities available for exchange at any given time. This finite number of options nevertheless offered a far greater number of combinations and it was this seemingly infinite number of combinations or options that was the mainstay of consumption and of the construction work that created the built environment at its micro-level. For the complete set to be a viable sales proposition, two scenarios are conceivable and they may well have existed simultaneously. Either, there already existed notions of a complete set in the first place, and the Company were showing themselves to cater for a demand that was already there. Alternatively, and even more manipulatively, Stone & Co. like Elwell and Taylor, were trying to convince their readers of the existence of such a notion and were in fact creating it in the process. By implication, another fiction was created; the fiction as to what is needed in a kitchen to turn it into a complete kitchen. Under such circumstances, 'complete' can easily come to stand for 'necessary'; a family's kitchen that did not contain all these items was by analogy lacking, incomplete and deficient. Associations with 'complete' would be positive, rounded, perfect and whole, while the implications for incomplete were their opposite: broken, faulty, imperfect and lacking. Stone & Co. did not even suggest that single items could be bought; they were marketing completeness. Completeness inevitably contains the threat of being incomplete and the challenge to achieve completeness, and the reassurance that all this takes place in a circumscribed and limited sphere. In other words, the aim must be definite and attainable. The right to define just what is complete, for example when a set was complete, was of course always reserved. But the nominal aim was outlined, and the carrot was never hung so high as to cease to be desirable. In addition, and also helpful to the consumer, services like mending and tinning, where they were offered, provided the link with the old and the familiar.[13]

Frequently small and humble commodities were not named in detail, but subsumed in 'kitchen furniture' or 'brass and copper', hence assuming a certain tacit understanding on the part of the reader as to just what was meant but not named. Some advertising emphasized the more up-market part of their production and wares. Overall, the impression is one of a continuum spanning the gamut from small to large and from cheap to valuable. One advertising strategy that may have benefited mundane goods was to place them with more prestigious goods also for sale. The extent to which goods could acquire quality by association, through being linked with desirable but ultimately foreign qualities, is most obvious in the advertisements of a rather different salesperson, the auctioneer and organizer of house sales. Here deliberate haziness of implication and amalgam joined forces with the equally deliberate celebrity sale. Genteel provenance played a big role, as for example, in the phrase 'All the genuine elegant Household Furniture ... by Mr Thomas Pemberton at the Hill' or 'All the genteel and fashionable Household Furniture, Linen, Plate, China & other effects belonging to Mr Samuel Freeth at Summerhill'.[14]

A number of keywords and key sales messages can be discerned. They include multi-professionalism, quality, completeness, choice, range, continuity and reliability evidenced by official approval through patents and royal or aristocratic patronage, care, speed and punctuality in executing orders, safety, availability and accessibility. The much- and often-signalled claim to variety and range is striking. It is implied in the multi-specialism of the 'Brazier, Tin-man and Ironmonger', the range of services, the lists of goods and the use of the ampersand. To this overriding interest

13 The idea of the complete set endured. Warren cites the nineteenth-century example of 'Deane & Company of King William Street, London Bridge' who offered a complete set of kitchen equipment for £11 3s 10d. The company asserted the 'thoroughly good quality, ensuring economy, efficiency and durability' of the goods and for orders over £2 no charge would be made for delivery. See Geoffrey Warren, *Kitchen Bygones: A Collector's Guide* (London: Souvenir Press, 1984), p. 10. No indication of date is given.

14 See, for example, T. Warren in *Aris's Birmingham Gazette*, 26 November 1770 and *Aris's Birmingham Gazette*, 3 April 1780 respectively, for examples of late-eighteenth-century household sales.

such relative qualities like mundane and luxury are subordinate. They existed less as categories than as shifting markers on a sliding scale. The idea of completeness was not only an advertising coup but also the expression of an ideal extended into the heart of the household. This approach readily accommodated all goods down to the last spoon. Within this concept, as well as within this scale of goods, even the last and least sophisticated item, the cooking pot, rested quite comfortably. While advertisements never overtly challenged existing hierarchies of goods, they subverted them by creating an atmosphere that amalgamated and compounded the buzz-terminology referred to above. The best of them aspired to create an imaginary space in which sale and purchase of all goods could take place: a virtual extension of the shop floor to the customer's mind.

The discussion prompts the question of representativeness. Whilst similar examples, as well as stylistically very different ones, can be found for the period, it is important to remember that there is ultimately no such thing as a norm in advertising; its essence lies in projecting a unique scenario. Most handbills, we must assume, since they tend not to have survived, and most newspaper advertisements, were less detailed and less sophisticated. It would appear that in most cases there was no detailed list of kitchen utensils or of small and comparatively cheap goods and the small, more numerous goods were usually subsumed under the collective 'kitchen furniture' or 'assortment'. The focus was usually placed on a lead-article such as a patented stove and kitchen ranges and in later trade cards register stoves seem to have advanced to staples that rarely failed to get a mention or a picture. The phenomenon in operation could appropriately be called elevation through association, be it yet so tangential. By sheer association, by dint of being retailed by the same maker whose skill is made evident, or at least believable, through his patent, for example, all articles bask in the same warm glow of desirability and skill and in their very number constitute a new quality: variety. On the basis of the evidence it is impossible to argue for any change in advertisers' essential messages – the 'puffs' that underpinned their advertisements for this or that gadget – whether they were radically new messages compared with earlier ones, which were not recorded, since they were not made on paper. We have not got the material to compare, say, the early eighteenth century with the evidence from the late eighteenth century. On the other hand, one real difference was most likely their relative durability. Paper messages, rather than oral or hand-written communications, were exposed to a greater number of people, and with newspapers being read from cover to cover like books, advertisements, too, became the latest and freshest advice, whilst being sufficiently ephemeral to be superseded by the next generation of promises. The dilemma between what was 'claim' and what 'reality', with the second being so essential to historians' assessment of the past, cannot entirely be resolved.

By laying out the cornucopia of available utensils and by extending the promise of attainability before the eyes of their readers, advertisements pointed them in the direction of a spiral of movement: in to and out of the kitchen. Such were the workings of selection, acquisition, addition and replacement that the concept of completeness was not fixed, but part of an ongoing process.

Kitchen Realities and Cooking Practices

From representations of cooking utensils on paper we move to the home where their corporeal counterparts were needed, and where the items, freighted with the ideals created, promoted and extolled by the retailers, had to be embedded into the daily functioning of the household.

The literature spans a broad spectrum of interests relating to the preparation methods, and more specifically, the cooking techniques that involved the use of utensils. Foci are the 'kitchen', the 'household' and women's work relating to domestic tasks.[15] Historians have most readily embraced the idea that food is an important aspect of culture and consequently have expended interest and energy in investigating its role and metamorphoses.[16] What most actual kitchens looked like, their size, height, atmosphere, the number of windows, is relatively elusive, however. Surviving kitchens, whether grand or humble, depictions, and floor plans that exist for cottages and grand houses indicate the location of the chimney and fireplace, and references to the wash copper suggest another feature, and they can probably be considered indicative of only the most general trends. Like any other space in a home, kitchens reflected individuality, if not individual taste, and status, if not always in the expected fashion.[17] As Pennell has shown, kitchens were the

---

15 See, for example, J. Seymour Lindsay, *Iron and Brass Implements of the English House* (illustrated by the author, with an introduction by Ralph Edwards, revised and enlarged, London: Alec Tiranti, 1970, 1st edn Medici Society: London 1927) and John Seymour, *The National Trust Book of Forgotten Household Crafts* (London: Dorling Kindersley, 1995, 1st edn 1987).

16 See, for example, P.C.D. Brears, *The gentlewoman's Kitchen: Great Food in Yorkshire 1650–1750* (Wakefield: Wakefield Historical Publications, 1984); contributions to Peter Brears, Maggie Black, Gill Corbishley, Jane Renfrew and Jennifer Stead, *A Taste of History: 10,000 Years of Food in Britain* (London: English Heritage in association with British Museum Press, 1993); contributions to Irmgard Bitsch, Trude Ehlert,Xenja on Ertzdorff and Rudolf Schulz (eds), *Essen und Trinken in Mittelalter und Neuzeit* (Vorträge eines interdisziplinären Symposions vom 10.–13. Juni 1987 an der Justus-Liebig-Universität Gießen, Sigmaringen/Germany: Jan Thorbecke Verlag, 1987); Stephen Mennell, *All Manners of Food: Eating and Taste in England and France from the Middle Ages to the Present* (Oxford: Basil Blackwell, 1985); Sara Pennell, 'The Material Culture of Food in Early Modern England ca. 1650–1750' (Cambridge University: unpublished PhD thesis, 1997); and Sara Pennell 'The Material Culture of Food in Early Modern England ca. 1650–1750', in Sarah Tarlow and Susie West (eds), *The Familiar Past? Archaeologies of Later Historical Britain* (London and New York: Routledge, 1999).

17 See William Verral's comment on the poor array of cooking tools found in the kitchen of a country squire in *William Verral's cookery book* (original edn 1759, facsimile edn edited by Ann Haly, with an introduction by Colin Brent, Lewes: Southover Press, 1999), pp. 17–25. Verral was a male cook and trained in the French style of cooking. He served several masters but ended up running his own public inn. His narrative is marked by a common-sense approach to what the cook in question needed and a great amount of sympathy rather than derision for the hapless, badly equipped female cook.

scenes of much more than merely food preparation.[18] They could be multi-functional places and serve as living room, sleeping place, a place of congregating, socializing – amongst fire and food – warmth and energy. In an obvious way, kitchens straddled the divide between 'home-making' and 'work place', until 'home' in the Victorian sense at least notionally became a sanctuary from work and ceased to be perceived as a place of work. For the majority of people in the early-modern period, kitchens were central to 'household *oeconomy*'.[19]

Like other raw materials, food and foodstuffs came into the household in a far less processed state than today, and consequently required a considerable amount of physical work to fulfil the needs and requirements of that particular household. A fair amount of preparation and organization was needed to provide the day's fare, as well as ensuring provisions for the seasons to come. In this respect, the number of servants employed in even poorer households and their kitchens, smacks less of striving for convenience and status as of necessity; the requirements of housekeeping involved a substantial amount of hard labour, which kept the persons involved in it fully occupied.[20]

Cleaning routines are a prime example. Not only do they represent the reclaiming of the object from use and disintegration in the form of having become 'dirty' through use. Through cleansing it from use and its traces, the functional object – whose entire *raison d'être* is its repeated use – is reinstated to its ideal state of object in pristine condition. It also means readying it for the next occasion of use.[21] Moreover, the act of cleansing in western culture is deeply imbued with notions of moral cleansing, of coming clean and of washing off sin. Use equates with sin, the clean and pristine surface equates with purity and untarnished and untainted saintliness. Most religions advocate ritual washing, and the cleansing rituals extend from the human soul and body to everything that surrounds the body and comes into the sphere of human influence and control. To that extent cleaning stood for moral reclaiming and for creating the moral conditions under which the cleansed person or item could be readmitted into the household. In pure, Protestant ethic, frugality and prudence were

---

18 Sara Pennell, '"Pots and Pans History": The Material Culture of the Kitchen in Early Modern England', *Journal of Design History*, 11/3 (1998), p. 207.

19 See Pennell, 'Pots and Pans History', p. 216, who points to the duality of meaning contained in *oikos* and *oeconomy*.

20 For the mid eighteenth century Weatherill estimates that the time spent daily on meals and their preparation amounted to three to four hours, that keeping the fire going took an hour per day, whilst getting food and water took another hour daily and one additional hour per week. Three hours were spent each week on baking and brewing respectively, and two days per year were given to preserving food. See Lorna Weatherill, *Consumer behaviour and material culture in Britain 1660–1760* (London and New York: Routledge, 1996, 1st edn 1988), pp. 142ff for an assessment of time spent on domestic work, and p. 143, Table 7.1: 'Household activities: stimates of time spent doing them'. Additional time and effort would have gone into activities, such as organizing the fuel supply.

21 See for example, Susanna Whatman, *The Housekeeping Book of Susanna Whatman 1776–1800* (edited by Thomas Balston, London: Geoffrey Bles, 1956), p. 16; and Samuel and Sarah Adams, *The Complete Servant* (edited by Ann Haly, with an introduction by Pamela Horn, Lewes: Southover Press, 2000, 1st edn 1989, original edn 1825), p. 105.

regarded as a housewife's virtues. Reintegration of objects does not carry the same moral weight. However, western notions of hygiene and propriety are influenced by this morality of washing. In a commentary on set scenes for amateur painters of picturesque scenes of industry, the author digresses to praise the clean appearance of pottery: 'There is something so cleanly in the vessels made by the potter, that it is no wonder they have, in a very considerable degree, superseded those of wood and of the various metals ...' and how 'its cleanliness and elegance will, perhaps, for ever secure to it an universal [*sic*] use'.[22] Elsewhere in an article designed to sing the praises of copper-smithing the same author includes a comment on the dangers of that metal: 'Unfortunately unless great care is taken, it [copper] is far from being innocent with respect to health.' He considers the dangers sufficiently great and widespread to consider it 'worth while [sic] here to notice the following case ... M. Gallet, formerly apothecary in the armies ... discovered a remedy for the poison communicated by verdigris in ill-cleaned copper vessels ... he drank a strong solution of sugar in water ...'.[23]

Another important aspect that pertains to workshops were routines and their effects on efficiency. For effective functioning, kitchens, like all workshops, relied on a range of routine activities since routines presage skills that are frequently needed, and that therefore should take up as little attention as possible. Routines facilitate good performance. The positive feedback and the reduced need for worry or fear explain why routines are something positive and indeed healthy. Their psychological effect extends further. Routines contribute to and bolster a person's sense of self-worth, wellbeing, comfort and confidence with regard to everyday tasks as much as the sense of achievement derived from tackling exceptional tasks does. Regarding the tools that routine uses require, it is through use that these objects retain their place (and space) and through use that their status, role and function are constantly re-confirmed, tested, assessed and – at the end of the object's life cycle – denied. Only use of an object – and uses can change over the course of its life cycle – ensures its place. Through routine tasks involving a given object, such as cleaning, maintaining and using, objects are recreated and tied to the present and the past alike.

Cooking demanded knowledge of heat, fire, fuel, the tools, their different properties, the foodstuffs, and indeed timing to synchronize preparation and serving times. A mid-nineteenth century manual contains the observation that '[i]n comparing roasting with boiling ... I have observed that though the latter appears to be a more simple process it is not so in reality, because it requires a greater advance in the mechanical arts, to procure the saucepan or pot in which the water must be contained'.[24] Warren notes the very probable and very ephemeral practice

22 W.H. Pyne, *Microcosm: Or, a Picturesque Delineation of the Arts, Agriculture, Manufactures, &c. of Great Britain ... Part 1 Early Trades and Industries* (London: William Miller, 1808, republished Luton: Luton Museum, 1974), p. 11. According to the original introduction (n. p.) the *Microcosm* had a double purpose, first, to present students and amateurs with 'picturesque representations of the scenery of active life' and second, to show them accurate depictions of the various sorts of instruments and machines used.

23 See C. Gray's explanations in Pyne, *Microcosm*, n.p.

24 J.H. Walsh, *A Manual of Domestic Economy: Suited to Families Spending from £100 to £1000 a Year. Including Directions for the Management of the Nursery and Sick Room, and*

of poor households where one large pot was used. For example, a perforated piece of wood acting as a divider half way down inside the vessel supported earthenware jars containing different foods, made watertight and weighed down. Other foods, such as cereals and beans, were placed in little bags of cloth and suspended into the pot hanging from a cord that was stretched across the mouth of the vessel.[25] These practices of the poor did not necessarily enter the written record, and its wooden and cloth implements rarely survive. Indeed, inscribed only on the moment, all these routines were ephemeral, and therefore in large part impossible to retrieve. However small and insignificant each act was on its own, it was nevertheless demanding and in their co-ordination and sequencing mentally challenging.[26] And it is the sum of a large number of small acts, each insignificant on its own, is what differentiated the successful from the less successful workshop.

A fundamental change occurred regarding the source of heat. The 'kitchen revolution' of the eighteenth century lay in the replacement of the main source of heat, from open, down-hearth fire to coal grate and to the enclosed range. This fundamental development was conceptual, because like so many other fashions, its spread was very uneven. The down-hearth fire did survive in pockets until the early twentieth century.[27] Even so, many cookery writers who produced instructional books for the middling sort and their servants assumed at the very least a chimneyed hearth, if not already an enclosed stove.[28] The difference between down-hearth and range was considerable. Open or down-hearth cooking was simple, and it was most effective if the heat of the cooking fire also served to heat the dwelling place. The down-hearth fireplace was open and contained a live fire, giving warmth and brightness; it had therefore many of the features associated with sitting around a fire or a fireplace. The range raised the source of heat, enclosed and harnessed it. It was still warm, but not bright. Working at it was like working at a machine for cooking. Over a period of two hundred years the process of cooking was thus moved from an open and down-hearth to an enclosed and raised facility, from being in the centre of the room to the sidewall, into a recess, from the 'hall', which served as a central gathering place, to a 'kitchen' separated from the rest of the house. Although enclosed forms of cooking were recognized for being more economical with fuel, the lesson was never

the Preparation and Administration of Domestic Remedies (new edition, London and New York: G. Routledge & Co., 1858), p. 454.

25 Warren, *Kitchen Bygones*, p. 56.

26 Oral communication from Debbie Buckson, but see also Sara Pennell 'Pots and Pans History', p. 212, who insists on the degree of expertise and specialist knowledge that is inherent in any independent physical activity.

27 A picture of a Devon kitchen in the 1930s shows down-hearth cooking. It is reproduced in Roderick Butler and Christopher Green with a contribution by Roger Brownswood, *English Bronze Cooking Vessels and their Founders 1350–1830.* Handbook to accompany a loan exhibition 23 September – 11 October 2003, Marwood House, Honiton, Devon (Honiton: Roderick and Valentine Butler, 2003), p. 17, A Devon kitchen in the 1930s with hanging cast-iron cauldron (from the Beaford Archive).

28 See, for example, the frontispiece in Eliza Smith, *The Compleat Housewife or Accomplish'd Gentlewoman's Companion* (1758, facsimile edition, London: Studio Editions, 1994).

translated into better stoves rather than ranges, and fuel economy did not become an issue with manufacturers until the early twentieth century.[29]

Changes in cooking technology, where it took place, had lasting architectural consequences. Less obvious were the consequences for the users' behaviour and actions, which were transient and not captured directly in the fabric of the house and its fixtures. Routines involving everyday objects create familiarity, value and patterns of doing things that structure life itself. The retrospective account of the Lancashire governess, Miss Weeton, relates the loss of a dinner because it was knocked off the oven by a child rushing past. It highlights the irony of changing design and the question of progress. The recollection dates from the early nineteenth century and suggests that enclosed cookers were not in all respects perfect, since the accident she describes could not have happened with a down-hearth fireplace.

> One day, [...] I bought some potatoes, boiled and mashed them with milk (which I paid for half yearly). 'Well, I *shall* have a dinner to-day!' thought I. I was *too* sure, and accordingly, punished for my presumption. When they were ready for eating, I placed them on top of the oven, whilst I fried some bacon and eggs for some of my pupils, who generally brought their dinner. One of them in passing the oven hastily, threw down the dish of potatoes on the floor amongst some ashes, so that they were utterly unfit to eat. I can *never* forget what I felt at that moment. I hastily placed the frying pan on the floor, and without speaking, ran upstairs into the parlour where, shutting myself up, I gave vent to my disappointment in a violent fit of crying.[30]

It would be unwise to follow a mechanistic relationship between form and function. Uses frequently resist categorization, and moreover, users may display a 'troubling irregularity' in the way they use objects, which means that how people actually and really utilize and use things is 'extremely resistant' to being presented and described accurately.[31] For the most part, eighteenth-century cookery books were not prescriptive regarding the tools to be used.[32] They assumed that the cook had some equipment, and perhaps in precisely what is not said expressed a certain arrogance and presumptuousness, but they make no further demands with regard to the range or set of tools available to the reader/user.

Just as the 'technologies' employed in making domestic tools were a mixture of incremental, yet fundamental, and gradual, yet radical change, in the same way the workshop 'kitchen' underwent change. However, as Davidson has pointed out, the

29 See Yarwood, *The British Kitchen*, p. 86.

30 From *Miss Weeton's Journal of a Governess*, a reprint of *Miss Weeton: Journal of a Governess* (vol. 1, 1807–11, new introduction by J.J. Bagley, New York: Augustus M. Kelley, 1969), p. 26, with italics as given in the source. The context is turn-of-the-century Lancashire, and the incident moreover illustrates the importance of even the simplest food, prepared in a simple manner. Note also that prior to running off the unhappy Miss Weeton placed the frying pan, still hot and with a handle prone to the same kind of accident, on the floor.

31 Neil Cummings, 'Reading Things: The Alibi of Use', in Neil Cummings (ed.), *Reading Things* (Sight Works vol. 3, London: Chance Books, 1993), p. 18 and p. 14 respectively.

32 This is a marked contrast to later cookery books and cookery literature, where the reader is told how to equip a kitchen, suggesting that the idea of the essential set had set firm roots.

changes were not initiated by those whose workplace it was. Nor did households generate any measurable power that could have enforced change in other sectors, which in turn would have benefited them. As the presumed end-consumer, the household was not regarded as a unit of production that created measurable value; the value it created did not count since it was focused and directed to those living within it, and in many cases consumed immediately.[33]

Buying between Ideal and Reality

Not surprisingly, advertisers' agendas were very different from that of the buyer and user of kitchen equipment. In contrast to the second group, advertisers did not focus on direct, physical use of an object but on giving reasons for 'furnishing' and consequently, the sales proposition could be wildly exaggerated or far-fetched. On the other hand, this does not gainsay the possibility and indeed likelihood that something about the perception of kitchens was filtered through to the potential customer.

Paper-based advertising brought together the salesmanship and the promise of completeness, safety and convenience, as well as the reality of an expanding range of tools for domestic use to the end consumer and user. The promotional literature supplied the information, reliable or otherwise, in place of the physical goods, but it also supplied the words and terminology to shape demand enabling the potential customers in return to express their wants. All bear the hallmarks of information, both manipulative and useful, which had the potential of expanding the consumers' minds and thereby the material world, despite the fact that at that stage the objects only existed on paper and were consequently not part of a visible, displayed materiality. Advertisements put into manageable and accessible terms concepts like accessibility, service, repair and maintenance. They provided an assurance that continuity could be acceptable, as could be buying into the values of thrift and economy through reasonable and cheapest prices. In so doing they confirmed and validated co-existent values of thrift and economy alongside values of fashion, change and 'modernity'.

A set of interesting juxtapositions ensues from this. Retailers included kitchens and their furnishings in their discourse of aspiring completeness, with ideas firming up as to what were regarded as proper, safe, healthy and hygienic surroundings. Kitchens were not therefore elevated spaces and remained workrooms that continued to be the work place of girls and women, and frequently paid domestic labour. Whilst the nature of this segregation may have resulted in the disregard for kitchen work, late-eighteenth-century buyers were exposed to the idea that a well-appointed kitchen was part of a complete house. Evidence for actual kitchens for the period is unfortunately sparse, and Verrall's example of the cook and her one sorry frying pan[34] an extreme just as the Prince Regent's show kitchen at Brighton was, with its rows of every conceivable cooking vessel. On the other hand, cooking practices, which percolated, however unevenly, through the social strata, came to embrace a

---

33 See Davidson's assessment in Davidson, *A Woman's Work is Never Done*, pp. 197–8.

34 See footnote 17. Verrall's example is intended to illustrate his point about necessary equipment. It is not intended to be representative of all (female servant) cooks.

growing number of utensils with increasingly specialized uses. Thus cooking pots and other kitchen tools were advertised as being part of the wider phalanx of necessary possessions that made a house complete, and by implication, their owners satisfied. The noticeable reluctance on the part of the advertisers to class kitchen furniture in a category that may have shown them to be less desirable than others signalled what is a truism in the language of the advertisements: everything is desirable and everything is essential. The fact that even the purchase of everyday goods would have been made against the backdrop of this kind of manipulation provides a corrective to investigations focused solely on luxury goods and contributes insights into notions of renewal, replenishment, modernization, completeness, hygiene, and even danger as imposed via the public language of advertising.[35]

Thus, in the example of cooking vessels, a concern becomes apparent that would be irrelevant in connection with most non-tool items of furniture: the concern about risk and danger. Rather than remaining a matter of private discretion, the awareness of the dangers inherent in the use of certain materials was made a public concern. Turned into a moral concern, responsibility could be laid at the door not only of cooks and servants, but also those buying and making the utensils. From now on, manufactured objects should not only please, perform well and be good value for money; they also had to be safe.[36] In connection with articles ultimately used in the preparation of food, however, and against a backdrop of dirt and general absence of food hygiene and standards, these were in fact 'modern'. The idea that a tool needed to be reliable and safe because users wanted assurance of their safety as well as of their compliance with the latest developments in this sector, is ample evidence of an expectation that all goods, and tools, should comply with notional standards regarding their performance.

---

35 The impact of the advertisements on sales figures and on the minds of the buying public cannot be quantified for the eighteenth century. This is not merely an issue of absent evidence. The effectiveness of printed media is difficult to assess for advertisers even today, and even in this age of surveys and statistical methods, advertising agencies struggle to quantify the increase in sales to which a specific advertisement or advertising campaign gave rise. Whilst quantification or even qualification with regard to the effect on consumers is elusive, it is nevertheless possible to make a few suggestions on the basis of the available advertising material as to the messages that were imparted to customers. The cost involved and the evidence of strategic devices support the argument that the examples reveal some of what the advertisers hoped would work in order to establish a dialogue between themselves and the public, to start the negotiation process that would ensure their success.

36 Although not an entirely new concern, it fits into a long-term trend towards risk reduction. Thus the late seventeenth century saw the advent of fire insurance; the late eighteenth century extended the need for safety and security to the use of materials in the creation of the interior. And with batch output as the precursor to proto-mass production, the trend for safety in products was itself on the way to attaining more general support and thereby critical mass. See for instance the argument for the development of risk reduction for a twentieth-century context presented by Mary Douglas and Aaron Wildavsky in *Risk and Culture: An Essay on the Selection of Technological and Environmental Dangers* (London and Berkeley: University of California Press, 1982).

The act of buying encompassed the paraphernalia of choosing and deciding, or, equally significantly, it included the absence of any sense of choice and proceeding to the local outlet that has them available, or buying from the tinker who came to the door.[37] As with all incidents of decision-making, however much it may have been subject to pressures to conform to established patterns of consumption, the decision underlying the users' actions would in each instance have been slightly different.

The important keyword in connection with tools is 'use'. No object was used in a vacuum just as no object was bought in one. Any object's existence, whether real or virtual, was always relative to a context formed by other objects and most uses of one object required or enjoined the use of others. Real or imagined, objects had gravitas, and their physicality triggered and perpetuated the choreography of their use. Far from all of the baggage acquired in the sales process was accommodated when the objects were transposed into the new context. In fact, the loss of some of the baggage was presumably a precondition for successful integration, which changed them from objects integrated into a matrix of implied or openly vaunted aspiration into objects of use and purpose in everyday cooking tasks. On the part of the buyer and user, whether they were one and the same or different people, the decision to remove the commodity from the commodity sphere through and for the purpose of using it, was a fundamental one.[38]

The decision to use an object was also the decision to engage in a gradual process of depreciation, be that in the sense of a smaller or greater loss of value or a total loss of use through damage, with only relatively small returns for scrap materials. In the case of cooking utensils use entailed continual wear and tear, with the heat of the open fire placing ongoing strain on them, and therefore increased risk of damage. On the other hand, and unlike objects that were useful in a decorative sense, depreciation on the grounds of datedness or looks was less important. By incorporating utensils into an array of such tools, and by using each one alongside others within different sets of use-routines, each utensil was given a place, which had to be negotiated by its user. At the same time, degrees of 'efficiency' were achieved, which, although they were always likely to be highly idiosyncratic, structured the space in which a given activity took place.[39]

---

37 One port of call for advice were household management books which praised thrift, taste and caution regarding the family's financial health. I would like to thank Barbara Caddick for this piece of information.

38 See Igor Kopytoff, 'The Cultural Biography of Things: Commoditization as Process', in Arjun Appadurai (ed.), *The Social Life of Things: Commodities in Cultural Perspective* (Cambridge: Cambridge University Press, 1986), pp. 64–91, for a discussion on the commodification and decommodification of objects. The move to using an object is not dealt with by Kopytoff.

39 This investment, contained in time–space structures of a repeated occurrence, does not lend itself to being expressed in monetary terms. Indeed, since servant time was cheap, and the mistress of a house unwaged, a time–price calculation would probably result in infinitesimal amounts. The housewife's input has not been calculated and given a scale, and whilst the injustice, discriminating mainly against women, is deplorable, there is also ground for maintaining that the home was not a work place like any other. In her preface Daphne Spain expresses the hope 'for a future society that equally values caretaking [*sic*] and moneymaking,

The choreographies created by using the tools were the acts of negotiating space, effectively of furnishing, a workroom. Here the effect to be created was not that of a set scene or a still life, but that of a running storyline of activity, repeated and re-enacted, and occasionally brought back to zero only to be restarted. Aspirations and the reality of spaces structured by activity and everyday actions forced the homemaker to conceive of the home in the ways suggested by the idealized presentations of retailers as well as in terms of their own, everyday requirements. In the case of the kitchen, the physical, dirty, and demanding labour of practically using the objects that had been obtained left the home maker with little room for manoeuvre between ideal and reality, or any satisfactory compromise. Whilst consumer practice can be investigated via selection and acquisition, possession totals are a fragmented picture of a reality that was always in flux. We sense, for instance, that the promotional puffs did not achieve total adoption, however hard advertisers tried. The example of kitchen utensils illustrates the fact that one of the key measures of how homemakers negotiated space was through the choreography of use. It is unfortunate but inevitable that this important aspect of the everyday negotiations performed in homemaking did not inscribe itself except in fragments; for instance, the worn down side of a spoon, the polished and worn sides of a pot through scrubbing, the worn feet of formerly three-legged skillets pushed about in the heat of glowing embers.

The choreography of use was not recorded, just as it was presumably never planned but developed through practice. The application of Taylorism[40] and the views of other students of efficiency such as Christine Frederick[41] came later, and added weight to an argument for turning informal, individually pursued processes into workplace routines. The relevance of eighteenth-century kitchens and the items contained in them to an assessment of the development of efficiency and economy cannot easily, if at all, be captured and measured in simple time-space models.

one that attaches as much importance to the activities occurring in private spaces as to those occurring in public places', but points out that 'The reality is that nonindustrial [*sic*] and industrial societies [alike] attribute greater value to the public forms of status defined as masculine' and that 'This system is not likely to change until women occupy the same space as men, and occupy it in ways that redress the existing distribution of knowledge and balance of power.' See Daphne Spain, *Gendered Spaces* (Chapel Hill and London: University of North Carolina Press, 1992), p. xv. Whilst the chapter has not addressed the position of women within the kitchen, it cannot but acknowledge that this most female workshop is a problematic space – it is uncontested and therefore ignored. Spain concludes, p. 235, her analysis of gendered spaces that the home is 'the spatial institution containing the least amount of socially valued knowledge'.. Spain's assessment is mainly based on her analysis of North American practice.

40 Scientific management or Taylorism is the name of the approach to management and industrial and organizational psychology initiated by Frederick Winslow Taylor in his 1911 monograph *The Principles of Scientific Management* (reprint, New York and London: W. Norton, 1967).

41 See Janice W. Rutherford, 'A Foot in Each Sphere: Christine Frederick and Early Twentieth-Century Advertising', *The Historian*, 22 September 2000, n. p., available online at http://www.encyclopedia.com/doc/1G1-68952035.html (last accessed May 2007).

Historians of consumption and material culture have a tendency to see goods as signals of status or affluence by the owners to their peers and others. However, the message, in particular of humble possessions, need not necessarily be transmitted to a vast audience. The most important recipient of whatever message an object may signal was the user. Objects provided comfort, security and ease in a tangible, physical sense and to the users they communicated a sense of structure and of order that went beyond accumulative material value.

Chapter Three

Guns, Horses and Stylish Waistcoats? Male Consumer Activity and Domestic Shopping in Late-Eighteenth- and Early-Nineteenth-Century England

David Hussey

Over the past three decades, interest in consumption has provided an ongoing critique of the classical theories of social and economic development in the eighteenth and nineteenth centuries. Whether this has been couched in reinterpreting supply-led or demand-driven models, with their associated cultural assumptions, attention has been drawn towards an awareness of gendered modes of consumer activity in the creation of a distinctive and historically-specific 'consumption ethic'.[1] Following Neil McKendrick's research, much work has equated the birth of a highly speculative 'Consumer Revolution' in the later eighteenth century with an expansion of female acquisitiveness as arguably one of the main agencies of cultural change. To McKendrick, female materialism found expression in frenzied personal spending. Frivolities, luxuries and the kinds of decorative and expressive goods that had been hitherto restricted to the elite, permeated the market in early industrial Britain seeping through a fluid and culturally permissive social order. The increased

1 See N. McKendrick, J. Brewer and J.H. Plumb (eds), *The Birth of Consumer Society* (London: Europa, 1982); C. Campbell, *The Romantic Ethic and the Spirit of Modern Consumerism* (Oxford: Blackwell, 1987); G. McCracken, *Culture and Consumption: New Approaches to the Symbolic Character of Consumer Goods and Activities* (Bloomington: Indiana University Press, 1988); and B. Fine and E. Leopold, *The World of Consumption* (London: Routledge, 1993). For studies rooted in an historically-specific canon, see the collection of articles in J. Brewer and R. Porter (eds), *Consumption and the World of Goods* (London: Routledge, 1993) and A. Bermingham and J. Brewer (eds), *The Consumption of Culture, 1600–1800: Image, Object, Text* (London: Routledge, 1995); P. Glennie, 'Consumption within Historical Studies,' in D. Miller (ed.), *Acknowledging Consumption* (London: Routledge, 1995); P. Glennie and N. Thrift, 'Consumers, Identities and Consumption Spaces in Early Modern England', *Environment and Planning*, A, 28 (1996): 25–45 and S. Pennell, 'Consumption and Consumerism in Early Modern England', *Historical Journal*, 42 (1999): 549–64. See also, T. Edwards, *Contradictions of Consumption: Concepts, Practices and Politics in Consumer Society* (Buckingham: Open University Press, 2000), pp. 32–51 and J. Storey, *Cultural Consumption and Everyday Life* (London: Arnold, 1999), esp. pp. 1–17, 36–60.

earning power and commercial presence of women was pivotal. It released a 'desire to compete with social superiors, a desire pent up for centuries or at least restricted to a very occasional excess'. Central to this conception was the emblematic, culturally transgressive presence of conspicuous female consumption: the déclassé 'mill girl that wanted to dress like a duchess' and whose unchecked, emulative expenditure 'helped to create the industrial revolution'.[2]

The theme of unregulated female consumer voracity with its Veblenesque undertones of emulative action and salivating cultural envy was a favourite bête noire of eighteenth-century satirists and conduct manuals. It is also an unhelpful archetype that has been subsequently extended and embellished. Elizabeth Kowaleski-Wallace, for example, has argued that 'with the birth of a consumer culture women were assumed to be hungry for *things* – for dresses and furniture, for tea cups and carriages, for all the commodities that indulged the body and enhanced physical life'.[3] However, recent important scholarly work has sought to identify and unpick the complexity of women's consumer activity in this period. As a result, a far more nuanced picture of female consumption has emerged. To be sure, the idea of an unconstrained, almost visceral female acquisitiveness remains pervasive, but it has been leavened by an awareness of the practical, affective, emotional, status-driven and symbolic motivations that were collapsed within the act of consumption.[4] These sorts of consumer stimuli have also been read into the process of material possession and shopping. As Cox, Berry, Berg and Edwards have emphasized, shopping represented both work – with its deeper resonances of skill, experience assiduousness and also quotidian drudgery – and pleasure, a diversion charged with pejorative associations with the ephemeral, the leisured and the compulsive.[5]

---

2 N. McKendrick, 'Home Demand and Economic Growth: A New View of the Role of Women and Children in the Industrial Revolution', in N. McKendrick (ed.), *Historical Perspectives: Studies in English Thought and Society in Honour of J.H. Plumb* (London: Europa, 1972), pp. 152–210, esp. pp. 200, 209. See also, A. Vickery, 'Women and the World of Goods: A Lancashire Consumer and her Possessions, 1751–81', in Brewer and Porter (eds), *Consumption and the World of Goods*, pp. 276–7.

3 E. Kowaleski-Wallace, *Consuming Subjects: Women, Shopping and Business in the Eighteenth Century* (New York: Columbia University Press, 1997), pp. 4–5.

4 Vickery, 'Women and the World of Goods', pp. 282–93; A. Vickery, *The Gentleman's Daughter: Women's Lives in Georgian England* (New Haven and London, Yale University Press, 1998), pp. 161–94; M. Berg, 'Women's Consumption and the Industrial Classes of Eighteenth-Century England', *Journal of Social History*, 30/2 (1996): 415–34; M. Pointon, *Strategies for Showing: Women, Possession and Representation in English Visual Culture, 1665–1800* (Oxford: Oxford University Press, 1997); M. Berg, 'New Commodities, Luxuries and their Consumers in Eighteenth-Century England', in M. Berg and H. Clifford (eds), *Consumers and Luxury: Consumer Culture in Europe, 1650–1850* (Manchester: Manchester University Press, 1999), p. 66 and passim; M. Berg, *Luxury and Pleasure in Eighteenth-Century Britain* (Oxford: Oxford University Press, 2005), pp. 234–42.

5 N.C. Cox, *The Complete Tradesman: A Study of Retailing, 1550–1820* (Aldershot: Ashgate, 2000), pp. 127–45; H. Berry, 'Polite Consumption: Shopping in Eighteenth-Century England', *Transactions of the Royal Historical Society*, 12 (2002); 374–94; Berg, *Luxury and Pleasure*, pp. 247–78; C. Edwards, *Turning Houses into Homes: A History of the Retailing and Consumption of Domestic Furnishings* (Aldershot: Ashgate, 2005), pp. 55–60, 104–43.

Yet, where does this picture leave masculine consumption habits? Whereas normative feminine behaviour has been routinely if problematically located in the construction of the domestic, men have been largely constrained to the notionally 'public' arenas of status expenditure – the guns, horses and stylish waistcoats and the clubs, dinners and homosocial bonhomie that commonly accompanied them.[6] Even though this neat binary divide translates imperfectly to historical experience, there is a dearth of work addressing male engagement with developing consumer markets: between the sensory hedonism of the dandy or the overblown 'effeminate' and 'foreign' decadence of the eighteenth-century fop and macaroni and Christopher Breward's 'hidden consumer' of late-nineteenth-century metropolitan male fashion, the field is especially barren.[7] In this chapter I wish to extend Margot Finn's initial forays into the area of men's articulation with the consumer market to examine the

---

See also, B. Lemire, *Fashion's Favourite: the Cotton Trade and the Consumer in Britain, 1600–1800* (Oxford: Oxford University Press, 1991), pp. 55–6; Berg and Clifford (eds), *Consumers and Luxury*; and R. Bowlby, *Just Looking; Consumer Culture in Freiser, Gissing and Zola* (New York and London: Methuen, 1985) cited in C. Breward, *The Hidden Consumer: Masculinities, Fashion and City Life, 1860–1914* (Manchester: Manchester University Press, 1999), pp. 5–6.

6 For a discussion of the fairly arid debate surrounding 'separate spheres', see L. Davidoff and C. Hall, *Family Fortunes: Men and Women of the English Middle Class, 1780–1850* (London: Hutchinson, 1987), esp. pp. 108–13, 180–92; M. Roper and J. Tosh, 'Introduction. Historians and the Politics of Masculinity', in M. Roper and J. Tosh (eds), *Manful Assertions: Masculinities in Britain since 1800* (London: Routledge, 1991), pp. 1–24; A. Vickery, '"Golden Age to Separate Spheres"? A Review of the Categories and Chronology of English Women's History', *Historical Journal*, 36 (1993): 383–414; L. Klein, 'Gender and the Public/Private Distinction in the Eighteenth Century: Some Questions about Evidence and Analytic Procedure', *Eighteenth-Century Studies*, 29/1 (1995): 97–109; R.B. Shoemaker, *Gender in English Society, 1650–1850* (London: Longman, 1998), pp. 15–58; J. Tosh, 'The Old Adam and the New Man: Emerging Themes in the History of English Masculinities, 1750–1850', in T. Hitchcock and M. Cohen (eds), *English Masculinities, 1660–1800* (London: Longman, 1999); J. Tosh, *A Man's Place: Masculinity and the Middle-Class Home in Victorian England* (New Haven and London: Yale University Press 1999); and W. D. Smith, *Consumption and the Making of Respectability, 1600–1800* (New Haven and London: Yale University Press, 2002), pp. 151–60, 175–8, 233–7. For a recent review of gender and sexualized spaces, see K. Harvey, 'The Century of Sex? Gender, Bodies, and Sexuality in the Long Eighteenth Century', *Historical Journal*, 45/4 (2002): 899–916.

7 For eighteenth-century modes of male consumption see P. Carter, *Men and the Emergence of Polite Society, Britain, 1660–1800* (Harlow: Longman, 2001), pp. 124–52 and C. Campbell, 'Understanding Traditional and Modern Practices of Consumption in Eighteenth-Century England: a Character-Action Approach', in Brewer and Porter (eds), *Consumption and the World of Goods*, pp. 40–57. The latter half of the nineteenth century is discussed by (amongst others) Breward, *Hidden Consumer*, pp. 54–99 and Brent Shannon, 'Re-fashioning Men: Fashion, Masculinity, and the Cultivation of the Male Consumer in Britain, 1860–1914', *Victorian Studies*, 46 (2004): 597–630. See also B. Lemire, *The Business of Everyday Life: Gender, Practice and Social Politics in England, c. 1600–1900* (Manchester: Manchester University Press, 2005), pp. 110–40.

means through which Hanoverian and Victorian men bought for the home.[8] The research focuses on the diaries and personal papers of five male consumers. These comprise two extensive, longitudinal collections of diary entries and three smaller selections of records. The two main sources are a business, family and social diary kept by James Oakes, a well-to-do yarn merchant, banker and alderman of Bury St Edmunds (1778–1827) and a more personal, and reflective journal compiled by John Thomas Brooks, a minor squire and amateur gentleman-horticulturalist of Flitwick, Bedfordshire (1829–58). These two sources permit the lifecycle and spending patterns of established male-led households to be analysed as the social, cultural and business associations of their writers matured over time. Three additional sources provide insights into the consumption patterns of single men. The bulk of the manuscript diary of the gauche if devout young Methodist and button manufacturer Julius Hardy of Birmingham (1788–93) and the work and social diary of the Chichester artist and portrait painter John Lush (1833) detail elements of a bachelor existence. In contrast, the diary of William Gitton (1866), an impoverished printer and occasional newspaper reporter of Bridgnorth, Shropshire, provides a diurnal of the everyday patterns of life of a sixty-five year old widower in straightened economic circumstances.[9]

Collectively, the diaries illuminate aspects of male consumption viewed through the lens of class, provincial society and religious affiliation. In particular, the records emphasize the range of mundane and expressive goods acquired, used and displayed by middle and upper-ranking men. The sources are not without interpretational problems. They were almost wholly devised for other purposes – mostly religious contemplation, the discussion of biblical exegesis, work-based *aides-mémoire* and miscellanies of social memoranda – and aggressive editing in all but the manuscript sources has excised the minutiae of everyday life; precisely the kind of information of interest here.[10] Even so, the diaries reveal not merely that the 'consumer market included highly acquisitive men as well as compulsively possessive women', but that men were active in negotiating the spaces between the acquisition of goods and the domestic arenas of Georgian and early Victorian households.[11] Through this, the work begins to uncover the ways in which male concepts of propriety, gentility and

---

8 M. Finn, 'Men's Things: Masculine Possession in the Consumer Revolution', *Social History*, 25/2 (2000): 133–55.

9 J. Fiske (ed.), *The Oakes Diaries: Business, Politics and the Family in Bury St Edmunds, 1778–1827* (2 vols, Suffolk Records Society, XXXII and XXXIII, Ipswich, 1990, 1991); Diary of Julius Hardy, Button-Maker of Birmingham, Birmingham Central Library, 669002, MS 218 (hereafter, Hardy, 'Diary'); Diary of John Lush, artist of Chichester, 1833, West Sussex Record Office, Add Mss 53,971 (partial transcript: Add Mss 19,026) (hereafter, Lush, 'Diary'); R. Morgan (ed.), *The Diary of a Bedfordshire Squire (John Thomas Brooks of Flitwick, 1794–1858)* (Bedfordshire Historical Record Society, 66, Hertford, 1987); M.D.G. Wanklyn (ed.), *The Diary of George Gitton of Bridgnorth for 1866* (Shropshire Records Series, 2, Keele, 1998).

10 For an interesting comparison see A. Fletcher, 'Courses in Politeness: the Upbringing and Experiences of Five Teenage Diarists, 1671–1860', *Transactions of the Royal Historical Society*, 12 (2002): 417–30.

11 Finn, 'Men's Things', p. 135.

politeness both in economic action and cultural sensitivity informed the construction of their homes.

Men at Home: Reconstructing Masculine Domesticity

Recent cultural history has sought to reposition Georgian and Victorian men as primary agents in the construction, articulation and life cycle of the household. As Tosh has argued, viewing male authority within a domestic and relational context throws open new ways of understanding the fault lines inherent in the idealized and rhetorical notions of the home.[12] Indeed, the orthodoxies of 'separate spheres' and a discrete female 'domestic ideology' which once held much sway now appear as conceptually problematic narratives. In particular, the hegemonic nature of masculinity meant that eighteenth and nineteenth-century men glided effortlessly between the notionally visible and active spheres of the public realm and the more occluded, opaque interiors of the home.[13] During the eighteenth century, the home formed one of the main arenas through which conceptions of polite masculine gentility – mannered deference, restraint, sensibility of thought and action, decency and the civilizing action of mixed company – were encoded. It was through these behaviours, located as much in the fabric of the bourgeois and elite home as the more discernible and studied arenas of masculine display, association and public deportment, that key male attitudes to the self, the body, sexuality and consumption were enacted. In this context, masculinity was a performance to be learned, refined and acted out: alongside the coffee house, the assembly room and the club, it was the home that framed the tensions inherent in male consumer activity. In parallel and in many ways in response to this, the household in itself became a contested arena of consumption. It was here in the dining rooms, parlours, dens and studies of the Georgian and Victorian middle class that the petty luxuries and new decencies – the leitmotif of polite material acquisition – were first apprehended and displayed. The linen, napery, china, porcelain and earthenware, silverware and tea, coffee and chocolate equipage together with the highly codified and gendered means through which they were deployed were thus gradually hard wired into the rhythms and choreography of the eighteenth- and nineteenth-century household. These goods freighted important socio-cultural inferences that served to describe the quality of the household and the discernment of its occupants and to give material weight to the wider discourses of politeness that were centred within the domestic milieu.[14]

12 Tosh, *A Man's Place*, pp. 1–8.

13 Tosh, 'Old Adam', pp. 69–71; J. Tosh, 'Middle-Class Masculinities in the Era of the Women's Suffrage movement, 1860–1914', in J. Tosh, *Manliness and Masculinities in Nineteenth-Century Britain* (Harlow: Pearson Longman, 2005), pp. 108–11.

14 This section is based upon a reading of Carter, *Polite Society*, pp. 53–87, 197–201; Smith, *Consumption*, pp. 181–3, 224–36; L. Klein, 'Politeness for Plebes: Consumption and Social Identity in Early Eighteenth-Century England', in A. Bermingham and J. Brewer (eds), *The Consumption of Culture, 1600–1800: Image, Object, Text* (London: Routledge, 1995), pp. 362–82; P. Langford, 'The Uses of Eighteenth-Century Politeness', *Transactions of the Royal Historical Society*, 12 (2002); 311–31; Berg, *Luxury and Pleasure*, pp. 199–219

The pervading ethos of a household dominated by concerns of masculine gentility and politeness is evidenced through the diaries of James Oakes and John Thomas Brooks. Both men were acknowledged heads of substantial and established families with grand houses at their disposal that they extended and improved to showcase their owners' quality and discernment. A high cultural premium was placed upon maintaining a household of leisured propriety through which a host of social equals, relations, neighbours, clients and friends were engaged. Key to this environment of casual opulence and mannered display was hospitality: an elaborated and codified version of what Davis has termed 'the chain of food-giving'.[15] Herein the status of company was measured not only in the perceived modes of correct deportment and conduct, based around formal and informal taking of food and drink but also in the reciprocity and generosity of behaviour. Mutual invitations and a seemingly endless round of tea-taking, polite conversational forms, visits, balls, musical soirees and dinners together with their material accoutrements punctuate the diaries. Impropriety in dress, conduct or, moreover, brusqueness of manner was met with opprobrium. Amongst the banking and estate business, the weather and market prices, Oakes's diary is littered with descriptions of domestic and civic amusements and longer sojourns in London, Bristol, Norwich, Manchester, Liverpool, the spas and at friends' residences. Indeed, evenings without domestic or extramural diversions are viewed as almost an emotional and psychic downtime, a hiatus to be endured between bouts of extended sociability. Similarly, Brooks actively courted social interaction: prolonged sequestration from company sparking bouts of incipient depression. He needed little encouragement to throw open Flitwick Manor and gardens for guests of quality. On 1 and 2 August 1848, for instance, 28 neighbours and assorted friends were invited to a day replete with fashionable diversions and lavish menus. As Brooks reported excitedly:

> We walked about the Grounds till dinner with which they were all much pleased, and after dinner till 12, dancing (in the old dining room and supper in the Library) and also Billiard playing, danced with the three Miss Smiths (Waltz, Polka, Quadrille and Country Dance) and enjoyed it exceedingly. A delightful Polka with *Sarah*. All went off well. At dessert 20 dishes on Table[16]

Brooks wore this geniality, gallantry and gentlemanly politeness easily: he dispensed an uncomplicated refinement and a genteel if largely feigned dismissal of 'worldly trifles' that was entirely in tune with his status as a High Tory, High Church rentier squire living very comfortably off the proceeds of his estates and commercial investments. On the other hand, Oakes, a well-to-do yarn merchant and banker, used his home not merely as an exercise in polite gentility, civility and informed consumption, although this figured large on his social compass, but as a means to further his economic and social interests and cement his position within the local

---

and J. Tosh, 'Gentlemanly Politeness and Manly Simplicity in Victorian England', in Tosh, *Manliness and Masculinities*, pp. 83–102.

15 N.Z. Davis, *The Gift in Sixteenth-Century France* (Madison: University of Wisconsin Press, 2000), p. 35.

16 Morgan (ed.), *Brooks*, pp. 95–6.

civic oligarchy. Oakes habitually met the Bury St Edmunds corporation 'at my House' before convening for official business. At the uncontested general election of August 1803, Oakes held a 'Dinner Company at home' consisting of the town's aldermanic bench, coroner, town clerk and the prospective candidate's agent. This meeting resolved upon using Oakes's house as the staging point for the subsequent, socially exclusive and wholly male post-election dinner at the nearby Angel Inn – a raucous affair, presided over by Oakes wherein the 'wine passd ab[ou]t very briskly [and] we had many loyal Songs'. This was followed by a general Ball, 'very full, suppos'd ab. 500. Very great plenty of Tea, Coffee, Cakes &ca &ca; Red & White Wine, Negus … Abt 8 or 9 Card Tables in the Card Rooms, Wine in plenty served there likewise' attended by the absent candidate's wife, Lady Templetown, who was escorted to and from the house by Oakes's acting proxy, his daughter-in-law.[17]

These anecdotes indicate how intimately Oakes and Brooks were linked into a wider social and cultural world and how the domestic locations of elite and bourgeois men emphasized and determined subtle distinctions of class and status. Of course, this veneer of relaxed social equanimity masked a real economic hegemony that both Oakes and Brooks exercised as landlords and magistrates over tenants, clients and, in a more paternalistic way, the resident poor.[18] In contrast, the Chichester artist, John Lush clearly had pretensions of gentility, in part a reflection of the nature of his clientele – the local landed aristocracy and urban bourgeoisie – and his core business, portrait painting and artistic instruction, where it appears a certain obsequiousness of manners secured custom. Yet Lush's home was only occasionally used for entertainment. This reflected less the Victorian, masculine ideal of the bourgeois home as sanctuary from an unpredictable and visceral other of the wider commercial world, but more a practical response to the proximity of work and domestic arrangements. To Lush, like many petty artisans of the time, 'home' was 'work': a factor lugubriously acknowledged in the terse diary entries 'painting at home'.[19] To this end, consumption patterns were geared to Lush's varied activities beyond the home: manly pursuits such as extempore singing at local hostelries, evenings whiled away at dinners and clubs, cricket matches, agreeable meetings with clients, and, as befitted his bachelor status, social liaisons, flirtations and visits with friends and mixed company.

The juncture of politeness and male domestic cultural forms meant less to the two other diarists surveyed here. From the humdrum social interactions described in George Gitton's journal of 1866, it is tempting to echo John Tosh's assertion that by the mid nineteenth century, politeness, far from being a permissive entry into genteel society, reflected mere affectation or pretension.[20] It is similarly persuasive to regard

17 Fiske (ed.), *Oakes*, II, pp. 44–6.

18 For the treatment of the poor, see Fiske (ed.), *Oakes*, I, pp. 10–11, 30, 115, 123–4, 151, 156–60, 304, 372, 382–6, 393–4, II, pp. 3, 114, 271, 277 and Morgan (ed.), *Brooks*, pp. 32–6, 43–6, 68–9, 77–9.

19 Lush, 'Diary', 24 July, 27 July, 29 July 1833. For an outline of Lush's career, see B. Stewart and M. Cutten, *Chichester Artists, 1530–1900* (Canterbury: Bladon Press, 1987), p. 32.

20 Tosh, 'Gentlemanly politeness', pp. 94–5.

the impecunious Gitton's household arrangements as an abbreviated version of the High Victorian bourgeois home: a personal bastion or bulwark from unwanted inspection and a cordon sanitaire from the extraneous and often harsh economic realities of everyday life.[21] Superficially, Gitton appears the very archetype of cosy Victorian domestic insularity. Days spent pottering around the town, conducting some print or journalistic business, meeting fellows and acquaintances at one of the many taverns were punctuated by prolonged escapes to home where Gitton indulged in his customary two very square meals – dinner at 2 and supper in the evening – habitually taken alone or in the company of his housekeeper-cum-servant. However, as Donald has noted, the middle-class household was not some private entity; it was subject to the intervention of a fleeting cast of plebeian tradespeople and the intrusions, whether invited, or transgressive in nature, of bourgeois friends, neighbours, relatives and associates.[22] This was policed by the scrutiny of domestic servants and maintained by their invisible toil. Gitton's domestic situation was no different except that his in straightened circumstances and widower status the syngeries of home and work were emphasized. Home was a functional workspace for editing reports, reading proofs and writing up shorthand accounts and yet was still a site of some leisure and comfort to which friends and outsiders were occasionally admitted.

In comparison, Julius Hardy, the young and devout Methodist, demonstrated all the 'prickly autonomy' of a committed evangelical.[23] Hardy had no time for the conventions of contemporary polite society and, although he cautiously observed Birmingham's fledgling cultural ambit and held minor local office, he absented himself from the rather limited and ersatz company that Birmingham afforded. Fleeing from inappropriate lodgings at the house of his erratic, violent and sporadically inebriated brother and co-partner, Josiah, in 1789, Hardy's first attempt at quasi-independent living was an austere space of thrift, communal prayers and intense spiritual cogitation, conditioned in part by his Wesleyan regimen and in part by the slow decline of the button-making business.[24] To Hardy, leading the household in prayer was the true 'duty of a Xtian man' and one he inflicted with regularity though with disappointingly diminishing returns upon his truculent workforce. Hardy's 'little household' and, by extension his wider social forays, were characterized by probity, moral rectitude and a steadfast plainness in both manners and material culture. Ostentation and display, or for that matter desire, emulation

---

21 See Davidoff and Hall, *Family Fortunes*, pp. 185–6, 364–9; J. Tosh, 'Domesticity and Manliness in the Victorian Middle Class. The Family of Edward White Benson', in Roper and Tosh (eds), *Manful Assertions*, pp. 48–51.

22 M. Donald, 'Tranquil havens? Critiquing the Idea of Home as the Middle-Class Sanctuary', in I. Bryden and J. Floyd (eds), *Domestic Space: Reading the Nineteenth-Century Domestic Interior* (Manchester: Manchester University Press, 1999), pp. 104–9.

23 See Tosh, 'Gentlemanly Politeness', p. 90. Both Quakers and Methodists admonished believers to guard against the incursions of worldly vice and material pleasure: B. Reay, *The Quakers in the English Revolution* (London: Temple Smith, 1985), pp. 118–20; W.R. Ward, 'Mirror of the Soul: the Diary of an Early Methodist Preacher, John Bennet, 1714–1754', *English Historical Review*, 118 (2003): 476–521.

24 For Hardy's wider business activities, see Birmingham Central Library MS 1342/144–148, Bills of sale, Hardy and Hardy and Company, 1785–87.

and hedonism – the notional engines of conspicuous consumption – bespoke of impropriety and a singular lack of substance. The object of his rather serious affection, Nancy Gardiner, was valorized as 'refrain[ing] from a worldly conformity in dress and conversation … an example to bye-standers, the giddy and unthinking [and] likewise an ornament to others professing godliness'.[25] In contrast, a friend's wife was chided for her forwardness and his workers were continually berated for their many petty infractions, indolence and slavish attachments to muscular forms of popular culture (drinking, dancing and lewd conversation especially).[26] His brother Joseph was dismissed as 'addicted to excessive talkativeness [and] also a disgusting confidence of expression', taciturnity being the mark of a serious, Godly man. In a similar fashion, Hardy's younger brother, Charles, a surgeon of Newport Pagnell, compounded an 'unnatural', over-emotional fondness for his daughter with scandalous indifferent 'conversation concerning our immortal state'.[27]

This did not mean, however, that domestic affairs did not feature prominently in Hardy's life or that his home was denuded of sociability. Like the other diarists, the domestic world, though clearly inferior to the wider callings of religion and work, remained an exercise in self-construction. For Hardy as much as for Squire Brooks, for example, home reflected the core attitudes of the man. Here he entertained a variety of fellow north-countrymen, occasionally indulging them in practices – smoking for instance – of which he disapproved.[28] Relatives, neighbours and co-believers were also received cordially into the Hardy abode. A slew of Methodist preachers passing through the Birmingham circuit were treated to meagre rations and earnest discussions on the lives of the early Dissenters, current politics, weighty points of scriptural debate and 'things eternal'. Less solemn conversations – the 'love-storys' of Richard Baxter, to which a Mr Cooper regaled a censorious Hardy and a much less affronted group of mixed company, for example – were worthless beyond simple immodesty.[29] In between times, the hesitant and God-fearing Hardy courted the equally solemn Nancy Gardiner at his home. With his solitary servant and housekeeper dismissed and suitably libated with tea, Hardy, reassured by the sincerity, piety and plainness of Gardiner's responses, even managed to propose. His new and sadly less reflective life, born in the testing fires of religious trial and providential delivery, began here.[30]

Buying for the Home: Male Consumption, Shopping and the Domestic

If the household was viewed as both an internalized extension of the public face of male activity and, conversely, a privatized retreat from the rigours of aggressive market

25 Hardy, 'Diary', 4 August 1789.

26 See, for example, Hardy, 'Diary', 10 June, 1789; 1 September 1789.

27 Hardy, 'Diary', 14 November, 1789; 3 March 1789.

28 Hardy, 'Diary', 28 November 1790.

29 Hardy, 'Diary', 20 May 1789.

30 See J. Tosh, 'Methodist Domesticity and Middle-Class Domesticity in Nineteenth-Century England', in Tosh, *Manliness and Masculinities*, pp. 148–69, esp. p. 166. Hardy, 'Diary', 10 December 1790.

capitalism, how did male consumers of the middle classes and lesser elites populate that space? Did they, for example, regard the home in a similar fashion to female contemporaries like Elizabeth Shackleton or Judith Baker, wherein the consumption of goods and the personal apprehension, codification and reinterpretation of material culture collided?[31] To an extent, such questions have been hamstrung by the 'pervasive mythology' of men hermetically sealed into a separate sphere bounded by the analytical straightjacket of patriarchal domination.[32] Viewed through this prism there is an uneasy tension between masculinity, domesticity and the acquisition of goods. Here, the work of Margot Finn is instructive. Finn's survey of four male diarists and spectacularly fastidious record keepers of the later eighteenth and early nineteenth century has emphasized that masculine consumption habits were eclectic and mirrored the acquisitive disposition traditionally if rather uncritically ascribed to women. Propertied men of the later eighteenth and early nineteenth century were skilful and assiduous consumers of goods. They invested a variety of personal, practical, domestic and affective cultural distinctions in the commodities they purchased from specialist and general shops, markets and itinerant hawkers and, in an imperfectly monetized economy governed by customary association, exchanged in quasi-ritualized forms of gift-giving. Far from being merely the agents of solid, substantial spending – the one-off, set piece focal items of household furniture bought by Shackleton's husband from Gillow's of Lancaster – or, for that matter obsessive hunters after fashionable *à la mode* clothing and trifles – the waistcoats acquired by Shackleton's foppish sons – such men navigated the embryonic consumer and retail markets with an easy, skilled familiarity.[33]

The diarists surveyed here serve to extend and contextualize these assumptions. James Oakes of Bury St Edmunds, for example, was well placed to comment upon consumer culture of the late eighteenth and early nineteenth century. Bury, itself, was a town of some social and cultural import: its markets, fairs, shops and wider amenities formed a convenient urban centre for Suffolk polite society.[34] Furthermore, Oakes was no backwater provincial with stunted, bucolic tastes. He was widely travelled. The diary records extensive stays at Norwich, Newmarket, Manchester, Liverpool, the spas and London, where Oakes indulged in the many metropolitan diversions – coffee houses, pleasure gardens, theatres, amusements – on offer. Opportunity did not, however, breed activity. Oakes displayed the eye of the bourgeois regulator rather than the acquisitive consumer: his compulsive supervision of Bury's various markets, for example, was undertaken to ensure that manipulative practices by denizen merchant and alien interlopers – regrating and forestalling of grain in the main – did not impact upon supply and thus foment popular disturbance.[35] The variety

31 Vickery, 'Women and the World of Goods', pp. 274–304; Vickery, *The Gentleman's Daughter*; H. Berry, 'Prudent Luxury: the Metropolitan Tastes of Judith Baker, Durham Gentlewoman', in R. Sweet and P. Lane (eds), *Women and Urban Life in Eighteenth-Century England: 'On the town'* (Aldershot: Ashgate, 2003), pp. 131–56.

32 See Breward, *Hidden Consumer*, pp. 9–10; Roper and Tosh, 'Introduction', pp. 8–16.

33 Vickery, 'Women and the World of Goods', p. 281.

34 Fiske (ed.), *Oakes*, I, pp. 191–6.

35 See, for example, Fiske (ed.), *Oakes*, I, pp. 319–20; II, pp. 43–4 and E.P. Thompson, 'The Moral Economy of the English Crowd in the Eighteenth Century', reprinted in

or quality of the goods available, save the purchase of a single turbot in June 1802, was not deemed fit to mention.[36] Similarly, although there is evidence to suggest that Oakes viewed shopping as not merely a practical exercise in material possession, but a means in itself, a lively diversion to be enjoyed and celebrated *en famille*, he was less concerned with commodity culture than with ensuring that Bury's retail sector maintained the traditional feasts and celebrations of the Anglican calendar.[37]

To an extent this ambivalence is an artefact of the source. Oakes's diary was designed to record his wider social and political activities, and where occasional items of personal consumption slip in – a set of new clothes bought in London, for example – they are often relegated to mere financial notation alongside the more serious business of work or levity. For example, the lodgings, amusements and carriages used in Oakes's frequent excursions are described in detail.[38] Stray references to discrete cash books and accounting schedules, sadly no longer extant, may well have added substance to these sporadic purchases.[39] The consumption habits that can be gleaned from the diaries, therefore, are almost wholly defined by acceptable 'manly' parameters. Oakes regarded himself a good judge of horse flesh and regularly attended local fairs at Stanton and Newmarket to acquire horses and ponies for both family and business use. In 1807, for instance, he paid the inflated amount of 80 guineas for a pair of highly decorative 'Phaeton Horses of Mountain: bright Bay, 14 H[an]ds' for his personal carriage.[40] In a similar fashion, Oakes demonstrated a refined taste in the consumption of table wine and fortified spirits which undoubtedly was connected with his desire, evidenced throughout the diaries, to provide a welcoming household of discernment and style to his neighbours and, particularly, his business associates and friends of quality. Oakes, often in co-partnership with immediate family and friends, bought in volume from wholesale merchants in London and King's Lynn, paying especial attention to the demands of shipping and personally supervising cellarage, bottling and subsequent use. This sense of connoisseurship was an essential accomplishment of correct gentlemanly behaviour and one that Oakes was keen to display. Like other men of his class – Parson Woodforde and Squire Brooks, for example – he invested a good deal of economic and cultural capital in acquiring the correct vintages, laying these down

D. Thompson (ed.), *The essential E.P. Thompson* (New York: The New Press, 2001), pp. 318–25.

36 Fiske (ed.), *Oakes*, II, p. 22.

37 On 13 June 1823, Oakes went 'Shopping for a couple of hours' with his son James and family (Fiske (ed.), *Oakes*, II, p. 283). For the regulation of shops see Fiske (ed.), *Oakes*, I, pp. 234, 327, 371; II, pp. 21, 249. See also Cox, *Complete Tradesman*, pp. 139–45; Edwards, *Houses into Homes*, pp. 55–60 and Berg, *Luxury and Pleasure*, pp. 263–70.

38 Fiske (ed.), *Oakes*, I, p. 272, Friday, 3 June: 'Include[in]g all Expences on the Road, Lodgings in London 6 Guineas, Glass Coach [£]44 2 9 ½ , include[in]g Amusements &ca. What Cloathes &ca we bo[ugh]t was an extra …'.

39 The particulars of an expensive visit to Bristol Hotwells in the winter of 1797–98 which included hire of furniture, servants, coaches, a harpsichord and library use were specified in a now lost 'Bristol Book': Fiske (ed.), *Oakes*, I, pp. 357–8.

40 For general horse purchases, see: Fiske (ed.), *Oakes*, I, pp. 228, 230, 237, 253, 301; II, pp. 21, 41, 55, 208. For the phaeton horses, see Fiske (ed.), *Oakes*, II, p. 97.

in proper fashion and securing them against inappropriate usage and occasional domestic pilfering.[41] As much as the ubiquitous tea, wine and port served as the social lubricant of distinction in the Oakes household, with common small beer, which was also brewed on the premises, used as an everyday and servants' beverage.[42]

Oakes certainly cared about the presentation of his domestic milieu and referred with barely suppressed pride to the refashioning and extension of his house in response to changing architectural style and domestic fashion. Indeed, it is interesting to note that Oakes directed rather more thought and diary space into the design and later fitting out of the banking rooms that adjoined his urban residence. In part, this reflected the retreat from direct mercantile activity and the need to secure and retain business from rival banking houses, but it is also telling that it was in this most public of arenas that the fiscal probity of Oakes's name, quite literally his credit, resided.

In contrast, the leisured lifestyle that his estates and commercial interests afforded John Thomas Brooks meant that the Bedfordshire squire was far less in thrall to imperatives of work and the necessary rhythms this imposed upon domestic activity and personal consumption. Brooks enjoyed an extensive range of pursuits geared towards self-improvement and self-gratification. He invested heavily in the normative consumption behaviours of nineteenth-century gentlemanly activity – fine wines and champagne, sourced directly from reputable London dealers,[43] live game for his parkland,[44] expensive horses and custom-built carriages,[45] an impressive and extensive library,[46] specimens of taxidermy, mineralogy and the collection of curios and miscellanies of objets trouvés.[47] Yet Brooks was also a practiced and assiduous shopper in his own right. The diary records regular trips to London wherein the ostensible reasons for travelling – horticultural shows, the opera, exhibitions, meeting friends and relations, or simply lounging around his club – were interspersed and, indeed, defined by extended bouts of luxury shopping at exclusive West End establishments. In February 1843, for example, Brooks described in fond detail how the uniform, equipment, weaponry and equestrian livery for his eldest son's army commission to India were procured from Nicholls of Jermyn Street and Moore of St James Street.[48] Guns were later sourced from Purdey's and Westley Richards in Bond Street.[49] In 1847 on his youngest son's entry to Oxford, 'all the necessary things for his outfit', plate, china and household wares were obtained in a similar fashion.[50] To an extent this can be read as a cultural extension of a wider form of economic

41 See for example, Fiske (ed.), *Oakes*, I, pp. 285, 354, 388; II, p. 40.

42 Fiske (ed.), *Oakes*, I, pp. 249–50. At the Christmas dinner (for servants) beer was served exclusively, whilst at supper immediate family and guests were entertained to beer, brandy and rum.

43 Morgan (ed.), *Brooks*, pp. 37, 82, 144, 152, 165.

44 Morgan (ed.), *Brooks*, pp. 1, 68, 176.

45 Morgan (ed.), *Brooks*, pp. 6, 61.

46 Morgan (ed.), *Brooks*, pp. 31, 113.

47 Morgan (ed.), *Brooks*, pp, 82, 83, 92, 96, 172.

48 Morgan (ed.), *Brooks*, p. 25.

49 Morgan, (ed.), *Brooks*, p. 49.

50 Morgan (ed.), *Brooks*, pp. 66–7, 73.

patrimony; Brooks setting up his sons in the kind of military and clerical preferment that were the required and desirable enhancements to a man of his station.[51]

However, Brooks's engagement with the pleasures of shopping was not merely constrained by traditional concerns. He delighted in adornments of the person and the home, displaying a commercial brio that reflected and to some extent antedated the refined consciousness and aristocratic style of male metropolitan expenditure in the later nineteenth century.[52] Up-market retailers were trawled for watches; gold chains (a staple item charged with personal and emotional significance and often procured as a gift); morning suits, regimental outfits and household goods and furnishings, like lamps and ottomans. These were combined with everyday market shopping and even bartering for second-hand goods where the quality and authenticity of the merchandize could be assured.[53] Similarly, as an uxorious, if somewhat overly flirtatious husband and a doting, heavily protective father, Brooks was tireless in searching out gifts for his immediate womenfolk, even if that led him to arenas and commodities of some feminine delicacy. In 1843, for example, he picked out silk for his wife, Mary, at Miss Linwood's Exhibition, a fashionable dress shop in Leicester Square.[54] Four years later, he amassed an ensemble of books, garters, cotton stockings, silk stockings and '6 pr thin shoes (2 kid, 1 Real Morocco, 1 French Russells, 2 silk)' for his daughter, Mary Ann, whilst in London.[55] In March 1848, he ventured to Harvey's of Ludgate Hill and Steel's of Oxford Street, a favourite source of goods, to obtain silk stockings and satin shoes for his wife.[56]

The proximity of London afforded the kind of shopping experience denied to more provincial men. Brooks revelled in acting as a somewhat mature flaneur cum spectator, drifting about the metropolis, nonchalantly accessing the many diversions on offer, and casting a vaguely sexualized, masculine gaze over the conduct of urban life. His encounters with women, whether they were acquaintances, friends' wives, or unfortunate workers – the 'very pretty and agreeable young' manager of the railway refreshment room, for example[57] – were subjects to be languidly graded on qualities of appearance, deportment and conversation. Even representational forms – William Salter's picture of a Flower Girl, a 'most graceful figure, dark face and eyes and superb bust, piquant',[58] viewed in London, did not evade Brooks's attention, although the presence of his sons or thoughts of his wife relegated such thoughts to whimsical daydreams. This Baudelairian image of a dandy-manqué, the flaneur

51 Brooks sought to advance his younger son by eventually acquiring the curacy of Flitwick parish church in 1855 at a cost of £2,850: Morgan (ed.), *Brooks*, p. 190; Bedfordshire and Luton Archives and Records Service, X21/732; Flitwick parish records, P59/0/2.

52 Breward, *Hidden Consumer*, pp. 27–51, Shannon, 'Re-fashioning Men', pp. 600–606.

53 In 1847 Brooks 'went to Nathan's, Smithfield Street and got a Cavalry forage Cap in exchange for an old pair of Epaulettes I found left of my Regimentals': Morgan (ed.), *Brooks*, p. 58.

54 Morgan (ed.), *Brooks*, p. 42.

55 Morgan (ed.), *Brooks*, p. 73.

56 Morgan (ed.), *Brooks*, 28 March 1848, pp. 88, 151.

57 Morgan (ed.), *Brooks*, p. 142.

58 Morgan (ed.), *Brooks*, p. 157.

for a day, however, hid a serious attachment to quality shopping in which Brooks's cultural geography of the city was clearly identified with the negotiations inherent in the shopping experience. His 'day out' in the capital on 2 September 1853 serves as fitting illustration:

> Went this day by the first train to Town. Walked from Euston Station to 33 Hunter Street to see Mr Harland the Artist … and then walked as follows: to the Club … Then went to the Strand and bought two reading lamps (for Palmer's Candle of two wicks) for Mary and I … and then to Covent Garden where I bought (for 6d each, small) 2 lbs of Gold Foil, and then to Brown Piccadilly to remonstrate about dear John's armchair, and then to the Club (Army and Navy, Pall-Mall) for lunch. Then (from 2 to ¼ before 6) walking about … I always enjoy very much a day in Town, and I find [it] the perfect change of scene for a day, and the exercise do[es] me much good.[59]

Despite such skilled and practised shopping excursions, consumption for Brooks was located firmly in the domestic sphere. Like others of his class, Brooks extended and beautified his residence. A new drawing and music room were added to Flitwick Manor in 1829 at a cost of over £272 and subsequent improvements were made to the structure and amenities of the house throughout the next three decades. By the time of Brooks's death in 1858, Flitwick boasted a specially commissioned organ, a refurbished billiard room, drawing room, bedrooms, library and study, new-fangled shower baths, and a range of modish furnishings including photographic equipment. Even the main estate cottage was extensively refitted with new plumbing, storage and a freshly wallpapered sitting room in 1853.

Much of this was, to borrow Celia Lury's phrase, simple 'positional consumption', in which Brooks used the array of goods acquired as emblematic and reified markers of his social position.[60] This is clearly demonstrated in his appreciation and acquisition of art. Brooks was keen to express a refined taste by exposing his collection of paintings to the approbation of both his peers and those of superior social standing or cultural knowledge.[61] Thus, in 1847, Brooks reported that a visitor, Mr Goodall, was 'delighted especially with the pictures in the Gallery amongst which he particularly admired a Breughel (of which Master he said it was a very fine specimen) and a Holbein'. Goodall, Brooks confided, 'is reckoned a very good judge of painting and *therefore his commendation is valuable*'.[62] Later, Brooks relayed how the Rev Henry Wellesley, nephew of the Duke of Wellington, was 'much pleased with [the] Picture Gallery, saying there were in it some very good Pictures' and drawing attention to the Parmigiano 'nearly over the door of the Best bedroom', two hunting and hawking pieces and a portrait of King William and Mary. Wellesley, notwithstanding his exalted social connections, was 'reckoned one of the best judges in the world

59 Morgan (ed.), *Brooks*, pp. 174–5.

60 C. Lury, *Consumer Culture* (Cambridge: Polity Press, 1996), p. 46.

61 For the artistic sensibilities of the Victorian bourgeoisie, see D.S. Macleod, *Art and the Victorian Middle Class: Money and the Making of Cultural Identity* (Cambridge: Cambridge University Press, 1996), especially pp. 88–91.

62 Morgan (ed.), *Brooks*, pp. 60–61. My emphasis.

of painting and engraving'.[63] If such consumption reflected the expressive nature of the goods Brooks chose to showcase,[64] it was leavened by elements of purely affective display and acquisition. Thus, alongside the Old Masters and the patriotic portraits of William and Mary, themselves loaded with ambivalent significance for such a High Tory, Brooks commissioned portraits of his family and house and spent an inordinate amount of time and expense acquiring a picture of his father of rather indifferent artistic worth.[65]

The manor house, however, merely acted as a fixed point, the physical framing to the continuing theme to Brooks's spending, the estate and, moreover, its gardens, arboretum, glass houses and parkland. This was not merely an arena of conspicuous consumption or fashionable deportment. Brooks was a serious practitioner, who took great pains to stay abreast of current horticultural trends. Although lacking the expertise of a Head Gardener between 1843 and 1852 – 'I cannot afford to engage a *first-rate* person … and I do not like to be troubled with an *inferior* person', he complained bitterly in his diary[66] – Brooks oversaw the buying in of seeds, cuttings and plants from renowned seedsmen in Kent and Hertfordshire,[67] exchanged practical gardening advice and specimens with like-minded friends, botanists and the gardeners of major estates[68] and spent much of his leisure time visiting country house gardens and horticultural exhibitions.[69] Naturally, Brooks was keen to display the creation of his manly labours to guests and passing cognoscenti. Yet beyond the modish interest in exotic plants – selective strains of Bourbon roses and rhododendrons in particular – the garden was an inexhaustible source of deferred pleasure. When Brooks was not actively planting and reshaping Flitwick's grounds, he was planning the next confection of horticultural excellence, or was holed up in his library transcribing and cataloguing new designs and phyla of plants gleaned from his extensive and fiercely guarded collection of specialist literature (itself procured from specialist London retailers at no little cost), or indeed was simply wishfully and imaginatively transposing the exemplars of Kew, Woburn or Chatsworth to his own reduced acreage.[70] Brooks's consumption of the garden thus became, in Colin Campbell's words, 'a happy hiatus between desire and consummation … filled with the joys of day-dreaming'.[71] For example, a visit to Capt. Boultbee's Chinese-inspired garden at Bedford in 1843, stirred Brooks to copy into his diary the intricate

63 Morgan (ed.), *Brooks*, p. 175.

64 M. Douglas and B. Isherwood, *The World of Goods: Towards an Anthropology of Consumption* (London and New York: Routledge, 1996), p. 38.

65 Morgan (ed.), *Brooks*, pp. 120, 161, 170.

66 Morgan (ed.), *Brooks*, p. 39. In May 1852, Brooks engaged Philip Wright as 'our new gardener': Morgan (ed.), *Brooks*, p. 156.

67 Morgan (ed.), *Brooks*, pp. 91, 93, 109, 113, 114, 116, 122, 166, 230.

68 For example, Morgan (ed.), *Brooks*, pp. 5, 10–11, 30–1, 35–6, 89–90, 170, 182–3, 217, 219, 238–9.

69 Morgan (ed.), *Brooks*, pp. 5–8, 41–3, 92–4, 117, 128–9, 156–7.

70 Morgan (ed.), *Brooks*, p. 112: Woburn's Evergreen Plantations formed the clear inspiration for Brooks's Evergreen Wood.

71 Campbell, *Romantic Ethic*, p. 189. See also Campbell, 'Traditional and Modern Patterns of Consumption', pp. 40–57, esp. p. 42–3.

arrangement of beds, gravel walks and borders, a design clearly shaped by Brooks's perception of his friend's more authentic and superior cultural experience. Later Brooks executed a facsimile of this in stages at Flitwick, placating himself from any charge of crass imitation by proffering Boultbee a selection of his own best hot-house specimens in lieu of his horticultural and intellectual poaching. He remarked triumphally that he had '[f]illed his [Boultbee's] carriage with plants'.[72] Thereafter, Brooks moved on to the next site of horticultural improvement in the pursuit of new experience and new emotional satisfaction. Novelty in this, whether measured in vistas of pine trees, perfect examples of mimosa or tenderly cultivated cyclamen, was not just a competitive quest for collection or a feverish desire for 'complete-ism', although this clearly informed Brooks's wider motivations. It constituted a key part in the cycle of anticipation, realization and disillusionment that provided the rationale that underpinned in Campbell's words, 'the restless and continuous pattern of consumption which so distinguishes the behaviour of modern man (*sic*)'.[73]

Flitwick's gardens also emphasize the importance of symbolic goods and affective experience to masculine domestic consumption. The garden provided Brooks with the space for 're-creation': it was a largely male showground wherein the physicality innate in accepted masculine tropes were performed and where Brooks could find solace and seclusion away from the vicissitudes of life, especially after the death of his daughter. It was also here that fondly imagined landscapes charged with emotional resonance – his daughter's British Garden, her passion for lilies, the frenetic and obsessive acquisition of new strains of roses, the heathland planted as a reified memento of his military experiences – were given substance and materiality.[74] The garden also acted as the means by which elements of uncertainty were disciplined through consumption. Like many Victorian landed gentlemen, Brooks's planting regime mirrored a wider Imperial project of subjecting the fractious exotica of colonial expansion to British, and especially English, hegemony. The enthusiasm Brooks demonstrated in acquiring seeds and specimens from the Americas, Africa and India can be seen in this light. It also coincided with the protracted absence of his eldest son on military service in India – a factor that hit Brooks, who was prone to bouts of tearful melancholia, hard emotionally which he played out through the one constant under his direct supervision and surveillance. Flitwick Manor, Brooks's imagined 'roof tree', was a segment of a fast-evaporating 'Merrie England'.[75] Protected by its woods, rivers and ha-has from the indigenous 'crowd of dirty, vulgar people' Brooks encountered at the Great Exhibition, the house and gardens formed the matrix through which strange or dissonant elements of the colonial experience, Cape bulbs from South Africa or Burmese poisoned arrows, a gift to the museum,

72 Morgan (ed.), *Brooks*, pp. 31–4.

73 Campbell, *Romantic Ethic*, pp. 89–93, 201. This point is expanded in C. Campbell, 'The Sociology of Consumption'. in D. Miller (ed.), *Acknowledging Consumption* (London: Routledge, 1995), pp. 120–1.

74 The diary is littered with such examples. See Morgan (ed.), *Brooks*, pp. 42, 172, 109, 114.

75 Morgan (ed.), *Brooks*, p. 159.

were preserved, sanitized, catalogued and emasculated.[76] Here the worlds of dream space in which treasured and endlessly deferred consumption practices were collapsed and the manly world of rigour, discipline and labour collided.

Men, the Everyday and the Home

As Michel de Certeau has argued, everyday life is that which 'holds us intimately, from the inside'.[77] The construction of the everyday and the consumption of the mundane are similarly intimate and defining processes and were no less significant for eighteenth- and nineteenth-century consumers. Traditional histories of the period have emphasized that the quotidian and circadian rhythms associated with the domestic were firmly rooted within a distinctively feminine mode of consumer practice. As Vickery has argued, the ordering and acquisition of mundane items of household use and the very process of shopping for the everyday 'was a form of employment and one that was effectively performed by women'. Whilst men were useful proxies in the absence of direct female superintendence and could be relied on to undertake specialized commissions for goods that could be more easily procured through their activity in the wider commercial world, 'husbands were not expected to interfere with the daily organization of household consumption'.[78] A similar, if rather more clearly demarcated picture between these notionally prescriptive gender roles, has been read into the normative domestic practice of the Victorian bourgeois household.[79] Of course, this is not an absolute historical orthodoxy. John Bohstedt's examination of male agency in late eighteenth and early nineteenth century food riots, for example, has led him to stress that '[n]owhere is there evidence for the frequent assumption that in this period women were the primary shoppers for their families', a view extended and amplified by Margot Finn's recent work on male consumption habits.[80]

Although some scholars remain ambivalent about the perceived 'extremity' of such assertions in relation to the wider feminization of consumer action, it is none the less important to test such assumptions of gender and the material acquisition of everyday goods through cultural practice.[81] Superficially, the male diarists reported here conform to the accepted masculine archetype of being only marginally associated

76 Morgan (ed.), *Brooks*, p. 152 (crowd at the Great Exhibition); p. 169 (planting of exotica); p. 96 (gift of poisoned arrows). See also P.J. Marshall, 'Taming the Exotic: the British and India in the Seventeenth and Eighteenth centuries', in G.S. Rousseau and R. Porter (eds), *Exoticism in the Enlightenment* (Manchester: Manchester University Press, 1990), pp. 46–65 for a cultural perspective on such practices.

77 M. De Certeau, L. Giard and P. Mayol, *The Practice of Everyday Life*, vol. II trans. T.J. Tomasik (Minneapolis: University of Minnesota Press, 1998) in M. Paterson, *Consumption and Everyday Life* (London: Routledge, 2006), pp. 1–2.

78 Vickery, *Gentleman's Daughter*, pp. 164–7.

79 See Tosh, 'Domesticity and Manliness', pp. 48–9.

80 J. Bohstedt, 'Gender, Household and Community Politics: Women in English Riots, 1790–1810', *Past and Present*, 130 (1998): 97 quoted in Finn, 'Men's Things', pp. 134–5.

81 See Berry, 'Prudent Luxury', pp. 133–4.

with the kind of mundane shopping and household management widely evidenced in the consumption practices and the attention to domestic accounting attributed to women. Both Oakes and Brooks clearly devolved household administration to their wives and assumed, as far as their diaries can confirm, that the management of purely domestic affairs and their primary agents, the small core of servants, was properly the preserve of their spouses or indeed designated housekeepers.[82] To be sure, both men were concerned with procuring food for the table. Like Parson Woodforde and William Holland, Oakes went to great lengths to secure supplies of fresh meat and, in particular, fish. Frequent gifts of freshwater specimens were supplemented by direct orders from London dealers and ample if somewhat less than fresh saltwater stocks brought back from Yarmouth, where Oakes took his regular constitutional.[83] Similarly, it is perhaps unsurprising that Brooks and Oakes were, as Vickery has commented, 'obsessively involved in the acquisition and distribution of game'.[84] Brooks, for example, used estate produce as a useful culinary standby and was not averse to picking up game at the public market if the occasioned arose.[85] However, such activities should be seen more in line with masculine gift-giving than an attachment to the procuring of mundane goods for the home. Gifts linked male consumers into a complex network of reciprocity, policed by unwritten codes of status and distinction that operated in parallel to more monetized forms of exchange. Thus, in July 1803, Oakes was pleased to acknowledge the receipt of a turtle as a fitting present from his Liverpool-based nephew James Bridge, but less contented by the fact the animal arrived dead from its ordeal of travelling 'full 270 miles on the roof of the Coach [in] such remarkably hot weather'. The turtle was quickly passed onto the clergy for their annual dinner.[86] With Brooks the subtle, ritualized hierarchies of gift-exchange were more pronounced. Game was habitually and gratefully received from friends of similar social standing. This was conveyed direct to table, or redistributed to social equals and, more specifically, the deserving members of Brooks's own domestic staff and estate workers. Gifts to superordinate parties; potential patrons to his sons' military, legal or clerical careers; cultured or learned associates; or people to whom Brooks owed a specific debt (the head gardeners of aristocratic estates in the main) were treated to the jewels of Brooks's own production, hothouse flowers, exotic plants, ice and, above all, seasonal fruit. Yet beyond this honorific gift-giving, the business of the everyday occupied a vague penumbra to Brooks's core consciousness and only intruded when extraordinary domestic situations demanded. The prolonged decline and death of his daughter in 1848 meant that Brooks, impotently secluded at home and 'of little use in the sick chamber of a Lady', was absorbed with domestic

82 Oakes employed Martha Melsome as housekeeper and 'super-indendent' to look after the daily running of the household, including minor domestic building works: Fiske (ed.), *Oakes*, I, p. 389; II, pp. 33, 169.

83 For Woodforde and Holland, see Finn, 'Men's Things', pp. 144–6. Fiske (ed.), *Oakes*, 27 August 1797, I, p. 356; 4 June 1800, I, pp. 389–90; 13 September, 1802, II, p. 28.

84 Vickery, *Gentleman's Daughter*, p. 167.

85 For example, Brooks purchased a 'basket of Game' at Leadenhall Market whilst on a trip to London in 1847: Morgan (ed.), *Brooks*, p. 57.

86 Fiske (ed.), *Oakes*, II, p. 41.

responsibilities.[87] Similarly, when his wife was gravely ill and housebound in 1856, Brooks was forced into the relatively menial task of ordering and unpacking the annual bulk delivery of groceries and 'store goods' (tellingly described as 'her Groceries') procured from Lucas and Harrington of London.[88]

Brooks and Oakes were heads of established, secure and highly structured patriarchal households and it might well be expected that the social and cultural distance from mundane activity this permitted rendered them rather more insulated from the necessities and even drudgeries of everyday life. What then of men whose domestic experiences were more fragmented and less consistently ordered than this? The jobbing artist John Lush and the Birmingham button maker Julius Hardy were for most of the surviving records bachelors dominated by an attachment to work and curiously impassive towards the demands and condolences of home. Lush's reported consumption practices, both of the mundane variety and the occasional indulgent acquisition, were almost wholly linked to the demands of his profession and the requirements of his client base. In particular, Lush was keen to maintain a certain sartorial bearing; purchases of items of personal clothing, jewellery and small grocery wares, like cigars, which he dispensed to his friends and sitters, recur frequently in his diary. Such goods were closely associated with the kind of mutual business transaction that tied Lush into the civic oligarchy of Chichester's main tradesmen and the landed elite of its environs. Thus, Mr Batch's portrait completed in May 1833 at a cost of £3 4s 4d partially offset the 'Mourning Ring to the memory of my father' that Lush had procured from Batch for £3 5s.[89] Between March and May 1833 Lush acquired two hats, one of 'Gossamere' and costing 14s 6d, some gloves and a pair of trousers from Mr Matthews whilst simultaneously completing the portrait Matthews had ordered in March.[90] Similarly, the commission for Mr Grey, the draper of North Street, Chichester, settled at £3 10s was sweetened by a prior purchase of 26 yards of linen at £2 8s.[91] Yet, information on Lush's purchases is dwarfed by the main concern of the journal, the tracking of the many commissions and petty repair work that Lush undertook to complete and the more pressing matter of the settling of accounts, to which Lush kept scrappy, but extensive notes of payments and outstanding debts.

A similar lack of detail pervades Julius Hardy's account. Here, the practice of personal or domestic consumption was less 'inconspicuous' as vestigial.[92] In part,

87 Morgan (ed.), *Brooks*, p. 86.

88 Morgan (ed.), *Brooks*, pp. 178, 192–3. See Vickery, 'Women and the World of Goods', p. 280 for the onerous tasks of unpacking and labelling normally attributed to female competence.

89 Lush, 'Diary', Saturday 18 May 1833, Cash Memorandum 13–19 May 1833; 'Diary', p. 55.

90 See Lush, 'Diary', Saturday 16 March 1833; Wednesday 15 May 1833, Wednesday 29 May 1833. There is no account of Matthews being charged for his portrait: 'Diary', p. 55.

91 Lush, 'Diary', Cash Memorandum, 5 October 1833; Friday 11 October 1833. See also the entry for Thursday 12 September.

92 For inconspicuous consumption see P. Burke, '*Res et Verba*: Conspicuous Consumption in the Early Modern World', in Brewer and Porter (eds), *Consumption and the World of Goods*, p. 149; Vickery, 'Women and the World of Goods', pp. 284–5; Vickery, *Gentleman's*

this reflected Hardy's conception of the Evangelical household as a moral bastion against the iniquities of the trivial, the worldly and the vain. As such, Hardy noted consumption events only if they freighted a wider discourse on the role of divine providence or if they served to illustrate the weaknesses of his too-pliant flesh set adrift amidst a sea of wickedness and temptation. For example, in 1790, Hardy's dilatory and much-delayed expedition to town to purchase the replacement for his 'somewhat threadbare and rather shabby' best coat, was happily abbreviated on the arrival of a travelling co-religionist selling cloth (presumably heavily discounted) in order to finance his journey to Liverpool. To Hardy, this was not acquisition per se, but speeding God's work.[93] A lack of basic household requirements – ale and newspapers in the main – also drove Hardy into the arms of nearby public houses, loci of foul conversation, drunkenness and boisterous humanity which Hardy routinely upbraided himself for going whilst, at the same time, accessing the desired services and commodities.[94] Indeed, such was Hardy's thirst for knowledge that it is worth emphasizing Douglas and Isherwood's 'false distinction' between the material world of goods and the realm of ideas as both were clearly conduits of cultural meaning for Hardy.[95] Although Hardy cared little about the adornment of the person or household goods beyond the strictly functional, he was a voracious consumer, if indifferent interpreter, of spiritual literature, history and current affairs throughout the span of the diary.[96]

Hardy's aversion to reporting acts of purchase (although, inferentially it is clear that goods were acquired from Birmingham), also proceeded from an inability to conceive of mundane domestic activity as anything other than an improper use of male time. Thus, the various stages of Hardy's existence as a 'sole house keeper' represent a series of ultimately unsatisfactory, ad hoc experiments in the creation of an appropriately centred household. This was viewed retrospectively as a necessary hiatus, a period of gestation and spiritual and moral trial before a mature and perfect married state was achieved. His first attempt at 'keeping a house' in 1788 involved a curious assemblage of Hardy, a servant girl-cum-drudge, the clerk of the button manufactory, James Stansfield and his wife. As Hardy dolefully reported: '[Stansfield] and his wife live in part of my new habitation; they live rent free, in consideration of the wife's cooking for me, etc.'[97] This domestic situation existed for over a year until Hardy piqued by Stansfield's 'malapertness unbecoming a servant' and 'Quakeristical' bearing abruptly ended their 'asylum'.[98] If religious antagonism, most probably arising from Stansfield's indifference towards the weekly gathering of Methodist-inspired instruction and improvement, provoked Hardy to reconfigure his domestic arrangements, his next choice as housekeeper, his longstanding servant

Daughter, pp. 183–5 and D. Kuchta, *The Three Piece Suit and Modern Masculinity* (Berkeley: University of California Press, 2002), p. 5.

93 Hardy, 'Diary', 17 February 1790.

94 Hardy, 'Diary', 23 January 1789; 16 March 1789; 24 June 1789.

95 Douglas and Isherwood, *World of Goods*, pp. 39–40, 49.

96 See, for example, Hardy's description of the Birmingham riots: 'Diary', 14 July 1791.

97 Hardy, 'Diary', 2 January 1789.

98 Hardy, 'Diary', 30 January 1790.

girl, was as injudicious as it was calamitous. The fact that she was soon pregnant by the landlord's dissolute son rendered the remarkably inobservant if incandescent Hardy liable to accusations of moral and physical complicity. Again, Hardy returned to Mrs Stansfield 'to super-intend my household concerns, and give the necessary directions to my new servant girl'.[99] One month later he was married.

In contrast, the diary of the Bridgnorth journalist and printer George Gitton illustrates a rather different and more permissive picture regarding male consumer activity. By 1866, Gitton was an old widower, and, having survived one formal bankruptcy and a number of financial scrapes, increasingly impecunious. In many ways Gitton represents an example of downward social mobility. Alienated economically from his principal means of subsistence – the printing press had ceased working in 1865 and he was forced to rely on the largesse and facilities of his former competitor, Edkins – and burdened by debt, Gitton was subsisting on an erratic supply of newspaper commissions and the occasional short run of print work. Despite or perhaps because of this comparative poverty, Gitton was, none the less, an active and thorough shopper for basic household goods and necessities, an activity he shared with his servant, housekeeper and occasional confidante, Susan Hayward. From his Diary, Gitton emerges as a slightly peripatetic, perambulatory figure, milling around the shops, markets and inns of Bridgnorth, passing the time in conversation or alcohol-fuelled meetings with friends and associates whilst simultaneously acquiring the mundane, quotidian commodities that served his small household. Gitton's extended shopping forays were thus enmeshed into the very fabric of his social life: they provided both the landscape for his journalistic work and the template through which his dealings with social superiors and erstwhile equals, Charles Deighton, the wine and spirits merchant of High Street and later mayor, for example, and persons of distinctly inferior status, Dick Jones the porter or Jem Davis the coal dealer, were contextualized within the somewhat restricted social ambit of Bridgnorth.

Gitton's routine purchases reveal that he saw no incompatibility or impropriety between his conception of himself as a man of some education and local prominence – central to the wider paradigms of middle-class Victorian masculinity – and the apparently highly feminized acquisition of everyday items for the home.[100] Indeed, in March 1866 – a fairly typical month in the Diary – Gitton recorded 64 'consumption events', the bulk of which were small, market-based transactions in which Gitton procured a weekly supply of meat, sausages, game, dairy produce and fish from a number of country butchers, dealers and fishmongers. Interspersed with these direct negotiations were regular visits to the town's principal fixed shops. Thus, tea, peppermints, Spanish juice, cough mixture and proprietary drugs were obtained through William Steward, chemist of 42 High Street, buns and cakes were bought from William Roberts, confectioner of Low Town, and candles, soap, stamps, salt butter, mustard, cheese and coffee were acquired from the grocer George Callant of 6 Waterloo Terrace.[101] There was also a clear gender demarcation in Gitton's

99 Hardy, 'Diary', 28 September–2 December, 1790.

100 See Breward, *Hidden Consumer*, pp. 6–9 and, in contrast, pp. 155–66.

101 Wanklyn (ed.), *Gitton*, pp. 22–31.

shopping routine. Gitton invariably frequented the high end trades, the grocers, chemists and wine merchants that passed as Bridgnorth's bourgeois, indeed the very places where male sociability was an important ingredient in the conduct of business. Susan, however, was entirely responsible for the key, everyday goods. She customarily settled the weekly bread account with the town baker, William Ormerod and organized the fortnightly sending out of washing to the laundress, Mrs Hughes. Furthermore, the buying in of fresh linens and, significantly, the acquiring of all new cloth purchased for both household and personal use fell to Susan.[102] Similarly, cooking was Hayward's province, with Gitton eating cold fare or at local hostelries when she was ill and fleeing the home when female cooking chores – the boiling down of a beef's cheek, for instance – created conditions incompatible with writing or quiet reflection.

From this, it is clear that Gitton was a skilled shopper. He kept running accounts, engineered discounts for ready money, secured extended credit lines, received and dispensed small gifts and gratuities to lubricate commercial dealings and, above all, was an accomplished haggler for goods. This business of the everyday may well have acted as an antidote – a functional salve – to the relative diminution in status suffered by Gitton in his advancing years, or indeed it be seen merely as a natural extension of an overarching male desire to control household expenditure during a period of relative impecunity.[103] However, it is also apparent that it animated and gave substance and purpose to Gitton's daily life: far from being an activity of minor importance and one habitually devolved to notionally lesser members of the household, as in the case of Hardy or even more so, Brooks and Oakes, shopping for mundane goods provided the main cultural discourse to Gitton's limited, but none the less surprisingly full social world.

Conclusion: Men and Buying for the Home

R.W. Connell has argued that '[t]he history of European/American masculinity over the last two hundred years can broadly be understood as the splitting of gentry masculinity, its gradual displacement by new hegemonic forms, and the emergence of an array of subordinated and marginalized masculinities'.[104] If, as Connell emphasizes, the dominant trope of masculinity was based on extended kinship and predicated upon institutionalized forms of class and gender violence, it is interesting to locate forms of eighteenth- and nineteenth-century male activity in areas traditionally ascribed to female competence. The journals of the men surveyed here – largely unremarkable individuals from the lesser provincial elites and middle classes – demonstrate an attachment to the active acquiring and display of goods and also the needs, comforts and refuges provided by the home. To be sure, the

102 Susan bought a 'white pocket handkerchief, ready hemmed for 6d' for Gitton from Thomas Corser the draper in March. In April, she returned to Corser for curtains for the parlour window. In December, she bought cloth for Gitton's 'clean flannel waistcoat': Wanklyn (ed.), *Gitton*, pp. 30, 40, 114.

103 See Lemire, *Business*, pp. 206–14.

104 R.W. Connell, *Masculinities* (2nd edn, Cambridge: Polity Press, 2005), p. 191.

repositioning of Victorian men within the domestic arena may well account for the home-loving attachments of the rentier squire John Thomas Brooks, keenly aware of the diminution of 'caste' that could befall his small estate and family, or the lowly, peripheral reporter and occasional printer, William Gitton, cheerfully cutting his toenails in his front room after a hearty supper.[105] Yet, all these diarists engaged directly with the market, through bespoke purchasing in fixed, specialist shops, haggling at fairs and weekly market spaces and via the ever present yet subtly gradated exchange of gifts and small gratuities, even if these activities were obscured by more prominently positioned events. Gitton's embracing of the mundane chores of everyday shopping – the basic foodstuffs alongside the more centred masculine purchases of tobacco and drink – may well have been exceptional and conditioned by age, creeping economic instability and his rather unique position within the peculiar microenvironment of a small and fairly insular Shropshire town. Yet even Brooks and Oakes, clearly superordinate members of local society, engaged in the necessities of buying goods for immediate household consumption: activities that were generally and routinely devolved to women. Overall, the diaries indicate the need to 'put the consumer back into consumerism'.[106] As highly individual documents they chart the minor acts of consumption and, in Julius Hardy's case a stoic aversion to consumption, that provided the cultural matrix upon which domestic and public lives were built. It is in these spaces that changing modes of masculine consumption can be found.

105 Tosh, *A Man's Place*, pp. 13–26; Tosh, 'Domesticity and Manliness', pp. 30–39; 48–51; Morgan (ed.), *Brooks*, pp. 163–4; Wanklyn (ed.), *Gitton*, pp. 27, 108.

106 Pennell, 'Consumption and Consumerism', pp. 549–64; Berry, 'Prudent Luxury', p. 134.

PART TWO
Shopping for Identities?

Chapter Four

Liberty and Lifestyle: Shopping for Art and Luxury in Nineteenth-Century London

Sonia Ashmore

While investigating fashion retailing in the mid twentieth century, I came across the catalogue for an exhibition held in 1993, entitled *Biba: The Label, the Lifestyle, the Look.*[1] Biba was a small, offbeat and romantic fashion boutique that by 1973 had expanded to fill an entire redundant department store on Kensington High Street in West London. Its owner, Barbara Hulanicki, brilliantly marketed clothing, accessories, home furnishings and even food in a coherently designed manner, used a palette of subtle colours and evoked particular historical moods with moments of exoticism. Biba's initially inadvertent success seemed to epitomize the waxing and waning of the popular 'swinging sixties' fashion movement. The exhibition catalogue proposed that 'Biba was the blueprint for the whole concept of the designer lifestyle, and the idea that it was possible to re-create an entire way of living, courtesy of the store.'[2]

This chapter suggests that Arthur Lasenby Liberty (1843–1917), founder of Liberty and Co. of London, instinctively understood and applied the concept of what is now referred to as 'lifestyle' retailing a century before this, even if not in the present sense of the commercial exploitation of segmented markets identified by increasingly sophisticated and detailed market research. Liberty effectively offered those attributes ascribed above to Biba; indeed it is likely that the Biba style owed some inspiration to Liberty. In presenting this argument, a brief account of the Liberty business is followed by an examination of the concept of 'lifestyle', and the Liberty enterprise is then reviewed in the context of these modern definitions.

The Liberty Business

Arthur Lasenby Liberty opened his first shop on Regent Street, by then a fashionable address in the West End of London, in 1875. Initially the shop sold distinctive, subtly coloured dress silks imported from the Far East, which were dramatically displayed by the standards of the day, in 'beautiful windows so well studied by Londoners that

1 The Laing Art Gallery, Newcastle upon Tyne, *BIBA: The Label, the Lifestyle, the Look*, (Newcastle: Tyne & Wear Museums, 1993).

2 Catherine McDermott, 'The BIBA Logo: the First Designer Lifestyle', in *BIBA: The Label, the Lifestyle, the Look*, pp. 16–25.

they hardly need description', according to a later report in the *Lady's World.* [3] (See Illustration 4.1.)

4.1 Liberty and Co., Chesham House, Regent Street, 1898, photographed by Bedford Lemere. The windows are framed in 'Moorish' fretwork, indicating the exotic atmosphere within

The business drew inspiration from both the Aesthetic Movement and the nineteenth-century 'art shop', and from the bazaars of North Africa and the near and Middle East, places which were being visited by an increasing number of European travellers including Lasenby Liberty himself. By the early 1880s, the first small shop had expanded into a labyrinth of premises along and behind Regent Street. It was divided into seven departments, selling 'Eastern Art Manufactures and Decorative Objects' which included furnishing fabrics, rugs and carpets, 'curios and antiques', oriental ceramics and metalwork, furniture and a bazaar full of incidental items as well as the key commodity, textiles, which became trade marked as 'Liberty Art Fabrics'. Increasingly, ranges of merchandize were developed which could contribute to a complete 'look' uniting clothes and furnishing, with a selling environment that enhanced the exotic and later historical, aura of the goods. By 1883, the business had a studio dedicated to interior design and custom furnishing, principally in 'eastern' styles, but later in a more 'English' idiom. A dress department was opened the following year under the supervision of the architect and designer E.W. Godwin, who in the spirit of dress reform favoured draped styles inspired by classical Greek dress. In general, subtle colours, exoticism and nostalgia were key concepts, yet with substantial injections of contemporary design.

3 *Lady's World: A Magazine of Fashion and Society* (London, 1887), pp. 98–9.

The company's success was quickly reflected in its balance sheet and later its share dividends, after it became a limited public company in 1894. The present Liberty buildings, built in the 1920s, reflected the financial and social status achieved by the company over half a century.[4] They evoked 'an almost bank-like strength and well-being … a top-hatted and fur-coated wealth, a directorate courteous, polished, very English and patriotic, always open for business on the basis of quality, trust and confidence'.[5] This was an image at odds with the 'artistic', even bohemian atmosphere sought by the earlier shop. Yet material success was reflected in a broader cultural context as the name 'Liberty', with its fortuitous suggestion of freedom, became not only a household word but also the name for a style. 'Stile Liberty' became a euphemism for 'Art Nouveau' and 'Jugenstil', perceived as a libertarian, even shocking artistic style at the time, not altogether approved of by Lasenby Liberty himself. Thus a family name became that of a business, a modern 'logo' and a carrier of varied meanings. (See Illustration 4.2.)

4.2 Liberty 'Lotus Brand' trademark 1883, based on Thomas Wardles' 'Tanjore Lotus' woven silk. The Trade Marks Registration Act (1875), and Patent Design and Trade Marks Act (1883 & 1888), which gave legal status to trade marks were timely for Liberty

4 In 2006, the business contracted to the 'Tudor' shop on Great Marlborough Street, off Regent Street.

5 Howard Robertson, 'Some Regent Street Details', *Architectural Review*, LXII (1927): 232–9.

Consumption, Lifestyle and the Department Store

In the modern literature of consumption, 'lifestyles' have been defined as 'patterns of action that differentiate people'[6] – at the crudest level, self-definition through consumption. Social theorists have borrowed heavily from ethnography where, as Mary Douglas and Baron Isherwood emphasized, 'it is standard … practice to assume that all material possessions carry social meanings'.[7] Rob Shields has argued further that the process of consumption actually becomes the lifestyle as, 'Consumption for adornment, expression and group solidarity become not merely the means to a lifestyle, but the enactment of lifestyle.'[8] The concept of 'lifestyle' has largely been used in the context of postmodernism and has also itself become a form of commodity; there are now hundreds of millions of internet sites offering to guide one through the possibilities of 'lifestyle'-related consumption, and indeed how to recover from lifestyles that are 'wearing you down'. Yet the essential idea of the lifestyle as something that could be marketed was clearly established by the late nineteenth century if not before; the history of both concept and practice could no doubt be traced to far earlier times. Even in the eighteenth century, the British aristocracy defined a distinctive class specific 'lifestyle' notably through a particular form of patronage of art and architecture informed by the 'Grand Tour', and emulated in their own way by the *nouveaux riches* mercantile classes of the next century. At another social level, and at a time when the production of manufactured goods was on an unprecedented scale, a consumer culture was developing as a market for new commodities, opening debate about the distinctions between luxuries and necessities, and between mere decoration and design.[9] As Rosalind Williams has noted, 'the historical examples of the late nineteenth century [are] valuable in discerning the origins of the modern obsession with lifestyle'.[10]

The anthropologist Grant McCracken has argued that 'the nineteenth century … saw the emergence of new "consumer lifestyles" and their novel patterns of interaction between persons and things … More and more social meanings were being loaded into goods through new and more sophisticated devices for meaning transfer.'[11] He has noted further that 'consumer goods were fascinating for consumers of the nineteenth century because they were increasingly the residence of cultural

6 David Chaney, *Lifestyles* (London and New York: Routledge, 1996), p. 4.

7 Mary Douglas and Baron Isherwood, *The World of Goods: Towards an Anthropology of Consumption* (London, Allen Lane 1979), p. 59.

8 Rob Shields (ed.), *Lifestyle Shopping: The Subject of Consumption* (London: Routledge, 1992), p. 16. See also Lauren Langman, 'Neon Cages: Shopping for Subjectivity', ibid., pp. 40–82.

9 See J. Mordaunt Crook, *The Rise of the Nouveaux Riches* (London: John Murray, 1999) and Maxine Berg and Helen Clifford (eds), *Consumers and Luxury: Consumer Cultures in Europe 1650–1850* (Manchester: Manchester University Press, 1999).

10 Rosalind Williams, *Dream Worlds: Mass Consumption in Late Nineteenth-Century France* (Berkeley and London: University of California Press, 1982), p. 203.

11 Grant McCracken, *Culture and Consumption: New Approaches to the Symbolic Character of Consumer Goods and Activities* (Bloomington: Indiana University Press, 1988), p. 22.

meaning and new opportunities for defining self and the world'.[12] The growth of advertising and proliferation of retailers' catalogues helped to invent such new 'meanings' for material goods by creating often spurious links between ideas and objects, such as the 'Mikado' trouser braces advertised in 1886, with 'elastic cable ends', their Japanese epithet entirely unconnected with western male dress, but clearly capitalizing on the popularity of Gilbert and Sullivan's operetta, which was in turn linked with the fashion for Japanese things marketed by Liberty and Co., and part of a wider *Japonisme* with its sources in both painting and trade.

The Liberty business developed in the context of the nineteenth-century department stores, which both responded to and drove burgeoning consumer markets, especially in the rapidly expanding cities such as London. As David Chaney and others have pointed out, this 'new era of consumer culture was inaugurated and institutionalised in the rise of department stores'.[13] Most of these stores were developing into expanded versions of their original drapers' shops; some, like Whiteleys of Bayswater, or the Army and Navy Stores, attempted to supply every material requirement of middle-class life, whether real or imagined, from pocket watches and picnic baskets to coal scuttles and maids' uniforms. In a sense, all of them helped to create and encourage aspirational 'lifestyles' predicated on the consumption of material goods and created a cultural role which gave form to the values of the bourgeoisie.[14] They became, in short, the new sites of consumption where images of the self could be constructed and acquired. Shields suggests that the stores themselves became 'key sites of cultural change'.[15] This could be explained both in terms of the goods that customers identified with and purchased, and of the modification of their social behaviour, particularly the new freedom that stores allowed women, one that both liberated them socially and also potentially enslaved them to consumption, a theme addressed by nineteenth-century novels of the department store.[16] As Rita Felski has commented, women could be seen both as 'objects of consumption' and 'consuming subjects, as … distinctively modern retailing strategies began to dramatically alter the everyday fabric of social relations between people and things'.[17] There was also a specific form of cultural change initiated at Liberty and Co., which had to do with shifting the frames of cultural reference.

12 McCracken, *Culture and Consumption*, p. 24.

13 Chaney, *Lifestyles*, p. 18.

14 See Michael B. Miller, *Bon Marché: Bourgeois Culture and the Department Store, 1869–1920* (London: Allen & Unwin, 1981).

15 Shields, *Lifestyle Shopping*, p. 16.

16 For a summary of work on the relationship of women and department stores see Mica Nava, 'Modernity's Disavowal: Women, the City and the Department Store', in Mica Nava and Alan O'Shea (eds), *Modern Times: Reflections on a Century of English Modernity* (London: Routledge, 1996), pp. 38–76, and Erika Rappaport, *Shopping for Pleasure: Women and the Making of London's West End* (Princeton, NJ: Princeton University Press, 2000).

17 Rita Felski, *The Gender of Modernity* (Cambridge, MA: Harvard University Press 1995), p. 63.

Marketing Culture at Liberty and Co.

The particular form of consumption promoted at Liberty and Co. emphasized the aesthetic over the functional qualities of material goods: decorative textiles and porcelain vases rather than bedsteads and saucepans. This was not a place where you would furnish a house for £100, as at stores like Shoolbred on Tottenham Court Road, but one where you could remake the image and style of both your home and your person in a particular, 'artistic' way. A review of the Liberty Company ten years after the founder's death made this continuing policy clear:

> The Company's goods appeal to a limited clientele and its business cannot be regarded from the angle of a big store such as Harrods, dealing in necessaries as well as luxuries and in goods which appeal to the vulgar as well as to the educated tastes.[18]

Thus, while Liberty and Co. was a large store with many departments, it aimed to be something other than a 'Universal Provider' of prosaic material needs.[19] Like other department stores, its social impact may have been, in Elizabeth Wilson's words, to assist 'the freeing of middle-class women from the shackles of the home', and permit, 'the concept of shopping as a leisure activity ... as a pleasure rather than a necessity'.[20] If the furnishing of basic material needs was not Liberty's promise, the refashioning of the self may have been an unstated one. In addition, there was a further agenda, the introduction of the British consumer to the material products of non-western cultures, as a means of reconnecting with the 'authentic' and handmade qualities of things lost in industrial processes.

This dichotomy of luxury and vulgarity – or perhaps necessity – in the culture of the department store echoes Pierre Bourdieu's concept of the struggle for cultural control and legitimacy, the 'distinction' of the cultural elite against the 'pretension' of an aspiring middle-brow culture, the recognition of that distinction and 'the effort to possess it',[21] and in particular the efforts of artists and intellectuals to define culture, 'the legitimate principle of domination'. In this site of symbolic struggle, according to Bourdieu, the taste-maker 'puts himself forward as a maker of higher rules', or new fashions.[22] In some ways this describes the efforts of Lasenby Liberty to suggest a new, non-traditional, non-western aesthetic, and to imbue the material goods sold in his shop with non-material, 'artistic' values.

Neither Liberty nor his contemporary, and in some respects competitor, William Morris, were working in a cultural vacuum in their attempts to redefine the parameters of taste. The late-nineteenth-century Aesthetic Movement created the intellectual justification, the artistic models and an audience with an appetite for 'artistic' goods. It also produced advice manuals on how to achieve an aesthetic home by authors such as Robert Edis, Lucy Orrinsmith, Eliza Haweis and even Oscar Wilde, with his

18 Liberty and Co, Internal Review, 1927. City of Westminster Archive.

19 'Universal provider' was the epithet adopted by William Whiteley of Baywater.

20 Elizabeth Wilson, *Adorned in Dreams* (London: Virago, 1985), p. 150.

21 Pierre Bourdieu, *Distinction: A Social Critique of the Judgement of Taste*, trans. Richard Nice (London: Routledge, 1986), p. 251.

22 Bourdieu, *Distinction* , p. 251.

notion of the 'House Beautiful'. Lasenby Liberty's undoubtedly genuine ambition was to assist the 'improvement' of taste by making goods with artistic integrity available to the public. His shop offered almost inexhaustible supplies of the key Aesthetic commodity, blue and white oriental porcelain, as well as Japanese screens, bamboo furniture, tastefully coloured textiles and clothing that harmonized with the furnishings. An essay in Liberty's 1887 catalogue made the powerful claim that, 'This is truly the home of aestheticism, and honour must be accorded to Mr Liberty for having fought the great "Art" battle for the present age.'[23] In 1896, the firm could boast that 'silk manufacturers are indebted to Messrs Liberty for their infusion of artistic feeling and spirit into the production of fabrics intended to satisfy a cultivated and reformed taste'.[24]

While Liberty, like Morris, reacted against the misconceived outputs of 'factory' production so blatantly exhibited at the 1851 and subsequent national and international exhibitions, his stated intention was to provide 'beautiful things' for a mass market, 'to secure the possibility of artistic surroundings being equally attainable by the patrician or artisan'.[25] This required intervention in the production process, which in terms of his key commodity, textiles, meant redeeming the primary product from the hands of irresponsible middlemen. 'Silken and stuff fabrics from the East were … being made for the European "taste"; gummed and stiff, cheapened and deteriorated in quality, glaring and fugitive in colours'.[26] His solution was to obtain naturally dyed, unstiffened silks that fell naturally, following the contours of the body. He reacted similarly against ostentatious Victorian furniture, favouring non-western models and hybrid or historically referenced pieces developed in Liberty's own workshops. Reacting against Paris-led fashions for women, the company developed alternative styles of clothing, dubbed 'permanent' or 'never out of fashion', and more suited to the soft fabrics and less formal surroundings of the 'Liberty' interior. Thus the Liberty woman was set above the merely fashionable one; she was confident with an alternative frame of cultural reference. It is not surprising that Lasenby Liberty admired the actress Ellen Terry, whom he claimed as both a customer and friend. The journal *Aglaia* had noted that a truly 'artistic' style of living did not stop at furnishings: 'The signs are many that the educated world is endeavouring to introduce beauty into its daily life; that the time is past when Art was supposed to mean pictures in frames. House decoration has made striking progress within the last thirty years ... but personal adornment very little.'[27] Liberty had already responded with its *avant garde* dress department and 'intention to make a continued and systematic attempt to establish an Educational School of Personal Adornment …

23 Liberty and Co., *Catalogue* (London, 1887), pp. 63–8.

24 Liberty and Co., *In Praise of the Needle* (London, c. 1896).

25 A. Lasenby Liberty, 'On the Progress of Taste in Dress: III In Relation to Manufacture', *Aglaia*, Journal of the Healthy & Artistic Dress Union, 3, 1 July 1893.

26 A.L. Liberty, 'On the Progress of Taste in Dress'.

27 *Aglaia* 3, 1893, Editorial.

indebted to M. Chevreul's admirable work *The Laws of Contrast and Colour*', thus appeasing the well-educated customer with both art and science.[28]

By 1905 the company felt it could claim that 'The extended knowledge of the laws of decorative art has reformed the taste of the nation … In the direction of refinement of taste in dress Messrs Liberty have had a powerful effect.'[29] Lasenby Liberty's approach differed from Morris's solution of selling hand-made and therefore expensive goods while attempting to provide meaningful work and decent conditions for their makers; he sought a wider market. Yet the company's attitude to mass production was inevitably self-contradictory, and comparable to the dilemma of today's luxury brands; while quantity was crucial to the existence of the department store or mass market, for competitive reasons, exclusivity had to be maintained. Lasenby Liberty argued that machine production was justified on democratic grounds as 'really artistic materials are now obtainable at modest prices, that there is no longer an economic excuse for the adoption of the vulgar or inelegant'.[30] Thus the Liberty store, as much as Morris and Co., was clearly intended as a site of cultural change. At Liberty the rare and beautiful was favoured over the showy or mass-produced goods which filled the catalogues of most department stores, but it could be bought at a variety of prices, 'from a shilling to five hundred pounds'; pieces of Japanese porcelain for a shilling each, or a sixteenth century 'Moorish' carpet.

In order to maintain an exclusive edge, there was a parallel suggestion that Liberty customers were buying something more than objects, they were buying cultural status, just as if they were patrons of fine art. In her discussion of Victorian art collecting, Dianne Sachko Macleod has noted that late-eighteenth- and nineteenth-century entrepreneurs tended to abandon aristocratic models of connoisseurship and 'recast the cultural system in their own image in an attempt to create a stable social category for their class'.[31] One model of alternative taste noticed by the ambitious young Liberty was the aesthetic embodied in the lives, indeed the lifestyles, of London's often wealthy bohemian and artistic social fringe, people identifiable by their ways of dressing and furnishing their homes, and with their 'Olympian' or superstar artists, Watts and Leighton, 'an irresistible magnet to press and public'.[32] Lasenby Liberty admired the unconventional tastes of artists in terms of decoration and dress, and capitalized on his association with them, admitting that 'My knowledge and appreciation of art were extended by prolonged visits to the studio of these [artists], where I was always made welcome.'[33] George Aitchison's Arab Hall for Leighton's

---

28 Liberty and Co., *Catalogue* (London, 1886–87). Michel Eugène Chevreul (1786–1889), was a French chemist; as director of the Gobelins tapestry works he turned his attention to the study of colour contrasts, which greatly influenced the Impressionist painters.

29 Arthur Fish, 'Dress and Decoration', Liberty and Co., *Catalogue* (London, c.1905).

30 A. L. Liberty, 'On the Progress of Taste in Dress'.

31 Dianne Sachko Macleod, *Art and the Victorian Middle Class: Money and the Making of Cultural Identity* (Cambridge: Cambridge University Press, 1996), p. 2.

32 Caroline Dakers, *The Holland Park Circle: Artists and Victorian Society* (London: Royal Borough of Kensington and Chelsea, Libraries and Arts Services, 1999), p. 2.

33 A.L. Liberty interviewed in the *Daily Chronicle*, c. 1913.

house in Holland Park, contemporaneous with the expansion of the Liberty shop, no doubt helped to provoke keen interest in its Middle Eastern merchandize. On his death, Lasenby Liberty himself was described in obituaries as a champion of unorthodox taste and an instigator of cultural change. He was 'The Man who Killed the Best Parlour', that bastion of Victorian domestic propriety with its antimacassars and overstuffed furniture, reflecting stuffy, conservative habits.[34]

Using Bourdieu's ideas, Macleod has suggested that Aestheticism offered an alternative cultural model to late-nineteenth-century collectors, who either could not compete with or rejected the elite cultural models of the aristocracy. Thus 'the Aesthetic interior was another route to establishing their middle-class identity ... Aestheticism's well-crafted and expensive looking objects served as easily identifiable markers for the socially mobile'.[35] These were the 'taste makers' proposed by Bourdieu, choosing the kind of objects retailed at Liberty, whether antique Chinese embroideries, silver designed by Knox or glass by Dresser. It could also be argued that Lasenby Liberty himself, like other Victorian merchants of modest social origin, was also redefining himself socially through cultural association, and discarding the taint of 'trade', enabled by his earned wealth and status to buy a large country estate and join the Buckinghamshire establishment as Deputy Lieutenant of the County, JP, and eventually achieve knighthood. Yet photographs of his own country house show a decorating style marked by its lack of ostentation, light colours and eclectic accumulation of objects.

Lasenby Liberty may well have recognized the 'fetishistic response of some collectors to Aesthetic works' suggested by Macleod,[36] for he encouraged the idea of connoisseurship. The Liberty catalogues, published from 1881, skilfully alluded to the possibility of providing access to the cultural elite by addressing potential customers as connoisseurs of rare artefacts. This was not shopping to buy status through ostentatious, expensive-looking objects, but through objects associated with art, antiquity and specialized knowledge. Merchandize was often, and justifiably, presented in the form of 'exhibitions', not as mere commercial displays of commodities; British silk, Burano fans, Indian embroideries were all given 'exhibitions' in the store, and Liberty sponsored other exhibitions in locations associated with contemporary art, such as the Hanover and Grafton Galleries. Among the *Ancient and Modern, Eastern and Western Art Embroideries*, exhibited at the shop in April 1894, for instance, was an 'antique Italian altar frontal' described as 'A unique example of the early XVI Century School. Taken by a French officer during the occupation of Rome by Napoleon in 1797, and afterwards sold by a member of his family, in 1873 to a gentleman residing in Madrid.' Furthermore, Liberty acquired patrons for these projects who had either cultural status, such as Sir George Birdwood of the India Office, or social cachet, such as the committee of aristocratic ladies persuade to join the campaign to promote English silk. This organization asked women 'to show their patriotism by refusing to wear, or use, anything but British-made dress silks and furniture brocades' and encouraged Liberty customers

34 Obituary of A.L. Liberty, *Daily Mirror*, 12 May 1917.

35 Macleod, *Art and the Victorian Middle Class*, p. 277.

36 Macleod, *Art and the Victorian Middle Class*, p. 289.

by emphasizing that they would be supporting 'The Ladies' Committee [which] numbers among its enthusiastic members and supporters the leaders of style and fashion in our nobility'.[37]

Although most of Liberty's merchandize was actually obtained through importers and wholesalers in London, the company gave the impression that it sourced the goods directly in 'exotic' locations and that they could not be obtained anywhere else. The company skilfully endowed its merchandize with meanings to the extent that some were represented as objects of veneration. Cashmere shawls, for example, were ascribed an incomparable heritage, described as 'some of the finest specimens of hand-work weaving that the world has ever seen … [they] may have been among the gifts presented to the Queen of Sheba by King Solomon'.[38] Examples of Kin-Kob, or cloth of gold, 'probably the most gorgeous material ever used for human apparel', were among the goods associated with particular cultural value, with ancient pedigree and association with both ancient and living royalty, 'extensively used at the present day by the Maharajahs and Rajahs of India for purposes of dress'.[39] This was not a question of truth but of emphasis. The word 'unique' appeared frequently in the catalogues, some of which resemble a fine art auctioneer's catalogue rather than that of a shop, implying specialized knowledge or appreciation on the part of the customer. The necessary background information was often helpfully suggested in the text; in turn, the goods available at Liberty were thus invested with the new kinds of social and cultural meanings suggested by Shields.

The challenge for Liberty and Co. was to retain this sense of authenticity and exclusivity for an elite market, while also appealing to a far broader one and supplying an ever-expanding shop with novel merchandize. At first this was achieved by sourcing unusual or 'exotic' goods in countries where hand labour was both skilled and cheap, namely India, Japan, North Africa and the Near East. Liberty effectively capitalized on the taste for the 'Orient' that was possibly 'the most important single external influence on the European decorative and applied arts in the second half of the nineteenth century'.[40] The artistic and commercial opportunities offered by the products of non-western cultures, were imbued in both shop and catalogues with the 'added values' of hand craft, rarity, ancient traditions, the image of the camel train and the faint odour of the harem. Oriental carpets were described as embodying, 'years of patient labour, deft and cunning workmanship, originality of thought, and centuries of artistic skill'.[41] Handcraft also endowed the merchandize with the uniqueness of art objects. The artisan nature of its range of Japanese pottery was emphasized: 'Few large factories, in our sense of the word, exist or indeed have never existed [in Japan]. The Potter in nearly all cases conducts *personally* the entire

37 Liberty and Co., *The British Silk Renaissance* (London, 1891).

38 Liberty and Co., *Ancient and Modern, Eastern and Western Art Embroideries exhibited by Messrs Liberty* (London, April 1894).

39 Liberty and Co., *Ancient and Modern*.

40 Elizabeth Aslin, 'Japanese Influence on 19th Century Decorative Arts', in Susan M. Wright (ed.), *Decorative Arts of the Victorian Period* (London: Society of Antiquaries of London, 1989), p. 74.

41 Liberty and Co., *Catalogue* (London, 1881).

process.'[42] Thus the Liberty customer, alluded to as discriminating and sophisticated, could become a patron of living artists and craft workers and at the same time, buy objects very similar to those favoured by well-known taste leaders, such as the blue and white oriental porcelain collected by the artists Whistler and Rossetti, who both shopped at Liberty, even though they did not actually pay their bills.

The Liberty Lifestyle

The merchandize at Liberty permitted McCracken's 'novel patterns of interaction between persons and things', and the shop environment certainly encouraged it. This was not just in terms of the physical experience of the store, or an invitation to sensual appreciation of the merchandize, but an invitation to experience cultural difference. Wearing a Liberty Japanese kimono, for example, was a significantly different experience to wearing upholstered Victorian dress, just as sitting on low cushions or the famous 'Thebes' stool, based on models from Egyptian antiquity, lacked the gravitas of Victorian drawing room furniture.

If 'lifestyles' are forms of personal expression achieved through the selection and use of certain commodities whose significance is recognized by one's peers, or how you live with what you buy, the Liberty store offered model experiences for rehearsing them. As Sean Nixon has shown in a more contemporary situation, customers are 'addressed and positioned' within shopping spaces designed to play on the narcissistic needs of the shopper.[43] With the Liberty merchandize offering a tangible experience of exotic, non-European cultures, the theatrical display environment of the store suggested an oriental *souk* or *harem* rather than a conventional department store with its orderly categories of gloves and hats and handkerchiefs. There was an inevitable emphasis on the self-image of the customer, with the potential of being different from the norm. The Liberty shop was described as a magical place, 'A veritable realisation of the palace of Aladdin, with the XIXth century supplemental advantage of brilliant electric illumination'.[44] A contemporary American journalist gave a vivid description of the shop in the 1880s, noting its apparently non-commercial otherworldliness, and the role of the shopper as a 'guest':

> The air is faintly perfumed with sandal and other scented woods … there are easy chairs and Turkish divans by the dozens and you are invited to rest yourself by a soft-slippered, noiseless young lady, who wears a pretty, draped apron of some art fabric, and has her head adorned with a silken cap or hair snood … No one even suggests that you purchase a single article and YOU ARE TREATED AS A GUEST.[45]

Thus shopping itself became a distinctive lifestyle experience; as Erika Rappaport has noted, 'Shopping was never synonymous with buying',[46] it was part of a new urban

42 Liberty and Co., *Catalogue* (London, 1881).

43 Sean Nixon, 'Have You Got the Look? Masculinities and Shopping Spectacle', in Shields (ed.), *Lifestyle Shopping*, pp. 149–69.

44 Press comment in Liberty and Co., *Catalogue* (London, c. 1890).

45 Annie Wakeman, 'The Opinion of an American Visitor', Liberty *Catalogues*, 1880s.

46 Rappaport, *Shopping for Pleasure*, p. 6.

experience, which both shaped and was shaped by shoppers. A century later, the Biba department store in Kensington offered a very similar experience to that described at Liberty, with an 'Eastern Casbah' on the ground floor 'selling exotic brass and other objects from the Near East', and where 'The comfortable velvet covered seating near the entrance was used by bored husbands and passers by, particularly Kensington's more elderly women, to rest on without making a purchase.'[47]

Both novelists and social historians have used orientalist metaphors to describe the seductive atmosphere of department stores; stores besides Liberty also had oriental-looking displays, but these were temporary affairs, passing attempts at novelty. The deliberately contrived and permanently exotic ambience set the Liberty store apart from its brasher competitors, even when it was rebuilt in the early 1920s. It was quiet, textured, and sensual – even the customer's sense of smell was appealed to, a feature now commonplace with our embrace of chemical 'fragrance' to evoke mood in commercial spaces. There was an 'Arab', later restyled as Tudor, Tea Room. This was an environment intended to sensually absorb the shopper and in which the shopper could re-imagine him or herself, for if the customer was to be transformed, this had to be done with calm and discretion.

The store also built up its own design studio, which, under the direction of Leonard Wyburd, trained as a fine artist, could execute complete interiors with 'Moorish arches, with fretwork tracery, across doorways and corridors'.[48] Room 'settings' enabled the customer to consider a variety of different 'looks': Japanese, Indian, Chinese, Arabian or Saracenic, and later a masculine Jacobean and other 'historical' styles. 'The adaptation of Eastern forms to English homes has been specially studied by Liberty and Co. and many beautiful rooms in town and country have been decorated by them', the 1895 *Handbook of Sketches* assured, announcing two drawing rooms in the Anglo-Arab style. 'The Galleries at Messrs. Liberty consist of a series of beautifully furnished rooms and represent an object lesson in period decoration.' Eastern or Saracenic designs could be 'modified to most European requirements.'[49] (See Illustration 4.3.)

Furniture made in the company's workshop, or designed by outsiders like Voysey, was complemented by the elegant if pseudo-historical ranges of silver and pewter ware named 'Cymric' and 'Tudric', designed by Knox and others. While nostalgic, these were also innovative in that they offered alternatives to the strict reproduction of old styles or the highly decorated surfaces associated with high Victorian style. 'Picturesque', or historically derived dress styles were introduced, many with a more 'English' theme, in harmony with the growing range of 'historical' furniture and interiors, such as *Henrietta*, a Charles II inspired 'home gown' of 1905. Liberty also developed a lighter touch in interior decoration with the use of plain wood, white paintwork and a restrained use of colour, also favoured increasingly by many Arts and Crafts designers. A Liberty employee recalled that the introduction

47 Anne Massey, 'Biba: Interior Lifestyles', in *BIBA: The Label, the Lifestyle, the Look*, p. 24.

48 Guy Bentley in *Liberty Lamp* (London, December 1930), p. 126.

49 Liberty and Co., *Catalogue* (London, 1912).

of lightweight curtain material was typical of the firm's revolutionary approach to home decoration.

> Stiff and starched propriety gave way to the soft draping of the Madras muslins which, first appearing in the early '80s, increased in popularity until they almost entirely ousted the older makes. At first they were always cream coloured, but by degrees soft pastel tints were introduced. Our firm became famous both for these goods and for the way they were draped and frilled.[50]

4.3 Liberty's 'Saracenic' Smoking Room suggested for a summer cottage, c. 1900. A 'Moorish' or 'Saracenic' style of decoration was thought to be masculine and suitable for the male preserves of large houses, such the smoking or billiard room; a 'Japanese' style was considered more feminine

'Own brand' goods of oriental appearance were increasingly produced in Liberty's furniture and garment workshops, or made by selected manufacturers. Work was commissioned from leading designers, giving the company an innovative edge in world markets, but the identity of these designers was almost always subsumed to the Liberty name. Thus, despite their disparate origins, and their widespread imitation, the goods sold by the company were recognizably 'Liberty', and not the equivalent of, say, a Jasper Conran range at Debenhams. A closer comparison today would be the anonymous use of designers by international fashion houses, where the identity of individual designers is usually sacrificed to the brand name and where fashion designers, or rather their brands, have expanded into cosmetics and home

50 Guy Bentley, *Liberty Lamp* (London, September 1930), p. 90.

furnishings, not only to subsidize the expensive couture trade, but to encourage consumers to buy in to a whole range of branded products.

So who bought into the Liberty 'lifestyle'? In 1889, the *Woman's World* characterized the Liberty store as, 'The chosen resort of the artistic shopper', depicted 'fingering … the art stuffs and fade silks shown her with a certain amount of reverence expressive of the artistic yearnings of her soul'. Her home is done out harmoniously and her clothes form an integral part of the picture:

> We may be tolerably certain that such an one has her drawing-room arranged in the very last scheme of colour – cool silver grey, possibly, in conjunction with yellow terra-cotta, or the new red-brown with the faintest, palest of olive-greens; the floor in parqueterre, with rich eastern rugs laid down on it, furniture in dark wood, Moorish style; three-legged tiny tables, yellow, white or pale green; graceful palms in huge pots of Eastern pottery in beaten iron stands, a fretwork arch in wood dividing the double rooms. Imagination further conjures up the lady herself in a tea-gown of silver-grey *pongee* cashmere, with full-front of yellow Surah …'.[51]

This was a customer defining herself as 'artistic' through the possibilities of consumption, an idea cultivated by the store; her deliberations about colour could be those of a painter with palette in hand, but also bring to mind advice in present-day decorating publications, endlessly advising on 'matching' colour schemes. Annie Wakeman's comment that 'The eye is rested on all sides with groupings and arrangements of goods worthy of the Studio of an Artist', was among many press comments reproduced in the store's catalogues, intended to reinforce this concept. Yet, despite this Du Maurier-ish image of desperate aesthetic aspiration, Lasenby Liberty, who subscribed in general terms to the naturalistic ideals of dress reform, suggested that women of independent mind might patronize his shop, women who might abandon tight lacing and experiment with unorthodox ways of dressing themselves and their homes. 'Personal choice is freely exercised, and grace and variety developed quite independently of prevailing fashions', he wrote.[52] (See Illustration 4.4.) One contemporary commentary expressed gratitude for this liberating possibility, with an intentional pun on the Liberty name:

> Think what slaves we were to the gentlemen who bought for us in the early seventies! They liked to see their own womankind in black satin brocade and bombazine … Then came Liberty, and can anybody be but grateful for that relief?[53]

The department store was often associated with various forms of depravity: debasement of taste, shoplifting, the questionable morality of female shop assistants, the destruction of family life through the practice of both live-in staff and the idea of women shoppers neglecting families in their quest for luxury.[54] But at Liberty,

51 A.E. Eliot-James, 'Shopping in London', *Woman's World*, II (1889), pp. 5–9.

52 A.L. Liberty, 'On the Progress of Taste in Dress'.

53 *Olivia's Shopping and How She Does It: A Prejudiced Guide to the London Shops* (London, 1906), pp. 50–1.

54 See Geoffrey Crossick and Serge Jaumain, *Cathedrals of Consumption: The European Department Store, 1850–1939* (Aldershot: Ashgate, 1999), p. 6.

quietness and respectability set the mood; the store provided a sober yet seductive framework within which conventions of taste could be subtly transgressed without moral or social reputation being at stake.

4.4 The educated Liberty woman, dressed in 'permanent fashion' in harmony with the contemporary furnishings, from *Dress and Decoration*, 1905. This catalogue, illustrated by A.E. Howarth, contained an essay by Arthur Fish noting that 'the extended knowledge of the laws of decorative art has reformed the taste of the nation'

The shop attracted an influential clientele, including men. Besides well-known artists, Liberty's (recorded) male customers included the philanthropist Andrew Carnegie, impresario Richard D'Oyly Carte, James Morton of the textile firm Alexander Morton and Co. and W.R. Cassels, a retired East India merchant. He commissioned 'Jacobean' interiors from Liberty for his house in Harrington Gardens, South Kensington, designed by architects George and Peto, with elaborate plasterwork ceilings and panelled walls. Aristocratic patrons included George Howard, Earl of Carlisle, artist and friend of the Morrises, and the Earl of Iveagh who bought a large number of carpets from the shop for his orientalized Suffolk mansion, Elveden Hall. The Maharajah of Baroda had the Brighton Pavilion decorated by Liberty for a ball in the winter of 1887–88. Politicians, diplomats and several generations of the royal family shopped there, confirming its fundamental respectability. Lord and Lady Aberdeen, respectively diplomat and philanthropist, commissioned an entire 'Eastern' music room for a charity bazaar at their house in Grosvenor Square.

While it is evident that the company did a good trade in complete, custom-fitted interiors during the late nineteenth century, the majority of customers are more likely to have bought individual objects, assembling something of a Liberty 'look' over a period of time. Illustrations in the catalogues suggested the equivalent of the 'cosy corners' popular in late Victorian and Edwardian Britain but done in exotic style, with *Musharabiyeh* latticework panels, *portières* created with oriental rugs or textiles, brass trays, brass hookahs, or Japanese fans and screens depending on the theme chosen. 'To those who like to be very Japanese' advised *Woman's World*, one of the many new magazines offering advice on how to choose from the bewildering array of cultural styles available in the shops, 'I may recommend a not unpleasing form of semi-transparent window-curtain of bamboo and coloured threads. The effect is quaint and thoroughly Oriental.'[55] The 'oriental' interiors available from Liberty were both literally and metaphorically a construct, just as the merchandize became increasingly hybridized. More suggestively than actually oriental, they satisfied the taste for exotic surroundings while remaining acceptable in an English, middle-class home.

From Lifestyle to Brand

Despite the inevitable changes and differences of meaning over more than a hundred and fifty years, it seems clear that the modern concept of 'lifestyle' was effectively being marketed on Regent Street by the 1880s. Liberty and Co. suggested the 'novel patterns of interaction between persons and things' suggested by McCracken; through its displays and its catalogues it was loading new social meanings onto goods, with 'sophisticated devices for meaning transfer' and 'new opportunities for defining self and the world' through new styles of luxury. The shop, in short, can be seen as one of the 'key sites of cultural change' of the expanding metropolis. Lasenby Liberty also understood how to initiate a wide spectrum of customers into an apparently elite store in the smartest shopping area of London, by providing something for everyone. In the same way, to expand their markets, the purveyors of luxury brands today, 'are all creating luxury products with price points that appeal to the growing market of middle-class consumers who … want to trade up'.[56]

In proposing alternative styles of dressing the person and furnishing the home, Liberty was recognizing the emergence of new middle-class consumers. Non-

55 *Woman's World*, May 1888, p. 96.

56 Kate Betts, 'Luxury Fever', *Time: Style and Design* (Fall 2004): 52–8.

European furnishings could bypass traditional class associations in furniture that underlay the popularity of imitation or reproduction furniture. The 'oriental' interior represented one form of experimentation with consumption, and at a moment when alternative 'styles' were subverting accepted rules of taste, there may have been a growing recognition that 'lifestyle' was a purchasable commodity. As the *Daily Telegraph* commented in the 1880s, 'We live in an age of Eastern magnificence without its history. We are as luxurious as Sultans without their faith … we ask Liberty to bring us the glories of soft colours imagined by the artists and Indian looms.'[57] Liberty was offering 'oriental' luxury to the middle class consumer, often at a relatively modest price. A warning against the *faux pas* of attempting to create the Liberty effect on the cheap, however, was sounded by the cartoonist George Du Maurier, whose 'Upper Tooting Housewife' gets her furniture (over) upholstered locally, in imitation of Liberty. Her visitor, undeceived, murmurs, 'Oh Liberty, Liberty, how many crimes are committed in thy name!'.[58]

Liberty and Co. outsold and outstayed many competitors. It was effectively run by the founder and a close-knit, reliable group of directors, it used up-to-date marketing methods such as advertising, catalogues and mail order, had a thriving wholesale business and paid attention to public relations. The company not only invested in design and merchandize, but in stocks and property, which enabled the redevelopment of the shops in the 1920s. While the business was in many ways conservative, running the same product lines for years on end, it was also innovative, to the extent of abandoning the 'native producers' it at first promoted so enthusiastically and by developing new design ideas. The benevolently patriarchal structure of the company was typical of many contemporary businesses including department stores. Until the 1920s, although the store was spread out among various premises on Regent Street, it provided an integrated atmosphere where the elements of an artistic and orientalized home could be acquired. It became a site for consumption in a modern sense, a century before Biba opened her doors on a department store with a *fin-de siècle*, 'Liberty' feel, combined with nostalgia for the 1930s.

During the last quarter of the nineteenth century, the company's financial success was matched by a very modern skill in managing its identity. The Liberty name became a trademark, defended by lawsuits where necessary, and specially designed typefaces were used. The man himself became so closely identified with both his business and his merchandize that he said, 'I have become a mere adjective.'[59] This anticipated the current association of family names such as Prada and Missoni with fashion brands today, and the business remained in the ownership and artistic control of the Liberty family for 125 years.

The twentieth century saw a more uneven development of the Liberty style. In the 1950s, after a period generally characterized by creative stasis, the company was committed to post-war modernist design, with a more contemporary 'lifestyle' on offer. In the spirit of the times, high-quality, modern Italian and Scandinavian design

57 *Daily Telegraph*, quoted in Liberty and Co. *Catalogue* (c. 1885), p. 55.

58 *Punch*, 20 October 1894.

59 Interview with A.L. Liberty, *Daily Chronicle*, c. 1913.

was emphasized. Around the time of its centenary, in the late 1960s and 1970s, Liberty was again notable for a brilliant revival in its textile designs.

In the twenty-first century, the store itself has, under new ownership, lost some this recognizable identity. The Liberty name as a brand still has worldwide recognition, but not in the sense of modern 'superbrands' such as Coca-Cola or Nike or Gucci. It is also questionable whether the merchandize offered by the company still has the aesthetic integrity and sense of purpose to support its historic reputation. While the shop continues to sell unusual and luxurious domestic goods in an atmosphere of exclusivity, the 'Liberty' brand tends to be limited to a nostalgic application of historic surface patterns. Whether the contemporary business can maintain its individual identity as a brand in a super-competitive global market and to continue to offer a distinctive 'lifestyle' is another issue. While continuing to trade on its 'difference', in 2002 the store committed itself to becoming 'a treasure house of new and niche designer brands'[60] – possibly at the expense of its own.

60 *Drapers Record*, 2 February 1902.

Chapter Five

'Artistic and Commercial' Japan: Modernity, Authenticity and Japanese Leather Paper

Yasuko Suga

Introduction

Interior design is a medium of cultural transplantation. In the late nineteenth century, when *Japonisme* was prominent in western art and design and, as John MacKenzie has argued, 'popular Orientalism' was at its height, 'pseudo-oriental' objects and furniture as well as 'authentic' oriental crafts filled domestic living spaces.[1] Yet the apparent distinction between the 'pseudo-oriental' and the 'authentic' was a nuanced and permeable association. Indeed, some notionally 'authentic' objects were the commercial outcome of 'pseudo-western' influences. The interplay between these cultural perspectives can be examined through the material culture of Japanese leather paper, a commodity that sought to combine Japanese craft techniques with western demand to produce a highly decorative and commercial material.[2] In this chapter, the production and retailing of Japanese leather paper is examined in order to illuminate how objects of cultural hybridity were perceived by both British and Japanese homemakers.

Initially, the production of Japanese leather paper was stimulated by two foreign imports: tobacco, first imported in the sixteenth century, and Spanish leather introduced in the first half of the seventeenth century. Both commodities were shipped through Nagasaki during the period of Japan's national seclusion and it soon became fashionable amongst the upper classes to have tobacco pouches, purses and small boxes made of Spanish leather. Spanish leather, however, was rare and expensive, and experiments to imitate it through traditional Japanese papermaking techniques were encouraged. The first successful 'pseudo-leather paper', Tsuboya-gami, was

1 John M. MacKenzie, *Orientalism: History, Theory and the Arts* (Manchester: Manchester University Press, 1995).

2 In Japanese, leather paper made with tin foil are called 'Kinkarakawa-gami' or 'Kinkawa-gami' (literally 'golden, foreign-origin leather paper'), and the rest, more generally, 'Gikakushi' (pseudo-leather paper). No distinction was made between the two commodities abroad, all being known as 'Japanese leather paper', 'Japanese imitation leather', or even more simply 'Japanese leather'.

made in 1684 in the Ise district.[3] By the beginning of the nineteenth century, there were firms in several parts of Japan.

After Japan was forced to open its doors to the world in 1854, western merchants eagerly looked for marketable Japanese products – trade was, of course, the most pressing reason why the western nations urged Japan to open up. In turn, the Japanese government promoted exports to gain foreign exchange and to encourage industry. The manufacture of imitation leather 'wallpaper' thus developed out of both sides' speculative interests. The product was mainly exported abroad and tapped into the demands of aesthetic-conscious western consumers looking for 'authentic' Japanese goods. From the outset, British companies forged the strongest links with the production of Japanese leather wallpaper. In contrast, domestic and public architecture in Japan utilized leather paper in order to project the legitimacy of westernization.

This chapter considers the influences upon process of designing and consuming Japanese leather paper in both Japan and Britain. It addresses the politics of national and international representation via domestic objects and discusses the notion of 'authenticity', which was associated with the domestification of Japanese leather paper in Britain and with the projection of 'modernity'.

British Responses

The first British diplomatic representative to Japan, Sir Rutherford Alcock, was greatly impressed by Japanese leather paper. He had, for example, 'difficulty in believing an imitation of the Royal Arms of Holland' executed in paper. Indeed, when Alcock volunteered to act as the charge person for Japanese exhibits at the International Exhibition of 1862, he selected many 'imitation leathers', emphasizing their potential domestic use and that British 'upholsterers might consult with advantage to themselves and their customers.'[4] This was the world debut of the paper craft.

After the exhibition, William Burges, William Godwin, Christopher Dresser, Frederick Leighton and others, who had developed a strong appreciation for oriental aesthetics, bought parts of the Japanese exhibit. Burges, a significant intermediary between British and Japanese architectural practices, considered the Japanese section to be 'most medieval'[5] and was especially attracted by Japanese paper which not

---

3 Kume Yasuo, Kinkarakawagami to Gikakushi [Kinkarakawagami and Pseudo-Leather Paper], (Kami-no-Hakubutsukan, 2003), p. 14. The first person who succeeded in making leather paper was Horiki Chujiro from the Ise district. He reinforced the existent paper with oil, strongly pressed it from both sides to make it deeply textured, and applied some colour and embossed patterns. This paper, known as Tsuboya-gami, was used for tobacco pouches that sold very well as souvenirs to visitors to the sacred Ise Shrine. As paper had no harmful connotations in Buddhist and Shinto culture, Tsuboya-gami pouches were ideal replacements for leather that was associated with killing.

4 Sir Rutherford Alcock, KCB, DCL, *Art and Art Industries in Japan* (London: Virtue & Co., 1878), pp. 229–30.

5 Toshio Watanabe and Sato Tomoko (eds), *Japan and Britain: An Aesthetic Dialogue 1850–1930* (London: Lund Humphries in association with the Barbican Art Gallery and

only imitated embossed leather but was also dexterously coloured in gold, bronze and other finishes.[6]

Although western consumers acknowledged the artistic quality and variety of use of Japanese leather paper as early as the sixteenth century,[7] commercially it remained of little importance. At the Second Paris Exhibition of 1867, Paul Balin, a French wallpaper manufacturer, produced a 'papier cuir repousse' that was widely acclaimed, whereas comparable Japanese and Chinese papers were generally criticized as 'imperfect', expensive and unprofitable.[8] It was only at the Vienna Exhibition in 1873 when the increased quality and variety of Japanese papers began to be a topic of interest and praise.[9] By then techniques had become more refined: stronger paper was used, the printing process was enhanced by the finer carving and printing of wood blocks, and very fine gold leaf and urushi lacquering was also applied.

Behind the success at the Vienna Exhibition was a critical change in the production of leather paper brought about by a British foreign expert, Arthur Stanhope Aldrich. Aldrich was in the service of the Meiji government [*oyatoi*] and worked for the Japanese Ministry of Engineering. In 1871 he suggested to a Tokyo-based paper-manufacturing company, Takeya, that larger sheets of leather paper would be fit for wallpaper use.[10] In Japanese traditional houses, there was no equivalent of European 'wallpaper', as framed and papered sliding doors [*fusuma*] were used as room partitions. The idea of wallpaper itself, therefore, was a western one. Following this advice, Takeya began producing sheets for use as carpet and wallpaper material: at the Vienna Exhibition, the firm exhibited 162 'leather wallpaper' sheets besides other types of leather paper. Several companies from Tokyo, Ise, Mutsu and other major papermaking districts also exhibited various kinds of leather paper and leather paper goods.[11] The British at once showed particular interest in it and it was reported in Japan that '1700 pieces of leather-like paper carpet were exported in Meiji 6 [1873] to Britain, at the price of 34 yen'.[12]

The production of leather wallpaper in Japan was energized as demand grew. This was encouraged by Christopher Dresser, a British designer and botanist, who, after visiting Japan in 1876 and noticing the use of Tsuboya-gami in the Ise

Setagaya Art Museum, 1991), pp. 17–22.

6 *Catalogue of the Exhibition: Japonisme* (Tokyo: National Museum of Western Art, 1988), p. 214.

7 Luis Frois, *Kulturgegensatze Europa-Japan, 1585* (Tokyo: Sophia Universitat, 1955).

8 *Bericht uber Die Welt-Ausstellung zu Paris im Jahre 1867* (Vienna: Wilhelm Braumuller, 1869), p. 262.

9 Sir Rutherford Alcock became a director of Japan Paper-Making Company Ltd established in 1873, but this company became inactive by 1879. Public Record Office BT31/1844/7216.

10 Takeya's leather paper goods were based on leather paper called Youkan-gami produced in Mito, Mutsu district.

11 Tanaka Yoshio, *Oukoku Hakurankai Shutten Mokuroku* [List of Exhibits at Vienna International Exhibition] (Tokyo, 1873).

12 *Yushutsu Bikou Daiissatsu* [First Volume of the Notes on Export], Okura-sho Kiroku-kyoku [Department of Recording, Ministry of Finance], Oct. 1885 (Meiji 18), p. 2124.

district, stressed the merit of its application as wallpaper. 'If this was to be used in Europe,' Dresser noted, 'it should be thinner and larger, and elegant patterns should be applied on the surface.'[13] With such international support, larger sized leather paper explicitly designed for wallpaper use began production in the Ise district.[14] Both at the Philadelphia Exhibition (1876) and at the Third Paris Exhibition (1878) where Japanese leather goods received several awards including a silver medal for Takeya's product, the characteristics of strong and beautiful leather paper were greatly admired. In the Japanese official report for the Third Paris Exhibition, the keen interest from Britain received a special mention: 'This kind of paper is exported to Britain in quantity, where, it is told, they use it for interior decoration.'[15]

Why Britain? Firstly, a main source of paper manufacturing in Britain had been old rags. However, by the mid nineteenth century, demand for printed media such as books, newspapers and magazines meant that there was a distinct lack of materials. Detailed research on Japanese paper manufactures using wood pulp and on the use of paper was commissioned in 1865, and in 1871 the British minister to Japan, Sir Harry Smith Parkes, submitted to Parliament the *Reports on the Manufacture of Paper in Japan*. In this report Parkes mentioned that 'imitation leathers' prepared by Takeya and another company were used for 'making boxes, purses, pocket-books, tobacco-pouches', as well as 'in the various modes of room-decoration', such as wall-papers (he must have meant papers used for *fusuma*), screens, panelling and covering boxes 'by the upper classes'.[16]

Why interior decoration? At that time, the population in Britain was steadily increasing and in the latter half of the century there was a housing boom among the middle class. Accordingly, demand for interior decoration for these new houses was created.[17] In addition, there was a desire for anything 'artistic' at home, largely because, as John Gloag has argued: '[o]rnament appeased the anxious appetite of the new rich and the prosperous middle classes for visible evidence of their social status',[18] Interior decoration thus increasingly became a mode of self-expression.

---

13 Ishida Tametake, *Eikoku Dokutoru Doresseru Doukou Houkokusho* [Report of the Accompanied Trip with Dr Dresser from Britain] (1877). Dresser later wrote on the making of Japanese leather paper. See C. Dresser, *Japan: Its Architecture, Art, and Art Manufactures* (London: Longman, 1882), pp. 174, 453.

14 The processes and designs differed in each district. In Ise, Horiki's firms were good at producing textured paper, with Japanese motifs. In Tokyo, cherry-wood cylindrical rolls were used, engraved with more westernized patterns. Horiki's firms sent some workers to Tokyo to learn the Takeya methods.

15 *Meiji Ju-ichi-nen Hutsukoku Hakurankai Shuppin Mokuroku* [List of Exhibits at the Exhibition in France in Meiji 11(1878)] (Hutsukoku Hakurankai Jimukyoku, Meiji 13 (1880)), pp. 30–1 ; *Les Marveilles de L'Exposition de 1878* (Paris, 1878), p. 242.

16 Sir Harry S. Parkes, *Reports on the Manufacture of Paper in Japan. Printed to both Houses of Parliament by Command of Her Majesty. 1871* (London: Harrison and Sons, 1871), p. 22.

17 See W. Hamish Fraser, *The Coming of the Mass Market, 1850–1914* (London: Macmillan, 1981).

18 John Gloag, *Victorian Taste: Some Social Aspects of Architecture and Industrial Design, from 1820–1900* (Newton Abbot: David & Charles, 1972), p. 136.

As the *Furniture Gazette* commented: '[t]he furniture, the carpet, even the curtains, express the people who use them'.[19]

The circulation of such significant domestic goods was supported by a new kind of retailing system – department stores such as Whiteley's (est. 1863) and Liberty's (est. 1875).[20] A.L. Liberty's shop was quick in importing Japanese leather. When William Godwin visited Liberty's in 1876, he remarked that Japanese leather was displayed on one of the walls 'since it was first imported, where it can be seen by any one', and that it was commonly 'used as a wall paper in new houses'.[21] The oriental material was located in what Godwin famously called 'a Japanese warehouse'. As Godwin continued:

> To an architect one of the most interesting modern imports from Japan is the leather-like embossed paper made in pieces twelve yards long and one yard wide … Among these papers there is one – a broad pattern of dark green meandering foliage on a gold ground – which is extremely beautiful, and, properly placed, might be well used in almost any style of building, and would of itself give a style to a house that had none.[22]

What he saw was in fact typical Japanese leather paper sheets. Whilst Godwin remained somewhat sceptical about the practicality of Japanese leather as widely employed domestic wallpaper, he was very quick in applying some smaller-sized sheets as inset panels to his renowned 'Anglo-Japanese' sideboard of ebonized wood.

In the same year as the Third Paris Exhibition, the Japanese government recognized Japanese leather as a profitable export industry and began production at its Printing Bureau. In 1879, the Printing Bureau factory exported '600 pieces of thick leather paper' and '300 pieces of thin leather paper' to 'Tiffany and Company in New York'.[23] This ushered in a period when the Japanese government sought to increase the production of export goods through the establishment of a network of national factories. The spirit of expansion was expressed by the politician Okubo Toshimichi, one of the key figures in Japan's modernization, who argued that national strength depended upon popular prosperity which itself related to the 'abundance of production'. To Toshimichi it was 'the duty of government officials, wholeheartedly and skilfully on the basis of actual conditions, to encourage industry and increase production and thus secure the foundation of wealth and strength without delay'.[24] The government decided to invest 18,000 yen in establishing a wallpaper factory for

---

19 'Household Art', *Furniture Gazette*, 24 July 1875, p. 38.

20 For department store culture, see Bill Lancaster, *Department Store: A Social History* (Leicester: Leicester University Press, 1995) and Erica Rappaport, *Shopping for Pleasure: Women in the Making of London's West End* (Princeton: Princeton University Press, 2000).

21 E.W. Godwin, FSA, 'I. A Japanese Warehouse', *The Architect*, 23 December 1876, p. 363.

22 Godwin, 'A Japanese Warehouse', p. 363.

23 *Insatsukyoku Koujou Dai 6 kai Hokokusho* [6th Report of the Factory of the Printing Bureau], (Meiji 13 [1880]), p. 45.

24 'Shokusan Kougyou ni kansuru Kengi-sho' [Proposal for Industrial Promotion] (Meiji 7 [1874]) in *Okubo Toshimichi Bunsho*, vol. .5, (Tokyo: Daigaku Shuppankai, 1968), p. 561.

the Printing Bureau of the Ministry of Finance (in charge of printing postal stamps and banknotes) in order to refine and improve the quality of further export. One of the main problems with the product was, as Sir Rutherford Alcock had noted, '[t]he difficulty of getting rid of the smell of the oil or varnish used in the manufacture' and this remained 'the chief obstacle to the substitution of this article in Europe'.[25] In addition, initial batches of leather paper were sullied with an efflorescence, what Godwin described as 'some whitish stuff', that appeared on the surface of the goods.[26] To counteract this, several printing machines were imported from France and Germany,[27] and in 1880 the production of leather wallpaper and the pigments for lacquer and metal-foil began.[28]

The government lost no time in sending samples of this newly improved Japanese leather paper to the Melbourne International Exhibition (1880).[29] Meanwhile, the *Furniture Gazette* in Britain soon reported on the 'Imperial Factory of Yokohama' and how 'the Japanese seek to turn their imitative faculties to account'.[30] Indeed, the production of leather paper was an attempt to make an authentic, national product out of 'imitation'. This may be analogous to the contemporary credit Japan receives as 'masters of theme parks', reproducing leisure and sightseeing spaces in some ways, as David Boyle observes, '*better* than real'.[31]

Mediating the Exotic: Rottmann, Strome and Co.

Many merchants, and especially British merchant houses, regarded Japan as a land that promised new business opportunities. More than half of the foreign merchants in Yokohama (the main site of foreign settlement) were from Britain, beginning with Jardine, Matheson and Co.'s operation at Yokohama 1. However, the combination of severe conditions and competitive markets meant that many merchants soon went bankrupt. Under these circumstances, Rottmann, Strome and Co. established in 1880 with offices both in London and Yokohama, emerged as the key dealer of Japanese leather paper.

The company started as a general partnership; a collaboration between a trade agent in Japan and a wallpaper manufacturer in Britain. C.J. Strome, who was 'very knowledgeable about Japanese goods',[32] came to Japan in 1877 starting

---

25 Alcock, *Art and Art Industries in Japan*, p. 229.

26 Godwin, 'A Japanese Warehouse', p. 363.

27 *Okura-sho Insatsukyoku Hyakunennshi* [A Hundred Years of the Printing Bureau of the Ministry of Finance] (Okurasho Insatsukyoku, 1972), p. 325.

28 *Insatsukyoku Enkakuroku* [History of the Printing Bureau] (Insatsukyoku, Meiji 40 (1907)), p. 176.

29 Information kindly supplied by Professor Miles Lewis, University of Melbourne, Australia.

30 'Japanese Wall-paper', *Furniture Gazette*, 21 February 1885, p. 150. This article was based on the information in the article 'Japanese Wall Paper', *Decorator and Furnisher*, February 1885, p. 163, published in New York.

31 David Boyle, *Authenticity: Brands, Fakes, Spin and the Lust for Real Life* (London: Harper Perennial, 2004), p. xiv.

32 Ishida, *Eikoku Dokutoru Doresseru Doukou Houkokusho*, p. 174.

C.J. Strome and Co. as the agent and manager of Londos and Co. of which Christopher Dresser was Art Director. Alexander Rottmann, a member of the Japan Society in London, was 'a man of taste' who was 'widely travelled in Japan', and knew 'how to distinguish the pretentious sham from the real meritorious work'.[33] Connoisseurship in art manufacture was a good sales point at this time as 'artistic' taste was greatly valued. As the *Cabinet Maker and Art Furnisher* commented:

> A most remarkable change has of late come over the English mind generally in respect of art ... The sense of being, as English people, at last alive to this thing called art is immensely exhilarating. Young ladies of both sexes and all ages, formerly the meekest of all meek Philistines, are now seen rushing about after a medley of fanciful design, Japanese, Georgian, advanced ecclesiastical, and much more, not only so wildly as to astonish their friends and admirers, but so courageously as to indicate the gravest social consequences. It is wholly unphilosophical to laugh at this aestheticism.[34]

In fact, the word 'art' was so overused in society that goods entitled 'art fabrics' and 'art wallpapers' were frequently advertised. With such prevailing conditions, a developed sense of artistic taste was considered necessary to judge correctly the quality and authenticity of art manufactures from shams.

Rottmann, Strome and Co. started discussing trade with the Printing Bureau when it began manufacturing Japanese leather wallpaper in 1880.[35] However, whilst other companies entered into direct trading agreements in these early years,[36] Rottmann, Strome and Co. preferred to ensure that adequate quality control mechanisms were in place. It was only in July 1884 that the company secured an exclusive contract with the Printing Bureau to sell 1,000 rolls of wallpaper every month for 6 years, thus gaining an absolute advantage over their competitors.[37] As well the government contract, Rottmann, Strome and Co. had links with a number of other independent factories and, although they were not the first to focus on leather paper,[38] their diversity and firm business grounding in Japan ensured their longevity. By 1885, the quality and quantity of leather paper marketed by Rottmann, Strome and Co. showed noticeable improvement. As an American trade journal commented, the market had

33 *Furniture Gazette*, 1 April 1885, p. 226.

34 'A Party of Taste', *Cabinet Maker and Art Furnisher*, 1 November 1891, p. 100.

35 In this year, Strome and Co. bought a large quantity of paper from the Printing Bureau factory. *Insatsukyoku Koujou Dai 8kai Houkokusho* [8th Report of the Factory of Printing Bureau], p. 707.

36 Between 1882 and 1883, a Dutch company in Yokohama, von Hemert, P.H. bought several thousands of leather paper pieces in 1882 and 1883; and a Swiss company, Siber and Brenwald (Yokohama) bought over 260,000 pieces. A London-based 'Jorushii aaru Uushii' (unidentified) that started trading leather paper in 1881 exported 13,500 pieces in 1883. See *Insatsukyoku Kojo Hokokusho*.

37 Insatsukyoku Enkakuroku, *Okura-sho Insatsukyoku Hyakunennshi*, p. 139. From 1883, C.J. Strome and Co. and Rottmann, Strome and Co. were both registered at the address of 'Yokohama 28'. By 1888 only Rottmann, Strome and Co. were active.

38 In Britain the Leather Paper Company was established in 1882 for manufacturing leather paper and parched papers etc., but it was liquidated after two years: Public Record Office, BT31/3053/17347.

grown to such an extent that 'some ten years ago small pieces of an oily smell were imported and sold at prices at which a whole roll of twelve square yards can be obtained for now'.[39]

Within a year of establishment, Rottmann, Strome and Co. was widely known for its specialty of 'Japanese leather paper'.[40] Their 'spirited catering for this department of art work' was 'recognized throughout the kingdom' and 'a large sale for such an admirable work of art' was predicted.[41] The company soon expanded its branches to Glasgow, New York and Kobe. The vigorous expansion of their business can be seen from the contemporary description of their five-floor London store. The third and fourth floors were used as stock and cutting rooms for Japanese wallpapers. On the first floor, Japanese bric-a-brac, Satsuma and Imari ware porcelain, lacquer ware and other oriental furniture were displayed, and on the second floor there was a collection of screens and leather paper rolls. It was estimated that on this floor, 'no less than two hundred and sixty miles of leather paper were stored in the racks'.[42]

This was certainly the time when leather paper, and Japanese art manufactures in general, were in great demand. Rottmann, Strome and Co. gained a gold medal at the International Health Exhibition (1884), and a silver medal at the Antwerp Exhibition (1885). Stimulated by this success, another company – Cocking and Co. based in Yokohama – commissioned 20,000–30,000 rolls of leather paper from the factory of the Printing Bureau in 1886, the year in which the art dealer Siegfried Bing opened a branch office in Yokohama.[43]

Charles Holme's Visit to the Printing Bureau Factory

Rottmann, Strome and Co.'s leather paper was shipped to London and supplied directly to a host of retailers.[44] One notable retailer was Holme and Co., a company established in 1879 by Charles Holme, a founding member of the Japan Society in London, the founder of *Studio* magazine and a good friend of A.L. Liberty. Holme and Co.'s direct trading with the Printing Bureau was first recorded in 1882 when several hundred pieces of Japanese paper were bought.[45] Although they were not recorded as 'leather paper', Holme seemed to have a particular interest in the product. At the 1883 Furniture Exhibition in London, the company provided a variety of oriental interior decoration packages presented in the form of generic room styles – 'Constantinople' for the Turkish collections and 'Canton' for Chinese examples, for instance. The Japanese exhibit, 'Yokohama', had walls decorated with 'stamped

39 'Japanese Leather Paper', *The Decorator and Furnisher*, July 1885, p. 114.

40 A.V. Sugden, *A History of English Wallpaper 1509–1914* (London: Batsford, 1925), p. 227. Rottmann, Strome and Co.was known in Japan as a major dealer of silk textiles (Habutae).

41 *Journal of Decorative Art*, April 1884, pp. 490–2.

42 Cabinet Maker and Art Furnisher, 1 February 1886, pp. 213–14.

43 *Okura-sho Insatsukyoku Hyakunennshi*, p. 325.

44 Retailers included the Decorators' Supply Co., Paper Stainers and Manufacturers of Cordelova and A. Sanderson and Co.

45 *Insatsukyoku Koujou Dai 11 kai Houkokusho* [11th Report of the Factory of Printing Bureau], p. 73.

leather paper and hanging pictures' and was equipped with an array of furniture and rugs.[46]

In 1889 Holme in the company of the Libertys and the painter Alfred East travelled to Japan. The highlight of his tour, the thing he was 'most interested in', was a visit made with Liberty to the 'government papermaking factory'.[47] C.J. Strome showed Holme around, and he spent some time examining and sketching the process of its production in detail. Holme's account of the Printing Bureau factory, with some sketches of his own, is significant because it is the earliest account of the processes of leather paper manufacture. No contemporary Japanese record survives.[48] His observation was precise, and matches with the description illustrated in an article on 'Japanese Leather Paper and How They Are Made' in the *Journal of Decorative Art* in 1890. (See Illustrations 5.1 and 5.2.)

5.1 Manufacturing Japanese Leather Paper: beating the pulp into the roller

46 'Guide to the Furniture Exhibition', *Cabinet Maker and Art Furnisher*, 23 April 1883, p. 12.

47 Charles Holme's Japan trip diary, manuscript, p. 330, Archives of Art and Design.

48 See also Félix Régamey's visit to the Yamaji Wallpaper Company in 1899: F. Régamey, *Japon* (Paris: P. Paclot, 1903).

5.2 Manufacturing Japanese Leather Paper: stencilling the colour

First, sheets of coarse paper were steeped in alum water until thoroughly soaked, then in rice water. An engraved wooden roller was placed upon a rack, and the steeped sheets of paper were placed upon the top of the roller. A couple of boys with a long-handled brush in each hand hit the paper with very rapid strokes until it was embossed thoroughly in the hollows of the wooden roller. The sheets of paper were arranged to overlap each other, and in this way a continuous roll of any length could be made. The paper was then dried in the sun, and was placed upon a table where the surface was lacquered with a large brush. While still tacky it was covered with sheets of tin foil, which was first rolled by a hand roller and then dabbed with a soft brush until it lay well within the cavities of the design. After drying in a damp room, the tin foil was lacquered giving it a golden hue. The paper was then coloured, either by hand, or by placing stencils over the pattern and any imperfections in colour were amended manually. Finally, the paper was thoroughly dried before it was ready for market. Holme emphasized the efficiency of the well-organized division of labour at the factory where, importantly, the workers looked 'very clean' and 'artistic'.[49]

In 1885 Holme and Co. changed ownership to become Mawe and Co.,[50] although Charles Holme himself retained a close relationship with the business. Mawe and Co. also dealt in Japanese leather wallpaper. In 1888, for example, they advertised a 'heavily embossed Japanese leather paper in new designs and colourings', and in 1889, 'highly embossed leather paper screens for dining rooms'.[51] George Sale, who had worked for Holme and Co.'s Yokohama branch office from 1881, continued to work for Mawe and Co., before establishing his own trading company in 1892 in Japan. Sale greatly helped Holme when he travelled in Japan, and later visited Holme at the Red House, the former home of William Morris. In fact, Holme may

49 Holme's diary, pp. 329–33.

50 William Mawe bought Holme and Co. for his son Frederic H. Mawe in 1885.

51 See Mawe and Co.'s advertisements in the *Journal of Decorative Art*, 1888, 1889.

have applied Japanese leather paper to one of the drawing room walls at the Red House while he lived there: one of the photographs he took shows that the wallpaper used for the drawing room on the first floor was heavily embossed.[52]

Editing 'Japan': 'Authentic' Craft, Cultural Representation and Exotic and Domestic Modernity

By the late 1880s there was already criticism that the quality of Japanese goods had dropped.[53] It was observed that: 'Japanese art has, in some branches, undergone in recent years a decided deterioration, in consequence of the demand in Europe and the United States for cheap and abundant art products.'[54] Against these criticisms, Rottmann, Strome and Co. emphasized the 'authenticity' of their goods, and the quality control they exerted over their products. When Holme visited the government factory, Strome informed him that other makers did not lacquer their papers and that the unlacquered ones were therefore not as durable as the company's products.[55] Their sales point was that their products were 'hand-made' and that 'no machinery [was] employed either in the fabrication of the paper itself, or in the printing'.[56] In addition, and a crucial consideration for the European market, Company factories were 'all worked by natives'.[57]

However, the emphasis on an 'authentic Japan' was deceptive, as it was constructed from a decidedly western and, moreover, British perspective. Whilst traditional Japanese motifs such as flowers, birds and fans were applied, the patterns most frequently used included typical Spanish leather motifs such as angels, grapes, birds and acanthus leaves. It was proudly reported that:

> They [Rottmann, Strome and Co.] have entered into special arrangements, by which the Government factory at Tokio is worked under their special supervision, while even the patterns, although designed by native artists, are not carried out until they have received Messrs. Rottmann's *imprimatur*.[58]

In essence, Rottmann, Strome and Co. wanted 'native' quality in material and handicraft production, but a mixture of oriental and western influences in design. In 1887, for example, the company was praised not only for preserving an authentic Japanese-ness, having 'wisely … determined to take advantage of the native taste

---

52 See Y. Suga and S. Ashmore, 'Red House and Asia', *Journal of William Morris Studies* (2006).

53 Edward Burne-Jones deeply lamented the deterioration of Japanese traditional art brought about by British bad taste. E. Burne-Jones's letter to Arthur Liberty, 1897, Liberty Archives, Westminster City Archives, 788/164/6/1/.

54 *Furniture Gazette*, 1 January 1887, p. 2.

55 Holme's diary, p. 333.

56 *Furniture Gazette*, 1 April 1885, p. 225.

57 *Furniture Gazette*, 4 April 1885, p. 226.

58 *Furniture Gazette*, 4 April 1885, p. 226. A similar view is expressed in the *Journal of Decorative Art*, April 1884, p. 490.

and talent', but also for an ability to 'direct it into grooves more in consonance with our Western notions'.[59]

Japanese art manufactures were, from the early stage of production, *edited* by British merchants for the singular tastes of the British market. As the *Cabinet Maker and Art Furnisher* announced, 'a careful appreciation of British requirements has caused them to educate their native artists and workmen into producing things which, beside adding beauty to our English homes, are really useful adjuncts to furnishing'.[60] Similarly:

> A knowledge of British requirements has enabled them [Japanese producers] to bring not only papers, but all sorts of other things, into accordance with our insular taste – without sacrificing essential Japanese characteristics – and thus many articles which were at one time purely ornamental have been brought within the range of utility.[61]

Thus, it was found that in practice a design which was 'Japanese but not "too Japanese"'was what was most desired by architects and decorators.[62] Whilst authorship was assured in terms of authenticity and provenance, the visual appeal of this design was firmly set beyond the country of origin.

The somewhat patronizing tone of such British trade magazines implies an imperialistic, hierarchal perspective. But how did it fit with the quest for 'authenticity'? David Cannadine's argument in *Ornamentalism* (2001) sheds an interesting light on the matter. Cannadine points out that Said's conception of 'Orientalism', dealing with the formation of the image of the other, cannot fully explain British imperialism. Britain wanted to retain some similarities with its colonial territories, and the Empire sought to replicate a familiar and domestic element within architecture and town planning. The system of Empire was supported by this power to domesticate the aspect of representation.[63] Yet, whilst the Empire expanded, a xenophobic tendency developed concurrently in Victorian society.

Cannadine's argument can be applied to the visual culture of Victorian Britain, in which diverse and competing 'styles' – not only Gothic but also Anglo-Greek, Anglo-Japanese, Anglo-Chinese, and even Anglo-French influences – were incorporated. This process of nominally anglicizing style may be considered as a political act of domestication through cultural representation. These styles revealed a desire to identify Britain with foreign and exotic elements, whilst simultaneously projecting the inequality of power relations inherent in imperialistic association. The expansion of Britain's imperial power was thus literally experienced in the 'domestic' setting of interior decoration at home.

This can be associated with what Richard Grove has termed 'green imperialism'. When new plants were imported from colonial habitats and planted in Kew Gardens,

59 'Japanese Leather Papers and Modern Wall Decoration', *Supplement to the Journal of Decorative Art*, March 1887.

60 *Cabinet Maker and Art Furnisher*, 1 February 1886, p. 214.

61 *Cabinet Maker and Art Furnisher*, 1 September 1888.

62 Japanese Leather Paper', *The Decorator and Furnisher*, July 1885, p. 114.

63 David Cannadine, *Ornamentalism: How the British Saw their Empire* (London: Penguin, 2001).

for example, they were bred and 'improved' so as to take root in British soil, thus physically completing the act of appropriation and possession.[64] At a more domestic level, the boom to grow plants at home or to have scenic wallpaper with exotic designs disciplined and sanitized foreign nature.

How is Japanese leather paper to be contextualized in the process of domestication? Firstly, from the beginning the product was created to identify itself with the West both by Japan and by the West. Also, its luxurious golden colour and motifs based on nature matched the contemporary aesthetic trend that introduced many oriental elements not in themselves restricted to Japan. In Rottmann, Strome and Co.'s strategy to retain 'nativeness' in material and that of 'mixed blood' in design, a will to domesticate was recognizable.

Secondly, Japanese leather fulfilled not only the feeling of domestic imperialism but also the practical conditions of modernity. Unlike fans and screens, Japanese leather paper was not simply a handicraft; it was also designed as a product that would stand the western measure of what was modern civilization. Japanese leather was advertised as 'clean', 'strong to damp', 'washable' and also 'non-arsenic' – a precondition for a health-conscious modern life. Hygiene and health were key features promoted by Rottmann, Strome and Co. at the 1884 International Health Exhibition in London. As the *British Architect* reported:

> The claims of the exhibit on the judges were not alone the artistic effects of their work, but also the ingredients of the manufacture, and the wall-hangings of the firm were pronounced to be absolutely free from arsenic and non-poisonous materials. The Hangings are washable, and permanent in colour effect.[65]

The company was awarded Golden and Copper medals at the exhibition and gained an international reputation by representing modernist ideas of 'practicality' and 'cleanliness'. (See Illustration 5.3.) Besides such features, another modernist ideal was 'economy'. The company's highly embossed papers were 36 inches wide and retailed at around 55 shillings per piece. This ensured 'a handsome profit to the decorator' and yet remained 'extremely reasonable in price compared to materials of a like nature'.[66] With this in mind, the *British Architect* was effusive in its praise:

> We wonder how the practicability of using these Japanese leather papers comes home to middle-class householders. Do they realize that, at a cost of 2s. per yard, a yard width of this admirable wall-covering may be obtained retail? Thus a small room is provided with a dado, which is about everlasting in wear, at a cost of some 36d. or 40s.[67]

At the Centennial International Exhibition in Melbourne (1888–89), Rottmann, Strome and Co.'s exhibits were commended as 'in all respects unique' and were awarded a First Order of Merit for the 'great variety of highly-embossed designs

---

64 See Richard Grove, *Green Imperialism: Colonial Expansion, Tropical Island Edens and the Origins of Environmentalism, 1600–1860* (Cambridge and New York: Cambridge University Press, 1995).

65 'Some Japanese Wall Coverings', *The British Architect*, 7 November 1884, p. 224.

66 *The Journal of Decorative Art*, April 1884, p. 492.

67 'Some Japanese Wall Coverings', *The British Architect*, 7 November 1884, p. 224.

of rare artistic merit as to depth and brilliancy of colours, combined with several economic qualities as to price and durability'.[68] Such attractive economic features ensured that the product was widely adopted. In Whiteley's catalogue of 1885, for example, 'leather paper' was priced from 5 to 60 shillings per piece. In Liberty's advertisement of 'Japanese Furniture and Decoration', 'Leather Paper for Wall Decoration' was available at the highly affordable rates of between 2 shillings to 2 shillings and 6 pence per yard.[69]

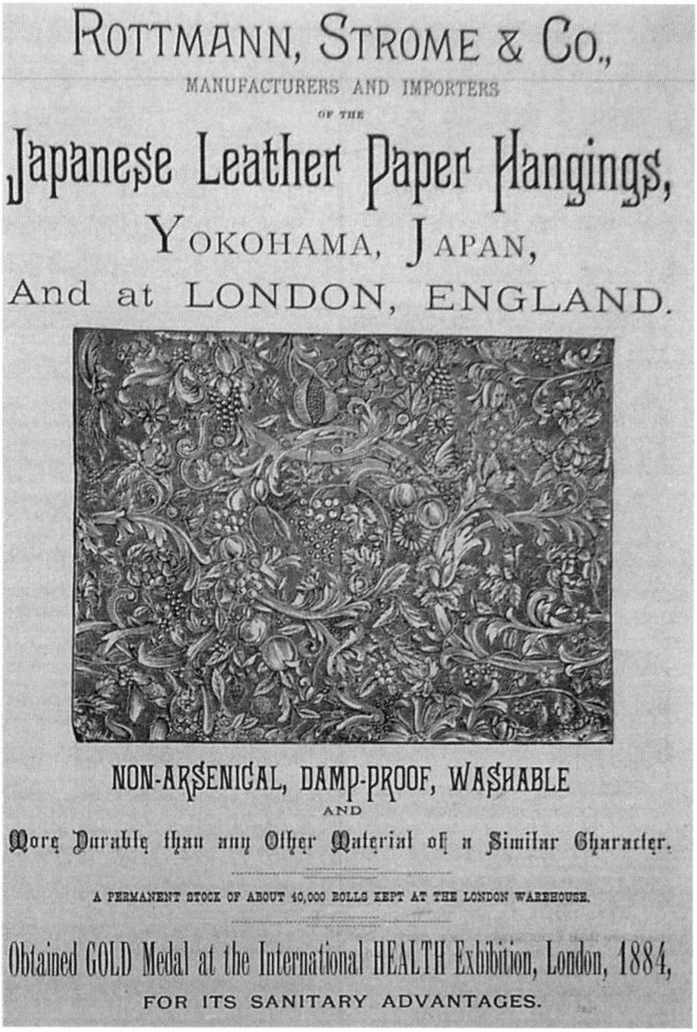

5.3 Rottmann, Strome and Co., advertisement for Japanese Leather Paper Hangings

68 *Official Record of the Centennial International Exhibition, Melbourne, 1888–1889* (Melbourne: Sands & McDougall Ltd, 1890), p. 728.

69 Liberty Archive, 788/36/1/10.

Authentically Western-Minded: Representing Modernity in Japanese Buildings through Imported Japonisme

When artefacts domesticated abroad are in turn utilized in their country of origin, the cultural signs forged by this multi-layered process of transplantation are complex. This was the case with Japanese leather paper, which was increasingly used to freight notions of 'modernity'. In essence, Japan wanted to improve the tariff situation and to stand on equal terms with western countries. In order to project Japan as a modern and civilized country, western-style architecture was used as a prominent political medium in the Meiji period (1868–1912) and Japanese leather wallpaper was frequently utilized in such spaces. For Japan, the fact that the leather paper industry gained recognition at international exhibitions symbolized the country's growing modernity as measured by western standards.

Representing westernized or modernized Japan again needed a British foreign expert. Josiah Conder, an architect and a member of the Japan Society who worked as a foreign expert in Japan, was pivotal in this context. Conder came to Japan in 1876 after study at the University of London and a short period working for William Burges. Conder was commissioned to plan Rokumeikan [Deer Cry Pavilion], a socializing hall for domestic and foreign celebrities, which was completed in 1883 at 40,000 yen over the original budget of 100,000 yen. This building, 'a representational limbo' in Toshio Watanabe's phrase, symbolized the period of 'pseudo-westernization' [Giseiyoka].[70] One newspaper reported that the interior was 'impeccable' and 'supremely decorated, with much dexterity'.[71] Charles Holme visited this hall, mentioned in his diary as 'the club', several times at Conder's invitation. The original interior is not known, but when Conder refurbished it in 1897 Rottmann, Strome and Co.'s leather paper was used.[72] In a similar fashion, Conder also employed the company's leather paper to add touches of the western to other projects. For example, the guest room of the former Iwasaki residence (completed 1896) – a group of buildings that contained both western (Jacobean) and Japanese-style design – was papered with the company's products.[73]

It was not only Conder, but also his Japanese students who took the initiative in using Japanese leather paper in their architectural projects. In this, a British-Japanese association was again evident. For example, the important Japanese

70 Toshio Watanabe, 'Josiah Conder's Rokumeikan: Architecture and National Representation in Meiji Japan', *Art Journal*, 55 (Fall, 1996): 21–7. Also see Cherie Wendelken, 'The Tectonics of Japanese Style: Architect and Carpenter in the Late Meiji Period', *Art Journal*, 55 (Fall, 1996): 28–37.

71 'Yubin-Hochi Shinbun', 17 Sept. 1884 (M16), in *Meiji Nyusu Jiten* [Meiji News Encyclopedia], vol. III.

72 The rolls used for this building are now in the Paper Museum, Tokyo. On one of the rolls the letters 'R.&Co.' are engraved.

73 The building was designed for Iwasaki Hisaya, the third lord of the Mitsubishi Financial Group. The rolls used for the building are also kept at the Paper Museum, and on one roll the letters 'R&Co.', and on the other, 'R.S.&CO' are engraved.

architect, Sakurai Kotaro,[74] was highly influenced by Conder's work. When Sakurai rebuilt the earthquake-hit Kure Commander-in-Chief's residence in Hiroshima in the English half-timbered style in 1905, he applied Japanese leather paper on the walls of the guest room, dining room and drawing room as well as along the corridor from the entrance to the hall. Another of Conder's students, Satachi Shichijiro, also used Japanese leather in his masterpiece, the Otaru Branch of the former Nihon Yusen Co., Ltd. (1904–06, Hokkaido) in the Renaissance style.[75] Interestingly, these Japanese architects experienced British Japonisme and absorbed a western orientalist perspective through Conder and Burges, re-applying such elements to Japanese architecture in pseudo-western architecture. It was, in a way, a re-importation of British-style Japonisme, through which Japan professed itself as authentically western-minded. (See Illustration 5.4.)

5.4 Kure building: designed by Sakurai Kotaro

When expensive Japanese leather paper was used in private buildings, it was often for the upper and upper-middle classes who had opportunities to entertain

74 Sakurai Kotaro initially worked under Tatsuno Kingo and Conder before graduating from the University of London in 1893 with the highest mark, and becoming the first Japanese ARIBA. In 1893 he returned to Japan and briefly joined Conder's office before working for the navy. He is best known for the Marunouchi Building (1923) and Seikado-Bunko (1924).

75 The carved roll used for this building is also kept at the Paper Museum, with the engraving 'R.S.&CO'.

foreign visitors. For example, both Hakone Rikyu Palace designed for the Emperor's family and an 'uninteresting semi-European looking house' according to Charles Holme[76] and Hayashi Mansion (Nagano), built in a pure Japanese style in the late 1890s and early 1900s for a prosperous family with business interests in the filature industry used Japanese leather paper extensively.

Japanese leather paper continued to be a barometer of modern national power: an authoritative way of defining 'conspicuous consumption'. The ultimate example was Parliament. Established in 1936 after over seventeen years of construction, Parliament was built in the kind of neo-classical style that suggested simplicity and modernist straight lines and was much favoured by British official architecture in the early twentieth century. Tatsuno Kingo was partly involved in the design.[77] The building was made of top quality domestic materials (except for the stained glass, doors and a post which could not be manufactured domestically), amongst which Japanese leather paper was selected.[78] On one level, to use Japanese leather paper was to represent national identity; on another level, it was a product that could manifest the attainment of a desired western standard. Japan took it as a representation of westernization, while the West took it as a representation of Japan: exoticism working on these local and global levels was the characteristic of the product.

The Consumption of Japonisme in Britain

To Oscar Wilde, Japan was best understood as a virtual entity, 'a mode of style' or 'a pure invention', which emerged only through the consumption of arts and crafts.[79] Wilde admired Japanese leather paper for its richness and beautiful effects, praising it as better than any other English wallpaper in terms of beauty and utility. (See Illustration 5.5.) When in 1885 he asked Godwin to refurbish the interior of his 'House Beautiful', casting away Pre-Raphaelite and Morrisian effects, Japanese leather was used on the ceiling of the drawing room. The 'Japan gold paper' for the drawing room, the study, and the bathroom cost him £12.[80] Yet, apart from Wilde, who else were the actual consumers of Japanese leather, and how was the product used in domestic arenas?

One way to investigate consumption is to consult the business records of contemporary interior decorators. A major source for this are the daybooks of Holland and Sons, a firm of established London interior decorators who on average had around 450 customers in the late 1880s; precisely the period in which Rottmann,

76 Holme's diary, p. 313.

77 Tatsuno Kingo was another of Conder's students who had previously studied under Burges in England in 1880–81.

78 The roll used for this occasion is kept at the Paper Museum.

79 Oscar Wilde, 'The Decay of Lying', in *The Works of Oscar Wilde* (New York: AMS Press, 1980), vol. 10, pp. 53–4.

80 H.M. Hyde, *Oscar Wilde: A Biography* (New York: Farrar, Straus and Giroux, 1975), p. 99; R. Ellmann, *Oscar Wilde* (New York: Alfred A. Knopf, 1988), p. 256.

Strome and Co. was most active.[81] From these sources, it is clear that well-to-do, bourgeois customers were prominent in ordering Japanese leather paper products. In 1883, a single reference to 'leather paper' ordered to decorate a screen, is recorded, although the country of the product's manufacture is not stated. By 1884, however, orders for specifically 'Japanese leather' become more distinct. For instance, Ker Seymer expended £16 10s on 6 pieces of Japanese leather paper at 55s each, and also acquired 1 piece of English leather at £5 5s for the entrance wall. In the same year, another customer bought French leather paper at 21s per piece to be used for the wall of his library.[82] In 1885, the Duchess of Buccleuch bought 14 yards of Japanese leather for £3 3s, whilst an unnamed customer ordered French leather paper for the dados of a staircase and library. In 1886, a company at Piccadilly used two types of 'Japanese paper' which was most probably leather paper judging from the prices. Also in 1886, Prince Edward bought a leather paper screen for £16 18s. In 1887, Lady Caroline Turner used 7 pieces of 'heavy embossed Japanese paper' at the price of 42s per piece for her dining room wall.

5.5 Rich interior decoration with Japanese Leather Paper

81 See Archives of Art and Design, AAD/1983/13, Holland and Sons, Cabinet Makers and Upholsterers Records.

82 Usually, the price range of a piece of wallpaper (21 inches in width and 12 yards in length, equal to 7 square yards) was from around 1s 6d, and flocked or partly gilt wallpaper was around 36s.

The customers of Holland and Sons who ordered leather paper for interior decoration purposes tended to live in exclusive residential or commercial areas like Hyde Park or Piccadilly. This was mirrored elsewhere. For example, a Mr Watts of Springfield used Rottmann, Strome and Co. wallpapers in his main entrance hall, the walls of which, it was reported, 'from the skirting to the cornice are covered with a rich and highly-raised Japanese leather ... in buff and old lacquered gilding.'[83] Indeed, such was the demand for Japanese leather paper outside the metropolis that Rottmann, Strome and Co. opened a branch in Glasgow. From the example of Watts's use of Japanese leather paper, it is also noticeable that the product was almost exclusively limited to the more public areas of the house. The *Journal of Decorative Art*, for example, recommended the application of Japanese leather paper for the ceilings of entrance halls, a most conspicuous domestic space.[84] In addition, the product was often used in dining rooms, libraries and studies. Such areas formed either 'front stage' locations where people commonly entertained friends and visitors and showcased their most refined goods, or were, occasionally, more private chambers where male members of the family dominated.[85] (See Figure 5.1.)

Figure 5.1 Country of origin of leather paper sold by Holland and Sons, 1883–93

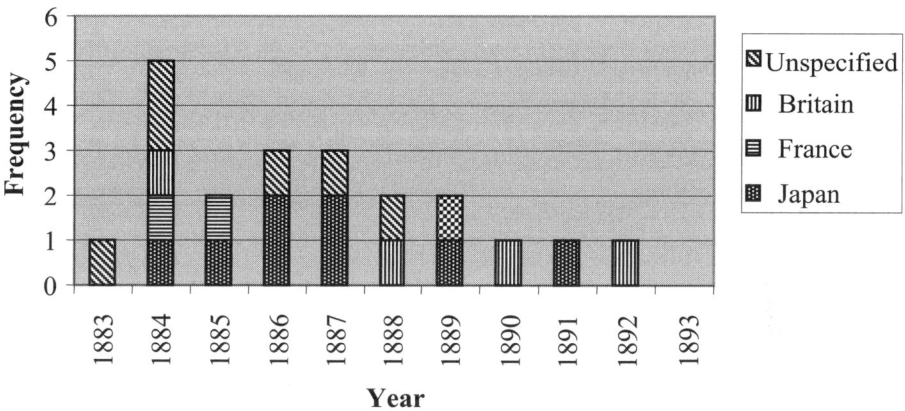

83 *Furniture and Decoration*, 1 May 1891, p. 69.

84 'How to Decorate a House, with Use of Materials. The Entrance Hall', *Journal of Decorative Art*, March 1888, p. 33.

85 For a discussion of 'gendered rooms', see Juliet Kinchin, 'Interiors: Nineteenth-Century Essays on the "Masculine" and the "Feminine" Room' in P. Kirkham (ed.), *The Gendered Object* (Manchester: Manchester University Press, 1996).

Table 5.1 Japanese manufactures bought through or repaired by Holland and Sons, 1883–93

Year	Sales	Repairs	Freq.
1883	Panelled cabinet Panel	Screen panelled with leather paper	3
1884	Walnut teapot stand with Japanese lacquer work panels Panels (x2) leather paper screen (x3)	Stands	8
1885	Japanese leather paper Japanese paper 1 roll Japanese hand-painted paper (4 kinds) Japanese flower stand Japanese metal vase		5
1886	Screen Japanese paper 2 kinds (white and gold; yellow and gold) Window screen panelled with real Japanese nets 4 fold Japanese leather screen A circular base for a Japanese vase Japanese paper for ceiling,	Japanese chair Cabinet	8
1887	Japanese paper Screen (x 2) Japanese paper panel Japanese imitation leather screen Leather screen, backed with leather paper Japanese paper Embossed Japanese paper Paper	Screen in Japanese paper Japanese painting in silk	11
1888	4 fold screen A fancy bamboo screen Own Japanese paper on walls as frieze Japanese plate Japanese rug A bamboo screen	Japanese cabinet (cleaning and re-polishing)	6
1889	Japanese rug 2 Japanese plates 8 Japanese vases A Japanese screen Screen in Japanese leather paper	Japanese blind (fixing) 4 fold screen (repair)	7
1890	2 pieces Japanese paper 2 Japanese trays		2
1891	Japanese carved stool with marble slab Japanese paper wall	Japanese embroidered table cover (lining)	4
1892		Japanese silk panels	1
1893			0

Holland and Sons's daybooks suggest that Japanese leather paper enjoyed a brief but intense wave of popularity. As Table 5.1 and Figure 5.1 emphasize, by 1886–87 Japanese leather paper had displaced French merchandize, a trend that coincided with a marked increase in the frequency of all types of Japanese wares ordered from Holland and Sons. However, this distinct taste for Japonisme in British middle-class consumer culture was progressively diluted by the impact of British-made 'leather paper' from the later 1880s. These goods were mostly produced by Jeffrey and Co.. The company had already commissioned a major Arts and Crafts designer, Walter Crane, to fashion an 'old Venetian leather' wallpaper which had attracted much critical attention at the Paris Exhibition of 1878.[86] In 1885, Jeffrey manufactured a new set of leather paper patterns designed by Crane that won a Silver Medal at the Invention Exhibition in the same year.[87] Lacquered or painted embossed leather papers in high relief cost from 8s a yard, whilst transparent lacquers on a metal background were from 3s 6d a yard.[88] The product duly found ready customers. In 1888, Lord Hindlip used Jeffrey's embossed leather paper for his dining room, as well as heavy embossed leather paper for the entrance hall. In the following year, too, Jeffrey's leather paper was used for a frieze. In 1892 Prince Edward also used Jeffrey's leather paper for his Salon and corridors at Sandringham Palace alongside more conventional English wallpapers.

The sales of Japanese goods through Holland and Sons fell dramatically in the early 1890s. By 1891, there is only a solitary reference in the day books to Japanese leather paper – a Mr Hunt being quoted for work including 'carefully sponging Japanese wallpaper' in the library, 'carefully sponging, stopping & touching up the leather paper on walls and Lincrusta dado under' in the entrance hall, and 'preparing for hanging with Japanese paper' in the drawing room. No purchase was recorded and there was no further reference to Japanese leather in 1892. By 1893, no Japanese objects at all featured in Holland and Sons' records.

The decline in trade implied by Holland and Sons's business records coincided with a change in Japanese economic policy. In order to curtail expenditure, government factories were privatized, and the country returned to protectionism. Accordingly, the trade structure of leather paper production changed. In June 1890, the Japanese government disposed of the wallpaper business when the six-year contract with Rottmann, Strome & Co. expired. The business was acquired by Yamaji Ryozo, Chief Manager of the factory, who rebranded the enterprise Yamaji Wallpaper Manufacturing Company.[89] Rottmann, Strome & Co. continued to trade with the new concern, until dissolving in 1892.[90] In 1893, Strome set up an independent company, registered as the 'Agent of Yamaji wallpaper company', which maintained an office

86 *Illustrated catalogue of the Paris International Exhibition*, 1878, p. 88.

87 *The Art Trades' Review*, June 1888, p. 7. Crane's leather paper, 'The Golden Age', was featured by Lewis F. Day in his article 'The Choice of Wall Papers', *The Decorator and Furnisher*, September 1892, p. 217.

88 *The 'Victorian' Wall-Papers, Embossed Leather-Papers, Staircase Decorations, Ceiling Papers Manufactured by Jeffrey & Co.* (undated).

89 The Yamaji Company stopped making leather paper in 1937 when it was amalgamated into another paper-making business.

90 *Insatsukyoku Enkakuroku*, p. 23.

in Yokohama.[91] Similarly, Rottmann and Co. continued in business, keeping a branch office in Yokohama until 1912, and moving its British base from St Mary Axe to Garlick Hill where the manufacturing and retailing of wallpapers continued.[92] In 1895, Rottmann and Co. enlarged their showrooms, building on their investment in fashionable Art Nouveau wallpapers, which were designed by Arthur Silver of Silver Studio, John Scarratt Rigby and Harry Napper.[93] I. Marians and Co., which took over the St. Mary Axe building, may also have acquired the stock of Rottmann, Strome and Co.[94] The company traded with Japan via their agents, Sale and Co., until 1897.[95] It is notable that the consumption of Japonisme in the West was largely supported by horizontal networks that existed between these small-scale companies, which were in terms of both human and material resources, based on the agency house system.

Conclusion: 'Artistic and Commercial Japan'

Both in Japan and in Britain, Japanese leather paper was used in interior decoration for the purpose of conspicuous consumption. The process of modification or the 'breeding' of the visual features of this product was layered with cultural connotations as it was transplanted reciprocally between the two countries.

Japanese leather fell out of fashion by the end of nineteenth century, because as soon as the government factories were sold off to private manufacturers, machinery was introduced, the quality of the production dropped and foreign demand accordingly declined. However, the peak of Japanese leather exportation was in 1898,[96] way after

---

91 The Strome family continued in business until 1934. The company diversified into silk, becoming Keen, Strome and Co. on the death of C.J. Strome in 1914. In 1923, the company reverted to the title Strome and Co., ceasing trading in 1934.

92 Rottmann and Co. moved again in 1906 to Lambeth Palace Road and at the same time closed the Barnes factory, selling the block tables and blocks to the Wall Paper Manufacturers Ltd. The company suffered a series of commercial setbacks during the First World War and thereafter Alexander Rottman became more preoccupied with town planning (see the *Times*, 16 September 1929). Rottman died in 1931.

93 'The Rottmann-Silver Studio Stencils', *Journal of Decorative Art*, July 1895, p. 152; 'Rottmann & Co. in 1896', *Journal of Decorative Art*, January 1896, pp. 35–6; Sugden, *History of English Wallpaper*, p. 227.

94 I. Marians and Co. opened a Japanese branch office in 1877 at the same address with Londos and Co. and C.J. Strome and Co. (joined there by Sale and Co. in 1893). See *Cabinet Maker and Art Furnisher*, October 1896; *Furniture and Decoration and Furniture Gazette*, 16 November 1896; and *Furniture and Decoration and Furniture Gazette*, 16 August 1897. From 1897, I. Marians and Co was succeeded by M. Marians and Co., and from 1901 this became Priest, Marians and Co. They continued to trade in Chinese and Japanese fancy goods into the twentieth century.

95 Sale and Co. started to deal with machines and became an importer of American machinery especially after they became Sale, Fraser and Co. in 1904. By 1909 the company was a major importer of Ford automobiles.

96 *Shigyou Zasshi* [Journal of the Paper Industry], 5 April 1919 (Taisho 8), cited in Kume Yasuo, *Kinkarakawagami to Gikakushi*, p. 48.

British consumption, as suggested from the Holland and Sons's daybooks, had been satiated. The demand for Japanese leather paper remained buoyant in North America and Australia until the beginning of the next century, and it is likely that the export peak may have mirrored robust consumption in those areas. By then, other countries such as Russia, China, Germany and Canada had begun to import the product not via London, but directly from the Yamaji Company in Japan.[97] Also, within Britain, whilst the fashion for Japonisme waned amongst the upper-class clientele who patronized Holland and Sons, it was still found to be desirable amongst more lower-class customers looking for cheaper decorative versions. Around this time, the number of advertisements for cheaper leather paper screens appearing in *The Times* increased, suggesting easier availability and more routes for consumption, but not necessarily products of the same craft quality.

There were some other major reasons for the decline in demand of Japanese leather paper in Britain. One factor was the emergence of powerful competitors. In 1877, Lincrusta wallpaper, which was cheap and easy to emboss, was introduced. Oscar Wilde used Lincrusta, alongside Japanese leather, and Dresser even provided the Lincrusta Company with a design that looked like Japanese leather.[98] There were also the competing products of Jeffrey & Co. The situation was not limited to Japanese leather paper: from the late 1880s to the 1890s, many artists and designers influenced by Japanese forms produced similar patterns for wallpaper, such as for Crane and Day. The wide availability of standard pattern books of Japanese design, such as William Watt's *Art Furniture from designs by E.W. Godwin, F.S.A. and others* (1877), Thomas Cutler's *A Grammar of Ornament and Design* (1880), and Siegfried Bing's *Artistic Japan* (1888), as well as trade journals carrying related articles and designs, encouraged this trend. Thus, British artists and manufacturers became adept at utilizing a 'domesticated' Japanese style that rivalled and even excelled the original objects.

Indeed, the matter of design was significant in this industry. In 1884, the designs were considered novel: it was reported that there was 'such a fecundity of fancy and imagination shown that the interest in them does not flag on the first or second glance, but is constantly discovering some new point of beauty', and the use of colour was so praised that 'these leather papers occupy a position entirely their own, and stand quite apart from their English or Continental rivals'.[99] However, at the fifth National Industrial Exhibition (Naikoku-kangyo-hakurankai, 1902), weaknesses were pointed out by even Japanese critics. Designs were described as 'limited' and the patterns in general were dismissed as 'within cliché'.[100] Despite this, Yamaji's products still received medals at the British–Japanese Exhibition (1910), and the San Francisco Exhibition (1913). However, with regard to the British consumer, the decline in quality was a key factor. This emphasized Rottmann, Strome and

97 Kume Yasuo, *Kinkarakawagami to Gikakushi*, p. 64.

98 Widar Halen, 'Christopher Dresser, the Centennial Exhibition, and the Anglo-American Dialogue', *The Magazine Antique*, 160/3 (2001).

99 *Journal of Decorative Art*, April 1884, p. 492.

100 *Dai 5kai Naikoku Kangyo Hakurankai Shinsa Hokokusho* [Report of the Judges of the 5th National Exhibition for the Encouragement of Industry] (Tokyo, c.1903).

Co.'s initial decision to closely supervise design and gear production to the British market.

In addition, within the context of Japonisme, objects like fans, screens and bamboo furniture, which were easier to produce in cheaper versions, stimulated wider mass consumption.[101] These goods became a requirement for projecting Japanese-ness in a room *a la Japonais*, and smaller leather paper objects (boxes, tobacco pouches, purses and so on) remained good business.[102] In contrast, leather wallpaper remained firmly linked to its craft origins and, as a result, was rather ironically fettered by its core authenticity in both materials and skilled production. This tended to limit the wider appeal of the product. By the end of the 1880s, Rottmann, Strome and Co. started to diversify, with more emphasis placed upon leather paper 'draught screens'. As the *Cabinet Maker and Art Furnisher* argued, 'Japanese leather paper is now largely used for making up strong dining-room screens'.[103] Tellingly, these were considered the very essence of 'artistic and commercial Japanese art'.[104]

'Artistic', and yet 'commercial' Japan reflected the real demand of the consumer: interior decoration, which allowed one to project packaged exotic spaces at home. 'Artistic' merit was necessary to produce the sense of authenticity, and 'commercial' merit was equally necessary to encourage economic accessibility. Rottmann, Strome and Co. and other foreign tradesmen who supported the infrastructure of Japonisme in the West had to judge the balance between the two elements and the transitional conditions that surrounded them.

The consumption of Japanese leather paper as wallpaper had a dual aspect. The West appreciated it for its notional qualities of authentic Japanese-ness: Japan took it for a mark of westernization and wanted to sell the craft tradition in a commercially viable way. At the same time it wanted to show, by creating official, western-style buildings that Japan could replicate western standards of living. Japanese leather wallpaper was, therefore, an exotic object to both sides. 'Authenticity' – an important sales point for this unique paper craft – was moulded by the Japanese themselves, but it was ultimately shaped by western perspectives, western parameters and western speculation.

101 In the 1890s, companies such as Model and Co., P. Bastendorff, Caspar & Co., The Mikado Bamboo Co., and J.B. Kohn frequently advertised bamboo furniture in trade and domestic journals.

102 At the 1889 Paris International Exhibition Tsuboya-gami was featured. See *Exposition Universelle internationale de 1889: Rapports du Jury International* (Paris, 1889), pp. 388, 391. At the beginning of the century Horiki's firm exported more than 12,000 yen, and received a Bronze Medal at Paris Exhibition (1900) and a Gold Medal at the British–Japanese Exhibition (1910). '"Sanchu" Horikike no Gikakushi' [Pseudo-Leather Paper at 'Sanchu' Horiki Family], *Furusato no Nenpo*, p. 135.

103 'Japanese Draught Screens', *Cabinet Maker and Art Furnisher*, 1 April 1889. Leather paper screens were specially referred to again in the 1 October 1890 issue.

104 *Cabinet Maker and Art Furnisher*, 1 April 1889. The company's screens were again featured in *Furnisher and Decorator*, 1 September 1891, p. 122.

PART THREE
Fashioning the Domestic: Making and Re-Making the Home through Consumption

Chapter Six

Desirable Commodity or Practical Necessity? The Sale and Consumption of Second-Hand Furniture, 1750–1900

Clive Edwards and Margaret Ponsonby

> Deep in the gloom of a sort of narrow avenue winding through a bizarre forest of wardrobes, with an undergrowth tangle of table legs, a tall pier glass glimmered like a pool of water in a wood.[1]

A new development within consumption studies has been an interest in second-hand goods. During the last twenty or so years consumption has largely taken over from production as an area for research in both humanities and social sciences.[2] The first wave of interest took account of class and gender (ethnicity has yet to be fully addressed), for contextualizing the consumption of goods. Now aspects that might be considered on the margins of consumption practice, including purchasing second-hand goods, are receiving attention. The disciplines of anthropology and cultural studies have explored how people in modern day western societies make meaning out of industrial mass produced objects.[3] How such commodities are subverted by consumers to make expressive individualized and customized goods have been studied. Consumption theory of this kind has shown that second-hand goods are often purchased in order to incorporate them in a sophisticated recycling process. However, most of this work has focused on contemporary society.[4] And clothing has been the most examined of commodities since it is the most obvious means of expressing taste and opposition to acceptable forms of behaviour. This chapter situates itself within material culture studies as a means of extending the

---

1 Joseph Conrad, *The Secret Agent* (London: Penguin, 1994), p. 121.

2 See, for example, Neil McKendrick, John Brewer and J.H. Plumb, *The Birth of a Consumer Society* (London: Europa, 1982); Rosalind Williams, *Dream Worlds: Mass Consumption in Late Nineteenth Century France* (Berkeley: University of California Press, 1982); Chandra Mukerji, *From Graven Images: Patterns of Modern Materialism* (New York: Columbia University Press, 1983).

3 Daniel Miller (ed.), *Material Cultures: Why Some Things Matter* (London: UCL Press, 1998); Irene Cieraad (ed.), *At Home: An Anthropology of Domestic Space* (New York: Syracuse University Press, 1999); Alison Clarke, *Tupperware: the Promise of Plastic in 1950s America* (Washington, DC and London: Smithsonian Institution Press, 1999); Judy Attfield, *Wild Things: The Material Culture of Everyday Life* (Oxford: Berg, 2000).

4 N. Gregson and L. Crewe, *Second-Hand Cultures* (Oxford: Berg, 2003).

interest in second-hand goods to the earlier period of the eighteenth and nineteenth centuries. The focus of the paper is specifically on furniture. Therefore our central aim is to show how this type of object in its second-hand state, lent itself to particular consumption practices that were specific to the type of good and to the period.

Some work has been done on the trade and market for second-hand goods in the past but still furniture has not received as much attention as clothing, and the eighteenth century has taken precedence over the later period.[5] This chapter seeks to redress the balance. Certain assumptions have also been made about the consumption of second-hand furniture and this chapter will examine the evidence for these claims and suggest that a focused study on furniture and on the longer period that we have chosen point to other conclusions.

The most extensive studies to date on second-hand clothing have been undertaken by Beverley Lemire. Her argument suggests that apart from economic considerations it was the chance for the poor people to emulate the wealthy in society by consuming their fashionable cast offs.[6] Emulation has now been problemitized as an explanation for consumption.[7] In any case furniture requires analysis that takes account of how it was consumed, in the semi-private world of the home. Further, the value placed on the physical qualities inherent in it in its second-hand state need to be considered. There is no equivalent in clothing of antique furniture where the signs of age in its design and patina are valued.

Stena Nenadic suggests that second-hand furniture became less attractive to middle-class customers by the nineteenth century. Nenadic claims that in the later eighteenth century furniture produced for a middle-rank market was then recycled within the same market, but by the 1820s, the situation had changed. To purchase second-hand was, she says, an indication of a lack of interest in fashion and style, and 'it was much more likely that working people would be able to purchase second-hand goods that had once belonged to the relatively wealthy'.[8] However, there is plentiful evidence that an extensive trade continued in the nineteenth century and was specifically aimed at the middle section of society. Her remarks also do not

5 See B. Lemire, 'Peddling Fashion: Pawnbrokers, Tailors, Thieves and the Second-Hand Clothes Trade in England, c. 1700–1800', *Textile History*, 22 (1991): 67–82; S. Nenadic, 'Middle Rank Consumers and Domestic Culture in Edinburgh and Glasgow 1720–1840', *Past and Present*, 145 (1994): 122–56; J. Styles, 'Clothing the North: the Supply of Non-Elite Clothing in the Eighteenth-Century North of England', *Textile History*, 25/2 (1994): 139–66; B. Lemire, *Dress, Culture and Commerce: The English Clothing Trade before the Factory, 1660–1800* (Basingstoke: Macmillan, 1997); Miles Lambert, '"Cast-off Wearing Apparel": The Consumption and Distribution of Second-Hand Clothing in Northern England during the Long Eighteenth Century', *Textile History*, 35/1 (2004): 1–26.

6 See previous note.

7 See, for example, Colin Campbell, *The Romantic Ethic and the Spirit of Modern Consumerism* (Oxford: Blackwells, 1987); Grant McCracken, *Culture and Consumption* (Bloomington and Indianapolis: Indiana University Press, 1988); John Brewer and Roy Porter (eds), *Consumption and the World of Goods* (London: Routledge, 1993); Amanda Vickery, *The Gentleman's Daughter: Women's Lives in Georgian England* (New Haven and London: Yale University Press, 1998).

8 Nenadic, 'Middle Rank Consumers', pp. 132–3.

take into account the growth of the antiques trades at just the same time that she says second hand became less desirable. Grant McCracken too in his discussion of patina ignores the antiques trade.[9] He says that with the dissemination of the fashion system people came to value patina in objects less, preferring new goods. But again the adoption of fashion by most sections of society and the growth of interest in antique goods, by some sections with in it, happened at about the same time, the mid eighteenth century. These developments are worthy of closer scrutiny in order to understand the appeal of second-hand furniture throughout the period.

Consumption for the home also differed to that for personal adornment since a different code operated. Furniture was a large investment that people often made only once in a lifetime. Furniture was meant to last many years and even be passed on to the next generation. This does not mean that furniture was outside the fashion system, but that it operated in a different manner.

Specific consumption practices were associated with purchasing furniture second hand. Diverse methods made the goods available to the whole population, including those in the section that most concern us, the middling sort/middle class. During the period changes occurred in both the availability of furniture and in the attitudes to the home and therefore homemakers' expectations for their household furnishings. These developments provide the framework for assessing the reasons for purchasing second-hand furniture. The chapter will assess the context for this consumption practice in two sections that relate, to some extent, to the chronology of the period under consideration. The reasons are firstly practical, including economic considerations and the availability of furniture. For the lower classes purchasing old, often discarded, furniture was a financial necessity. In the case of the middling sort although there were some financial restraints, there were other benefits to purchasing used furniture, providing it was in keeping with their status. By comparing the various types of retailers of second-hand furniture, and the methods of distribution, the relative status of their wares may be gauged.

A second reason for purchasing furniture second hand developed during the period that related to its inherent material qualities. The patina of old furniture appealed to antiquarians who collected pre-eighteenth century artefacts. This, however, was only a minority interest. Aged furniture that was second hand but not antique took on a fresh appeal to middle-class homemakers. This was due to the changing nature of homes and homemaking from the early to mid nineteenth century when a distinct domestic ideology developed. Middle-class consumers increasingly valued the emotional aspects of homemaking. For these consumers second-hand furniture provided symbolic qualities that could be woven into their homemaking practices.

9 McCracken, *Culture and Consumption.*

Practical Reasons

Just Another Way to Buy Furniture

A thoroughly pragmatic approach is apparent in the variety of purchasing methods recorded in the diary of Parson Woodforde of Norfolk. He made a number of purchases of furniture over a few years in the late eighteenth century, which demonstrate buying second-hand goods from a cabinet-maker, a purchase at a house sale, and a part exchange. On 12 January 1788 for example, he noted the delivery of a sofa from 'my upholsterer Mr Horth'. On 13 November 1789 Woodforde recorded that he 'bought this day of William Hart, cabinet-makers on Hog Hill Norwich, 2 large second-hand double flapped mohogany [*sic*] tables also one second-hand mohogany dressing table with drawers also one new mohogany wash stand for all which paid 4.14.6'. A year later on 2 April 1793 Woodforde attended the sale of goods of Mrs Michelthwaite where he bid for 'a very handsome mahogany sideboard, a very good and large Wilton carpet and a mahogany cellaret', the first two of which he successfully purchased. The next day he noted that 'we brought home the carpet that I bought, and gave orders to Sudbury my upholsterer to send home my sideboard by 2 men'. Six months later, he again employed Sudbury to supply new tables. The upholsterers 'took my two large tables and smaller one in part of exchange for the others and he is to allow me for the three, only 2.18.0'.[10]

It is possible that in the early modern period people were less likely to make a distinction between first and second hand – it was simply another means of getting goods that were desirable. For many goods, second-hand items, providing they were not too damaged by age, were a readily available source of furnishings. Although examples of consumers making such purchases are difficult to find, a much later example of a purchase of a second-hand item is provided by Matthew Robinson Boulton, the son of the entrepreneur, and appears also to illustrate the same pragmatic approach as that of Parson Woodforde (see above). In September 1837 Boulton's housekeeper, Mrs Wilkinson, wrote to Mr Westley, the agent at Soho House, that the family needed a sofa: 'we will look out for another at a sale, and should one be met with in this neighbourhood first we will appraise you – and you must do the same, should you find one that is reasonable. It is wanted for an ordinary room and provided it is a good length to lie on say 6ft, no matter for the fashion of it.'[11]

In November, Mrs Wilkinson wrote again on the subject: 'Do not look out for a Sofa – we have just heard of one at Banbury which will suit our purpose and comes over next week.' Although only for an 'ordinary' room, this sofa was intended for the family's use rather than for servants. Boulton was a wealthy man with a well-furnished home and yet he resorted to second-hand goods on occasion and went to some trouble to acquire the right object.

This apparent willingness to include second-hand furnishings in a wealthy interior suggests that goods had a function and use-value that were often more

10 J. Beresford (ed.), *The Diary of a Country Parson* (Oxford: Oxford University Press, 1929), pp. 148–51.

11 Birmingham City Archives, MBP 438.

important than style, at least in the lesser rooms of a house. Fashions in furniture changed at a slower pace than the seasonal ones for clothing. Despite an increase in changes in fashion from the eighteenth century, it was still customary for furniture to be purchased occasionally. Amanda Vickery says of the gentlewoman Elizabeth Shackleton's acquisition of furniture, in 'those categories of goods which were at the very core of the eighteenth-century fashion system – furniture, tableware and clothing – the extent to which fashion influenced her purchasing decisions was different in each category'.[12]

A practical and thrifty approach to homemaking meant that consumers kept items in their homes that had been repaired and altered and therefore long after they had been at the height of fashion. Throughout the period homemakers were ready to make over items and re-use the materials. The work of cabinetmakers and upholsterers often included repairing and altering furniture and furnishings. And it was not only provincial firms working for the middling sort but also fashionable and prestigious firms in London, who carried out repairs to both large and small, and smart and mundane items for their customers.[13]

In addition to cabinetmakers and upholsterers performing repair work it was common for second-hand furniture dealers to employ a 'handy-man' to repair and rebuild broken furniture for re-sale.[14] If a professional job was not possible then homemakers lower down the social scale could do repair work themselves and increasingly magazines provided instructions.[15] At all levels then a certain amount of 'make do and mend' was practised. Furniture, whether bought new or second-hand, was seen as a long-term investment both as objects to be kept, and cared for or as a source of materials.[16]

However, fashion was becoming increasingly widespread by the later eighteenth century, even in middling-sort homes. Therefore, the availability of new and fashionable furniture needs to be taken into consideration to ascertain whether consumers had a choice between these two classes of good.

Availability of new fashionable furniture

During the eighteenth century bespoke cabinet making became established as the desirable means of constructing furniture for the middling sort and above.[17] By the mid century knowledge of fashion was increasingly disseminated, even in the provinces

12 Vickery, *The Gentleman's Daughter*, p. 168.

13 See, for example, John Foden account book, Staffordshire Record Office, Stafford, 1361; Samuel Peat account book, West Sussex Record Office, Chichester, Add Mss 2239; and Hindley and Son day books, Guildhall Library, London, MS 10,883.

14 J. Thomson and A. Smith, *Street Life in London* (London: S. Low, Marston, 1877), p. 21.

15 Cassell's *Household Guide* suggested more ideas that are 'makeshift', such as making furniture out of barrels sawn in half, and reusing packing cases as furniture frames. *Household Guide* (London: Cassell, Petter and Galpin, 1874). Vol. 3, p. 212.

16 Nenadic, 'Middle Rank Consumers', pp. 132–3.

17 See Tables 6.1 and 6.2 for numbers of cabinet makers in London and Birmingham 1820–1890s.

and in smaller towns. Previously most furniture outside the large urban centres was produced by carpenters and joiners but gradually such regional/vernacular goods came to be seen as clumsy and vulgar and only acceptable for the service areas and perhaps bedrooms. The towns high up the urban hierarchy were well served for consumer goods and could support luxury trades such as cabinet making but in smaller towns there continued to be a scarcity, or at least a patchy availability, of fashionable items. Outside London timber shortages, and the high cost of materials, especially imported smart timbers such as mahogany, added to production problems. Thus for a time demand outstripped supply, rather than indicating a lack of desire for fashionable furniture outside the wealthiest 'upper ranks in society'. The difficulty of acquiring fashionable furniture provides a further reason for second-hand goods being popular at the outset of the period and encouraged 'recycling in the middle ranks'.[18] But Nenadic has suggested that once the supply and demand problem of the period was removed there was no longer any need to purchase furniture second hand. However, the example of Matthew Robinson Boulton purchasing a second-hand sofa confounds this analysis since he lived in Birmingham, which was extremely well served by cabinet makers by the 1830s, and he was sufficiently wealthy to commission furniture not only in Birmingham but also from London makers.[19] So, availability was not the only reason for purchasing goods second hand in the nineteenth century.

Quality Materials and Manufacture

Second-hand goods offered some middle-class customers the opportunity to purchase items that were of a better quality than they could otherwise afford. In particular, furniture made of solid wood and incorporating fashionable hard woods, such as mahogany, was seen as an investment. *The Magazine of Domestic Economy* recommended homemakers to purchase the best furniture that they could afford partly because such goods would fetch a reasonable price if resold.[20] So, quality furniture was seen as an investment that would hold its value reasonably well because it was perceived to be desirable within the second-hand market. This was an important consideration since many homemakers had to sell up their home furnishings when a move was needed due to economic problems or when a change of occupation necessitated it.

However, not all furniture produced in the nineteenth century was well made. Much of the increase in furniture making was in slop goods made to a low standard, even if superficially fashionable. The poor quality of such furniture is made clear, again in *The Magazine of Domestic Economy* which warned that when purchasing veneered furniture it was common for the two surfaces to part company and therefore homemakers should try to purchase that which had been made some time

18 Nenadic, 'Middle Rank Consumers', p. 134.

19 Bills and receipts show that he purchased furniture from various prestigious makers including George Bullock.

20 *Magazine of Domestic Economy* (London: W.S. Orr and Co., 1840), p. 65.

previously.[21] The east end of London became the source for much of this furniture by the mid to later nineteenth century.[22]

The acquisition of second-hand furniture made out of solid timber often posed less of a risk than the purchase of new. This is clearly demonstrated by the experience of James Hopkinson, a cabinetmaker in Liverpool who commented, in his diary in 1851, on purchasing goods at an auction. He wanted to fill his showroom and did not have sufficient items that he had made, so he went to an auction and bought what he thought were second-hand, good quality pieces, only to find that they were new, slop-made goods. The furniture had been darkened to look old and the auction room was poorly lit. He had difficulty reselling the furniture.[23] Therefore purchasing good quality second-hand furniture was in some ways more desirable than purchasing new in the latest fashion if that meant sacrificing on quality.

The location and status of the retailer has always been important to consumers of second-hand goods. For the middle-class homemakers in the nineteenth century some retailers more than others could provide them with furnishings that corresponded to their requirements and provided the status they needed.

Availability of Second-Hand Furniture: Status and Sites of Purchase

The quotation at the beginning of the chapter suggests 'shady dealings' and this is a recurring theme in contemporary descriptions of brokers of second-hand goods. The status of these goods was directly related to the nature of the outlet it came from. The division of the market between antique dealers,[24] auctioneers, cabinetmakers and upholsterers, furniture-brokers, pawnbrokers, and markets and fairs confirms a tentative hierarchy of furniture supply that was reflected in the locations of business. (See Tables 6.1 and 6.2.)

Table 6.1 Numbers of makers/retailers who might have dealt in second-hand furniture listed in London trade directories, 1820–90

	1820	1833/4	1854	1890
Antique Furniture Dealers	2	7	16	47
Auctioneers and Appraisers	125	385	462+102	697+91
Cabinet Makers	102	740	648	702
Furniture Brokers	2	632	567	390
Upholsterers	165	263	486	468
Pawnbrokers	13	284	324	302

21 *Magazine of Domestic Economy*, p. 345.

22 Pat Kirkham, 'The London Furniture Trade 1700–1870', *The Journal of the Furniture History Society*, 24 (1988): 1–219.

23 Jocelyne Baty Goodman (ed.), *Victorian Cabinet Maker: Tthe Memoirs of James Hopkinson 1819–1894* (London: Routledge and Kegan Paul, 1968), p. 36.

24 Antique dealers will be dealt with in the section on symbolic reasons for purchasing second-hand furniture. It is difficult to pinpoint the precise differences between brokers and antique dealers. It is also difficult to determine the characteristics of furniture that fell into these two categories. To establish fully the relationship between antiques and second-hand furniture would require a separate study.

Table 6.2 Numbers of makers/retailers who might have dealt in second-hand furniture listed in Birmingham trade directories, 1816–92

	1816	1830	1849	1892
Antique Furniture Dealers	0	0	0	0
Auctioneers and Appraisers	16	20	42	76
Cabinet Makers	39	76	146	130
Furniture Brokers	48	49	139	269
Upholsterers	19	87	61	50
Pawnbrokers	38	63	87	337

Auctioneers

On the whole, auctions offered a select method of acquiring second-hand furniture through sale rooms or on the premises of the vendor. Despite suggestions that the customer base changed by the nineteenth century, the wording of the advertisements for house sales in newspapers remained remarkably similar, at least until the later nineteenth century, suggesting that they appealed to a similar readership. The ambiance of the auction, whether at the house or in auction rooms, the quality of the furniture, described in seductive and expensive catalogues, and listed in detail in newspapers, all suggest that in many cases auctioneers provided middle-class people with quality furniture.

Cynthia Wall has described how auctions became part of the social scene in the later eighteenth century in London.[25] Gradually something of this position spread to auctioneers in the provinces. John Rodway's advertisement in a trade directory depicts the smart premises as well as the goods in which he dealt. (See Illustration 6.1.) Similarly, the location and style of premises of the firm of John Rodderick, auctioneers and appraisers in Birmingham, illustrate their status. They were located in New Street, the smartest street in the town for retailers. The premises were an imposing four-storey building with pilasters, and were called 'The Shakespeare Showrooms'.[26] All aspects of these premises point to a firm occupying a high profile within the urban scene. Both Rodway and Rodderick were clearly sources of quality wares. Auctioneers provided an attractive venue for acquiring furniture whether actually in the home being sold up, at a nearby inn where fires and refreshments were provided, or increasingly, at well-appointed salerooms such as Rodderick's Shakespeare Showrooms.

25 Cynthia Wall, 'The English Auction: Narratives of Dismantlings', *Eighteenth Century Studies*, 31 (1997): 11–23.

26 Birmingham City Archives, MS897, volume II, numbers 109 and 151 show Rodderick's old and new premises. The images are not dated but the move can be estimated as 1849 from entries in trade directories.

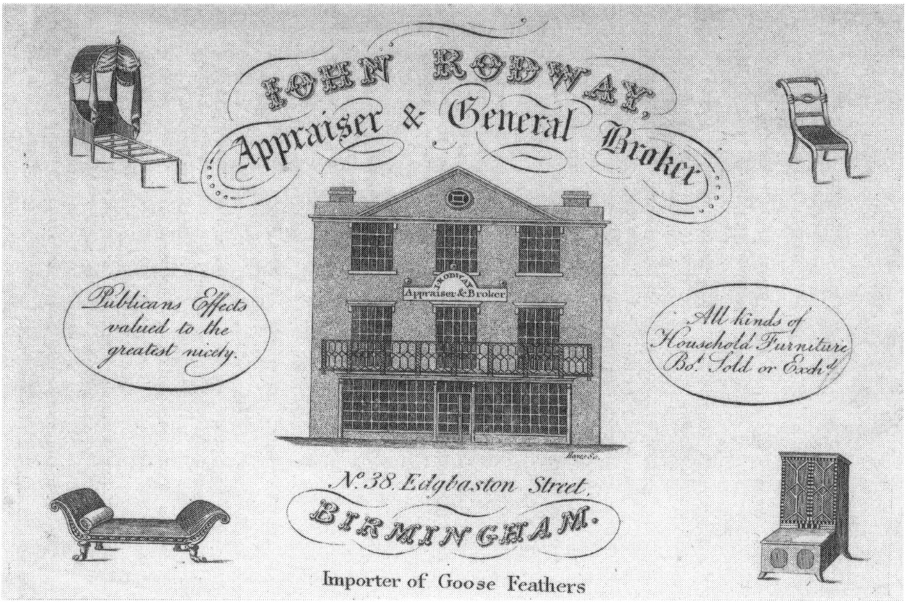

6.1 John Rodway, Appraiser and General Broker, Birmingham, 1823. Smart premises and fashionable goods were emphasized in this trade directory advertisement

Catalogues were a further means of advertising the contents of a sale and enticing prospective customers. The quality of the goods was established in the wording of the advertisement with comments on their newness, style, the quality of materials and sometimes the fact that they were 'London-made'. Although auctions were public affairs they could be restricted to 'respectable' prospective buyers and the catalogue was used to control admittance. The contents of the Lichfield home of Fairfax Moresby Esq., for example, were described in 'Catalogues price two shillings each from the Premises or Auctioneers, money will be returned to every Purchaser. The Furniture may be viewed one day previous to Sale; but no person will be admitted without a Catalogue.'[27] Purchasing the catalogue and going to view the goods was an end in itself for some people and was a popular pastime. But the auctioneer could regulate who was admitted by the high price of the necessary catalogue.

Although many of the auction houses were well run and genuine, some were less so. One correspondent to the *Edinburgh Evening Courant* wrote in March 1788:

> Tradesmen and shopkeepers complain much at this time of dullness in business, and want of employment … [a reason for this is] their customers going to sales and roups [auctions] with the ready money they ought to pay their debts with. It is notorious that at some late sales of furniture, higher prices were given than the articles cost a dozen years ago.[28]

27 *Aris's Birmingham Gazette*, 13 March 1815.

28 S. Pryke, 'A Study of the Edinburgh Furnishing Trade taken from Contemporary Press Notices 1708–1790', *Regional Furniture*, 3 (1989): 55.

Clearly people could be taken in by the auctioneers and dealers as in the example of Hopkinson, who as a cabinet maker, was better placed than the ordinary homemaker in judging the quality of furniture. Books and periodicals gave advice on how to avoid problems when purchasing at an auction. For example, in 1829, readers of *The Home Book* were told that if they thought that a house could be furnished 'in a superior style, at a very modest expense' by going to auctions, they should know that: 'a young person is in great danger of being drawn on, by the artful dealers who attend such sales, to continue bidding for an article which pleases the fancy, till at last it becomes his property at a price far beyond that for which it might be purchased of a regular tradesman'.[29] The author conceded that good-quality articles might be obtained in this way but that the homemakers would need a friend with some experience to advise them.

Not surprisingly, the 'legitimate' furniture trade took exception to auctions the popularity of which threatened their business. In a catalogue introduction, the Oetzmann Company republished an extract from the *London Mirror* of 16 September 1871:

> Attend any [furniture] sale you like either at a private dwelling house or an auction mart and you will find yourself out bidden in all directions by a knot of noisy clamorous, unwashed greasy looking individuals who dub themselves 'the trade.' [They outbid you, and then proceed to knock it out between themselves] … Depend upon it, a room – be it a dining room, drawing room or bedroom – furnished out of a saleroom has a saleroom look, which will cling to it as long as the articles hold together …. [30]

While goods sold in an auction room had no provenance or guarantee of their quality, the sale of house contents often made a feature of the owner's name and gave the name of the house. Indeed, the sale often took place on the premises. Holding the auction at the house had the benefit of sending a clear message to the prospective buyer, of the relative value of the goods and their authenticity. This was particularly important when the sale was for the house of a member of the gentry.

Cabinet Makers and Upholsterers

The involvement of cabinet makers and upholsterers, who were often representative of the better end of the trade in the appraisal and supply of second-hand furniture, was probably as much to do with providing a service to clients as a direct business proposition. When supplying new goods, old goods had to be disposed of or even part-exchanged, so a stock might be built up by default. The role of appraiser was a crucial one, and was naturally taken up by many furniture retailers as an adjunct to their business. The c.1790 trade card of Robert Mulligan of Mint Street, Southwark a well-known second-hand furniture location, demonstrates the range of services commonly offered by many eighteenth-century furniture retailers. Although he was

29 A Lady, *The Home Book: or Young Housekeeper's Assistant* (London: Smith, Elder and Co., 1829), p. 107.

30 Oetzmann and Co., *Hints on House Furnishing and Decoration* (London, c. 1871), p. 294.

primarily a sworn appraiser, bedstead maker and undertaker, he also: 'Buys and sells all sorts of household goods both new and second-hand. Makes cabinet and upholstery work in general and furnishes houses on easy terms, sells by auction household goods, estates and merchandise of every kind by commission or otherways and lends money on household furniture.'[31] The blurring between makers and retailers and of first and second-hand furniture again suggests that customers did not make a clear distinction between them.

The role of cabinet makers as appraisers was ambivalent, as in the mid-eighteenth century at least; 'they are obliged to take the goods if it is insisted on, at their own appraisement'.[32] On the other hand, there is evidence of simple trading. In 1760, George Browning, an upholsterer, appraiser and auctioneer noted on his trade card 'Ready money given for all manner of household goods'. In the same year, William Perry of Chiswell Street near Moorfields, London, another well-known second-hand furniture location, announced that 'the public may be supplied with every article of household furniture both new and second-hand'.[33] Similarly, the provincial cabinet and chair maker Richard France took out an advertisement in the *Salopian Journal* in July 1794, to tell customers that he sold both new and second-hand furniture and invited ladies and gentlemen to sell their furniture to him or exchange it for new.[34]

Although such practices continued into the nineteenth century selling second-hand furniture became increasingly the province of specialists, either auctioneers or furniture brokers.

Furniture Brokers

The brokers dealing with furniture tended to cluster together in specific areas, although the reputation of individual establishments varied.[35] In 1817, Johnston's *London Directory* listed Brokers Row as having twenty-eight premises housing ten brokers and appraisers, two furniture-brokers and six upholders/cabinet makers. While this suggests a mixture of makers and retailers, a description of the area in the 1820s confirms the second-hand bias of the businesses:

> When I remember Moorfields first [it had a] line of shops without fronts, occupied chiefly by dealers in old furniture, to the east and north. Most of these shops were covered in by screens of canvas or rough boards, so as to form an apology for a piazza … a broken down four poster or a rickety tent bed might be secured at almost any price … a tall stiff upright

31 A. Heal, *The London Furniture Makers from the Restoration to the Victorian Era, 1660–1840* (Edinburgh: Pryke, 1953), p. 55.

32 R. Campbell, *London Tradesmen* (1747) (reprint Newton Abbot: David and Charles, 1969), p. 175.

33 Ambrose Heal, *The London Furniture Makers* (London: Batsford, 1953), p. 116.

34 *Salopian Journal*, 30 July 1794.

35 The term 'broker' was used as far back as 1377 (OED) to describe a dealer in second-hand apparel and household goods. See Clive Edwards, *Turning Houses in Homes* (Aldershot: Ashgate, 2005), p. 27.

easy chair, without a bottom; a cupboard with one shelf left of three, and with half a door; here a black oak chest groaning to be scraped ...[36]

By the 1830s the evidence from the *London Directory* demonstrates the growth in this aspect of the furniture trade with a large number of dealers with the title of broker. Pigot's *Directory* listed 632 in London, with particular concentrations in the Borough/Southwark area, Soho, Old Street, Oxford Street/Tottenham Court Road area, Chelsea and Long Acre/Drury Lane. It is also likely that many furniture brokers who were at the bottom end of the market would not have been included in trade directories.[37] It was this image of second-hand dealers that became the most widespread. (See Illustration 6.2.)

6.2 Photograph of a second-hand furniture dealer in Holborn, London, 1877 by J. Thomson, depicts the popular image of second-hand furnishings

36 Aleph (pseudo.), *London Scenes and London People* (London: W.H. Collingridge, 1864), p. 35.

37 Shaw and Tipper suggest that agents for the directories did not venture into courts to collect information, resulting in the down-market traders escaping inclusion. Gareth Shaw and Alison Tipper, *British Directories: A Bibliography and Guide to Directories Published in England and Wales 1850–1950 and Scotland 1773–1950* (London: Mansell, 1989), p. 22.

A feature of furniture broking that distinguished it from other aspects of the furniture trade was the comparatively high number of women involved, particularly at the lower end of the business. This was partly because selling second-hand goods required less capital to set up in business than other forms of trading. In London, by the 1830s, evidence from the street directories shows a Broker's Alley, off Drury Lane, with twelve premises occupied by brokers; four of them run by women. Similarly, in the Worcester Street area of Birmingham, where many furniture brokers were listed in the trade directories of the 1830s and 1840s, a number, although still in a minority, were female. That these were small-scale enterprises is indicated by several of them sharing premises with other furniture brokers. However, another reason for the presence of female furniture brokers was that widows who took over their husband's cabinet making and/or upholstering business were not always in a position to continue the trade in the same way.[38]

While it is true that furniture broking clearly represented a less salubrious aspect of the second-hand trade than auctioneers and cabinet makers, still some firms had a good reputation and were frequented by wealthy customers. In April 1768 Lady Mary Coke 'went from the carpet manufactory [Moorfields] to a place called Brokers Row, where I bought several things: my coach was almost filled'.[39] Clearly, some firms here offered a respectable shopping location. This is also demonstrated by the insurance value of £800 for the house in Brokers Row of one Samuel Swain, an upholsterer and broker.[40] Similarly, Matthew Robinson Boulton made several purchases from furniture brokers in Worcester Street, the Birmingham equivalent of Brokers Row in Moorfields.[41] As Birmingham began to spread westwards with smart middle-class suburbs such as Edgbaston, so furniture brokers sprang up on the roads leading out of the city centre to cater for their home furnishing needs.

Other Sites of Purchase

Second-hand goods were also sold in large quantities in less formal ways than those already described. These methods included goods being sold through fairs and street traders. These methods were difficult to regulate at a time when retailing was becoming more organized, and together with items being remade, and bartering and exchanging old for new all contributed a disreputable image.[42] Although market stalls and fairs were popular ways of purchasing all manner of goods in the eighteenth century, their public nature was falling from favour by the nineteenth century and

38 Pat Kirkham, '"If you have no sons": Furniture-Making in Britain', in Judith Attfield and Pat Kirkham (eds), *A View From the Interior: Women and Design* (London: The Women's Press, 1995).

39 Clive Wainwright, *The Romantic Interior* (New Haven and London: Yale University Press, 1989), p. 34.

40 Wainwright, *The Romantic Interior*, p. 34.

41 Birmingham City Archives, MBP 479.

42 Beverly Lemire, *Fashion's Favourite: The Cotton Trade and the Consumer in Britain, 1660–1800* (Oxford: Oxford University Press, 1991), p. 68.

gaining a somewhat bad reputation.[43] The early-nineteenth-century depiction of St James's Fair, Bristol by Samuel Colman (Illustration 6.3) appears to be making a moralistic comment on the public spectacle of the proceedings. The scene shows all manner of household goods being sold on stalls and being auctioned, plus a peddler selling trinkets. As the nineteenth century progressed, it was only working-class customers who resorted to markets and fairs for purchasing furniture.

6.3 St James's Fair, Bristol by Samuel Colman, 1824. Dubious moral behaviour provides a backdrop for an auction and a stall selling second-hand furnishings

43 Nancy Cox, *The Complete Tradesman: A Study of Retailing, 1550–1820* (Aldershot: Ashgate, 2000), p. 85 and pp. 124–5.

Pawnbrokers were a further disreputable and difficult to regulate source of second-hand goods. They dealt in clothing extensively, and less commonly in second-hand furniture, nonetheless, this was still a source for such goods and contributed to the shady image.

Purchasing furniture second hand was practised throughout the period by a wide range of homemakers. The many practical reasons for doing so continued to make this source of furnishings desirable but by the nineteenth century it had become crucial to distinguish between sources and to only frequent firms located in the better sections of towns.[44] In addition, acquiring aged furniture for the home began to take on new meanings for homemakers that had more to do with constructing identity than the merely practical aspects of furnishing a house.

The Symbolic Associations of Aged Furniture

Collecting Antiques

Initially antique dealers were also known as brokers. The term 'antique furniture dealer' appears to be first mentioned in street directories from circa 1820. It is difficult to pinpoint the precise differences between brokers of second-hand furniture and antique dealers or to determine precisely the characteristics of the furniture in which they dealt.[45] It does seem clear though that there was an increase of traders in London, but less so elsewhere, who adopted the title of antique dealer from the early nineteenth century.

J.C. Loudon wrote in his *Encyclopaedia* of the dealers who would satisfy the taste for an antique interior:

> The exterior of chests or wardrobes might be rendered curious, and highly interesting, though we do not say in correct or architectural taste, by covering them with the Elizabethan, Dutch, Louis XIV, or Francis I ornaments which are now to be purchased in abundance, either at home or abroad. We have already referred to Nixon and Son [premises in Great Portland Street], for the two latter kinds of furniture; and we here observe that Wilkinson of Oxford Street, and Hanson of John Street, have extensive collections of Elizabethan and Dutch furniture and carvings, from which an judicious compiler of exteriors might clothe skeleton frames, so as to produce objects of curiosity and interest at a very trifling expense. Kensett of Mortimer Street has also some curious specimens of both Elizabethan and more ancient furniture.[46]

It is evident that the dealers concentrated in particular parts of town. Clive Wainwright has shown how Wardour Street, Soho developed into a centre of antique shops and traders. In 1817, there were no brokers but 13 cabinet makers or upholsterers. By

---

44 It was also in the early nineteenth century that towns were growing in size and distinct shopping areas for different sections of society were becoming more clearly defined.

45 It is probable that the distinctions were not clear or fixed and the situation was made all the more muddy by the increase in faking antiques or 'enriching' items to appear older.

46 J.C. Loudon, *Encyclopaedia of Cottage, Farm and Villa Architecture* (London: Longman, 1829), p. 1101.

1850, the numbers had increased to 23 brokers and 24 cabinet maker/upholsterers.[47] The reputation of the trade in this quarter is recognized by the term 'Wardour Street English' defined as a modern article with a sham antique appearance about it.[48]

The call for 'antique furniture' grew to such an extent that the regular furniture retailers also began to sell products under this description. Articles such as that published in the *Cornhill Magazine*, which, in 1875, declared that 'the art of furnishing must for the present moment be closely connected with the judicious buying of old furniture', stimulated this demand.[49] This would appear to relate to the taste for 'picking up' objects that would help to furnish an eclectic or artful interior. In the same year (1875), *The Pall Mall Gazette* wrote on the subject of old furniture:

> There are still great quantities of [eighteenth-century furniture] to be bought at a lower price than the same goods could be made for. These common chairs, tables, or cabinets only need the addition of appropriate ornament and exhibition in a fashionable dealer's rooms to take rank and value as fine old Chippendale or marquetry furniture. There are many workmen in London who are mainly employed in 'enriching' goods for the old furniture market.[50]

However, around 1871, the retailers Oetzmann and Co. warned their customers about the issue of appropriateness of furnishings, particularly concerning the antique:

> Of late years, a taste for antique furniture has developed … This taste may appropriately be displayed in the furnishings of a house, which is architecturally appropriate, but … for modern houses, we should prefer the comfort and elegancy of modern furniture to antique and for drawing rooms, antique furniture is simply inadmissible.[51]

Although Oetzman and Co. eschewed the sale of antique furniture in their business, other stores were not so concerned. Debenham and Freebody, better known for drapery and clothing, started to sell antique rugs and embroidery. In 1897, the company published *The Chippendale Period in English Furniture* by K.W. Clouston and then soon opened an 'antique furniture' department. In 1905, Harrods store opened a gallery for 'Antique and second-hand modern furniture'.[52]

The growth of interest in antiques, rather than merely second-hand furniture, began as a specialized antiquarian taste. It was about the mid eighteenth century that antique furniture along with other objects became identifiable as a collectable type of object for a minority, mostly wealthy people but also, according to Wainwright, some professionals such as clergymen and school teachers. Making a distinction between

47 Wainwright, *The Romantic Interior*, p. 34.

48 Wainwright, *TheRomantic Interior*, ch. 2.

49 S. Muthesius, 'Why do we Buy Old Furniture? Aspects of the Authentic Antique in Britain 1870–1910', *Art History*, 11/2 (1988): 234.

50 R.W. Symonds and B.B. Whinnery, *Victorian Furniture* (London: Country Life, 1962), pp. 82–3.

51 Oetzmann and Co., *Hints on House Furnishing and Decoration* (London, 1871), p. 293.

52 A. Adburgham, *Shopping in Style* (London: Thames and Hudson, 1979), p. 300.

purchasing furniture for furnishing a home and amassing a collection is useful for making the difference apparent between the two categories. Stefan Muthesius points out that 'What distinguished [these] interiors from earlier antiquarian ones was that there was no precise historical scheme.'[53] Collecting assumes knowledge and discernment it also implies method and purpose to acquire objects to form a collection that relate to each other in a particular way.[54] T. Dant neatly sums up the differences: 'collecting is a passionate rather than a functional form of possession'.[55] The nineteenth-century collectors of antiques wished to distinguish themselves as distinct and superior to users of 'reproduction' style furniture. While the idea of reproduction had not existed previously it was perhaps in the later nineteenth century that it began to acquire a pejorative connotation.[56]

McCracken has argued that patina on objects was no longer important once the fashion system became established in the eighteenth century. For furniture this argument does not hold up since it was at precisely the same time that antiques became desirable. Gregson and Crewe suggest, in their examination of current interests in second-hand merchandize, that such goods are consumed in order to 'capture difference'.[57] While their analysis can not be fully adopted for the period in question, the notion of expressing difference does apply to antique furniture during the period when it was of limited appeal; limited that is to a few wealthy patrons and somewhat eccentric or at least scholarly professionals.[58] In these cases, the 'old furnishings' expressed a passion for history looked at through the prism of Romanticism, but the underlying motives were still expressing wealth, education and taste as their forebears had done with the results of their efforts on the Grand Tour.

By the later nineteenth century the interest in pre-eighteenth-century furniture had increased although most of what was consumed was newly made 'reproductions' sometimes outright faked antique furniture.

For most middle-class consumers it was an antique look in newly made furniture rather than concerns with authenticity that prompted the demand. Collecting curios became more general, particularly for 'artistic' interiors. However, the move to

---

53 Stefan Muthesius' article makes this distinction. Muthesius, 'Why do we Buy Old Furniture?', p. 233.

54 On the subject of collecting see John Elsner and Roger Cardinal (eds) *The Cultures of Collecting* (London: Reaktion Books, 1997); McCracken, *Culture and Consumption*, pp. 41–2, on the modern practice of using patina as a method differentiation; P. Bourdieu, *Distinction: A Social Critique of the Judgement of Taste* (London: Routledge and Kegan Paul, 1984), on the theory of cultural capital and how it relates to antiques.

55 T. Dant, *Material Culture in the Social World* (Buckingham: Open University Press, 1999), p. 148.

56 Before the late nineteenth and early twentieth century the idea of reproduction furniture did not exist since copying was normal. See Attfield, *Wild Things*, for a discussion on reproduction furniture.

57 Nicky Gregson and Louise Crewe, *Second-hand Cultures* (London: Berg, 2003), p. 83.

58 See Margaret Ponsonby, *Stories from Home: English Domestic Interiors, 1750–1850* (Aldershot: Ashgate, 2007) for the example of David Parkes, a school teacher and collector in Shrewsbury.

furnish extensively in antiques remained a minority pursuit that continued to express a wealthy and educated taste.

Unlike antiquarians, homemakers purchasing second-hand furniture from a cabinet maker, upholsterer, auctioneer or furniture broker wanted goods that would blend with a vaguely fashionable scheme, not make a particular statement about their taste. While the lack of availability of fashionable goods might explain the purchase of second-hand furniture by middle-class customers in the eighteenth century, this explanation is inadequate for the nineteenth when cabinet makers were more widespread. To fully explain this homemaking practice the common physical attribute of second-hand furniture needs to be considered; this was its patina or signs of age.

Creating a Home: Domestic Ideology and Aged Furniture

The middle class, unlike the antique collectors, wanted to conform, to fit in and belong to society. They were newly rich and unsure of themselves. They were also perhaps the most home-loving section of society ever known. To understand how second-hand furniture complied with their homemaking, rather than merely house furnishing, the material qualities of these goods, and the cultural meaning that might have been associated with this kind of consumption practice, need to be considered.

An inevitable aspect about old furniture is that it has a past, a history. This past is manifested through physical characteristics; a general patina of darkened wood and faded textiles but also in minor blemishes such as scratches, scuffs, stains and pulled threads. Even furniture that was well cared for would inevitably have born testimony to its past use and its past owners. How did homemakers respond to these physical reminders of the past? Certainly antique collectors became increasingly keen on patina as a proof of authenticity.[59] But were such qualities ever valued in second-hand furniture that was not antique? Furniture, in common with other objects, can communicate meaning through a display of fashion or particular taste. This could be described as 'fixed meaning' since such cultural values must be shared by society for their meaning to be understood. Objects can also be invested with meaning on an individual level through associations with events in the life of the owner or with the lives of past owners.[60] This process is of relevance to the discussion of second-hand furniture since a means of acquiring it, not yet discussed, was through inheritance.

In the eighteenth century furniture was, according to Vickery, associated with the continuity of family life.[61] She suggests that furnishings of good quality 'carried family history down through time [and] were emblems of genteel status'.[62] References to furniture in eighteenth-century wills show the attitude that Vickery has noted. There are indications that similar ideas, of furniture as family history, continued into the

---

59 Muthesius, 'Why do we Buy Old Furniture?', especially pp. 244 and 251.

60 Characterized by Marius Kwint as the embodiment of memories, in the introduction to Marius Kwint, C. Breward and J. Aynsley (eds), *Material Memories: Design and Evocation* (Oxford: Berg, 1999).

61 Vickery, *The Gentleman's Daughter*, p. 192.

62 Vickery, *The Gentleman's Daughter*, p. 190.

nineteenth century and for people lower down the social order. Even more intriguing, and elusive, is the implication that furniture could carry emotional reminders of the testator to the recipient. Maxine Berg has argued that using wills rather than inventories tells us about people's relationship with their possessions. 'The goods mentioned in bequests were singled out for attention by the individual, and thus endowed with some emotional, familial or material value.'[63] Although furniture was not detailed in wills to the same extent as jewellery and pictures, especially portraits, objects that had obvious close associations with the testator, still furniture featured in some bequests in significant ways.[64] The gentlewoman Anne Cave, for example, left a detailed will in 1755.[65] She was a spinster and wished to be buried with her mother in Clifton upon Dunsmore. She left portraits of herself to several friends. Portraits were a favourite item for naming in a bequest and had clear associations with the testator and their wish to be remembered. Anne Cave, however, also left to a female relative, a spring repeating clock and her 'favourite armchair'.

In 1858 Fanny Downes, a spinster in Coventry, left instructions in her will for hair rings to be made and distributed to her female friends. Throughout the nineteenth century there prevailed a cult of mourning and rituals connected with death. The use of the hair of the deceased for making jewellery to be given to family and friends and worn in remembrance of them is a particularly strong instance of this.[66] Other objects could also have a strong physical association with the deceased: the favourite armchair, the writing desk used for writing letters every morning, the bed habitually slept in by them. So, with the rings that were to be made from her hair Fanny Downes gave attention to objects with strong physical associations by which her friends and relatives could remember her. However, she also left instructions that her brother Henry was to receive her writing desk; surely this was a piece of furniture that had important meanings for her and which she hoped Henry would share.

So, despite the growth in importance of fashion and therefore in replacing goods, there was still a continued expectation that substantial objects such as furniture were expected to last, not just a lifetime but several generations. Also that furniture could carry memories of individuals and family association down through the generations. For the new middle-class that was growing in numbers, particularly in urban areas, the material culture of the home expressed the moral and even religious values connected with homemaking. This is often referred to as a 'domestic ideology'. As *The Family Economist: a Penny Monthly Magazine for the Industrious Classes* stated, in 1851, 'We may keep with fondest care some article of furniture, some piece of silver plate which belonged to our fathers and grandfathers, which brings

63 Maxine Berg, 'Women's Consumption and the Industrial Classes of Eighteenth-Century England', *Journal of Social History*, 30/2 (1996): 415–34, p. 418.

64 Much of the research exploring the meaning of objects bequeathed or inherited has related to personal objects such as portraits and jewellery. See Berg, 'Women's Consumption'; Marcia Pointon, *Strategies for Showing: Women, Possession, and Representation in English Visual Culture 1665–1800* (Oxford: Oxford University Press, 1997); Vickery, *The Gentleman's Daughter*.

65 Will of Anne Cave 1 January 1755, Coventry Archives, 487/1.

66 See Marcia Pointon, 'Materializing Mourning: Hair, Jewellery and the Body', in Kwint, *Material Memories*.

memories of former homes and old familiar faces to consecrate the homes of the present.'[67] It is this attitude that is discernable in John Ruskin's letter to *The Times*, in 1854, condemning the interior illustrated in Holman Hunt's painting *The Awakening Conscience*. He made the comment that the immorality of the couple's relationship was expressed through the 'fatal newness' of the furnishings.[68] This extreme response was in part a condemnation of new styles in furniture that were thought to be bad design, showy with shiny veneers and lots of decoration but poorly made. However, Ruskin was also pointing out that if the couple depicted in the painting were married and had inherited family items, the interior would not be furnished with all new shiny and glossy objects.

Ruskin was from a privileged background. But for many newly middle-class homemakers there were either no furnishings to be handed down or they were too humble to acknowledge. To purchase all new furnishings risked being classed as upstarts, if not worse. Charles Dickens explores this theme in *Our Mutual Friend*, through the aptly named nouveau riche family, the Veneerings. In the eighteenth century cutting veneers was highly skilled work and used exotic rare timbers. It was therefore associated with expensive and smart goods and was highly desirable. But by the 1840s veneer cutting machines had been introduced that made the process far more economic. This led to veneers being used to cover up shoddy goods of poor materials and tacked together.[69] Although 'new' money had always been suspect, by the nineteenth century the layers of respectability had been even more finely nuanced. By calling this family Veneering Dickens was emphasizing their superficial hold on respectability. He expounds on this theme in a detailed description of the family:

> Mr and Mrs Veneering were bran-new people in a bran-new house in a bran-new quarter of London. Everything about the Veneerings was spick and span new. All their furniture was new, all their friends were new, all their servants were new, their plate was new, their carriage was new, their harness was new, their horses were new, their pictures were new, they themselves were new, they were as newly married as was lawfully compatible with their having a bran-new baby, and if they had set up a great-grandfather, he would have come home in matting from the pantechnicon, without a scratch upon him, French-polished to the crown of his head.[70]

Dickens clearly brings together the family associations, the emotional aspects of homemaking and the necessity for furniture that was not 'in a state of high varnish

67 *The Family Economist: a Penny Monthly Magazine for the Industrious Classes* (London: Groombridge and Sons, 1851), vol. 5, p. 182.

68 Ruskin's letter is reproduced in Caroline Arscott, 'Employer, husband, spectator: Thomas Fairburn's commission of The Awakening Conscience', in J. Wolff and J. Seed (eds), *The Culture of Capital: Art, Power and the Nineteenth-Century Middle Class* (Manchester: Manchester University Press, 1988).

69 See Clive Edwards, *Victorian Furniture* (Manchester: Manchester University Press, 1993), pp. 32–42 for technical details. Also Adrian Forty, *Objects of Desire: Design and Society 1750–1980* (London: Thames and Hudson, 1987).

70 Charles Dickens, *Our Mutual Friend* (Oxford: Oxford University Press, 1960, first published in 1865), p. 6.

and polish'. So, purchasing second-hand furniture perhaps offered a solution. The evidence of the popularity of house sales that took place on the premises suggests that people liked the idea of purchasing goods that had a known provenance, and associations with a wealthy person or family who was well respected in the community but perhaps there were also associations of 'pedigree' that are less easily quantified. In the early to mid nineteenth century, a few pieces of second-hand furniture in amongst a generally fashionable interior could be woven into the material culture of the middle-class home – indeed making it a home rather than just a fashionable interior.

Conclusion

The culture of consumption that revolves round the sequence of selling, buying, using, disposing and subsequent re-selling of possessions produced a life cycle of goods. Objects acquired a life history, which often represented a gradual decline in fortunes but that was not always the case. Some items continued to exist at an elevated status through a number of owners and could even eventually rise in fortune if they acquired the status of antiques. To understand the cultural value of second-hand furniture it is necessary to observe how it fitted into the wider cycle of consumption, and how the nature of the site of disposal, whether pawnbroker or society auctioneer, made a great difference to the image of used goods. These distinctions are often at the heart of how second-hand furniture was defined and understood by contemporaries. Such choices reflected the various cultural values placed by differing groups upon the comparative value of second-hand furniture. For the poorer groups purchasing 'part used' furniture was a necessity born out of financial pressures, and while to some extent this was also true for middle-class groups it was, more importantly, an opportunity to buy into an image of prestige and success through the better quality furniture sold. The patina of age became an increasingly valued characteristic and could express a particular taste to the collectors of antiques or simply a 'home' to the middle classes.

Chapter Seven

'A Pretty Custom' Updated: From 'Going to Housekeeping' to Bridal Showers in the United States, 1850s–1930s

Shirley Teresa Wajda

Buying for the home is, materially speaking, buying a dwelling and the goods for its creation, maintenance, and adornment. What generally makes a house a home, though, are the affective associations of specific, tangible objects acquired in preparation for what in the nineteenth-century United States was termed *housekeeping* and what by the twentieth century became *homemaking*. Though both terms were, and are, employed to describe woman's work, they together chart subtly a historic cultural shift recognizing the rise of mass production and mass consumption. *Housekeeping* referred to the utilitarian, quotidian processes of provisioning and maintaining a dwelling; *keeping* (like curatorship) was feminine, sometimes paid work in a culture in which endeavours of mastery and creation and production were coded masculine. By the advent of the twentieth century, *homemaking* had superseded greatly *housekeeping*, in recognition of modern women's power to make – create, produce – the set of values and affections associated with the selection and care of a house and its contents, both material and animal. At the same time, homemakers were unpaid wives and mothers who toiled about the house, often but not always without the aid of servants, their labour invested in the maintenance of an idea that subverted the possibility of economic equality. The establishment of home economics at the turn of the twentieth century endorsed women's knowledge as a form of mastery as it rationalized through sociology, economics, the natural and physical sciences, and architectural and interior design of the domestic dwelling – especially the kitchen – as not only a laboratory for modern living but a primary site of consumption.

American historians' discussions of women's housework have been focused on the meaning of labour, the impact of technology, and the instantiation of class and gender.[1] In addition, historians of marriage have rightly devoted attention to law, economics and the role of gender, while scholars of weddings have emphasized the

1 For the changing nature and meaning of women's domestic work see Jeanne Boydston, *Home and Work: Housework, Wages, and the Ideology of Labor in the Early Republic* (New York: Oxford University Press, 1990); Susan Strasser, *Never Done: A History of American Housework* (New York: Pantheon Books, 1982); Phyllis M. Palmer, *Domesticity and Dirt: Housewives and Domestic Servants in the United States, 1920–1945* (Philadelphia: Temple University Press, 1989); and Sarah Stage and Virginia B. Vincenti (eds), *Rethinking Home*

rite in and of itself.[2] Necessary as these studies are, they have often overlooked an important aspect of women's lives as housekeepers and homemakers: the gift economy surrounding marriage.[3] Gifting is often overlooked in studies of women as consumers. This essay explores that economy in the United States through two case studies: the first exemplifying the eighteenth- and nineteenth-century practice of 'going to housekeeping'; the second, the early-twentieth-century practice of 'showering' the bride with gifts useful to modern homemaking. I trace the continuities between these practices through their attendant material culture, seeking to understand the shifting relationship between the house and the marketplace.

'Going to Housekeeping' in Nineteenth-Century America

Since the colonial era, family and community members have endowed newlyweds with the necessities of maintaining a dwelling and managing a household. In the late eighteenth and early nineteenth centuries, marriage and 'going to housekeeping' were complementary but not necessarily simultaneous activities. As historian Laurel Thatcher Ulrich observes in her study of Martha Ballard and her family, weddings were rarely public affairs and often took place in private dwellings. Some six weeks after 'publication' of a couple's intent to be wed, the marriage took place. Six weeks more would pass for the wife to leave her parents' household and 'go to housekeeping' in a rented or purchased or gifted dwelling.[4] Parents often purchased some of the goods for the newlyweds' household; daughters sometimes had a 'portion', money or goods, with which to begin her married life. Marriage itself could incur a payment of dowry, but it was not the reason for gift-giving; setting up a new household was.

The amount of labour and expense in setting up a household of one's own were central factors in deciding when to marry as well as when to 'go to housekeeping'. Throughout the nineteenth century, young couples boarded before renting or purchasing a home. The English visitor Frances Trollope observed:

> For some reason or other, which English people are not very likely to understand, a great number of young married persons board by the year, instead of 'going to housekeeping', as they call having an establishment of their own. Of course this statement does not include

---

Economics: Women and the History of a Profession (Ithaca, NY: Cornell University Press, 1997).

2 On marriage, see Ellen K. Rothman, *Hands and Hearts: A History of Courtship in America* (New York: Basic Books, 1984); Nancy Cott, *Public Vows: A History of Marriage and the Nation* (Cambridge, MA: Harvard University Press, 2000). On weddings, see Celes C. Otnes and Elizabeth H. Pleck, *Cinderella Dreams: The Allure of the Lavish Wedding* (Berkeley: University of California Press, 2003); Vicki Howard, *Brides, Inc.: American Weddings and the Business of Tradition* (Philadelphia: University of Pennsylvania Press, 2006).

3 For an examination of British practices in the post-World War II period see Louise Purbrick, 'Wedding Presents: Marriage Gifts and the Limits of Consumption, Britain, 1945–2000', *Journal of Design History* 16/3 (2003): 215–27.

4 Laurel Thatcher Ulrich, *A Midwife's Tale: The Life of Martha Ballard, Based on Her Diary, 1785–1812* (New York: Alfred A. Knopf, 1990), pp. 134–61. See also Rothman, *Hands and Hearts*.

persons of large fortune, but it does include very many whose rank in society would make such a mode of life quite impossible with us.

Mrs. Trollope could 'hardly imagine a contrivance more effectual for ensuring the insignificance of a woman, than marrying her at seventeen, and placing her in a boarding-house'. Yet she also heard many ladies declare that it is 'just quite the perfection of comfort to have nothing to fix for oneself'.[5] Young couples saved money and perhaps enjoyed an easier life by boarding before establishing households of their own. The dislocations and relocations caused by the Industrial Revolution, beginning in the 1790s and accelerating unevenly with the economic 'booms and busts' throughout the century, made boarding with private families or in boardinghouses a common activity.[6] 'We are going to housekeeping!' exclaimed Helen Hunt Jackson to her sister Ann in a letter dated 12 November 1873, '... & I do long for private mashed potato!'[7] Desirable were the taste of one's own cooking and the ability to dine with family and invited friends. Couples lacked control over many aspects of their everyday lives, including privacy.

'Going to housekeeping' could be delayed for a variety of reasons. The decision could also be hastened due to the necessity of moving to a new town or city or state. Other couples went to housekeeping without boarding. Whatever the circumstances, they entered into marriage with a great deal of forethought, negotiation and work surrounding the new household. Securing and maintaining a house was a financial and physical commitment. During their yearlong courtship by letter, Sarah Lovina Plimpton of Sturbridge, Massachusetts, and Lucius A. Benham, residing in West Haven, Connecticut, discussed their future plans. Their letters reveal the difficulties of setting up a household. As well, these documents offer insight to the types of goods a bride required to begin her married life.[8]

Sarah Lovina Plimpton, born in Sturbridge, Massachusetts on 22 August 1825, was the daughter of Ziba and Hannah Marsh Plimpton. Ziba, a prospering farmer, miller and teacher, died in 1843. Later in that decade, Sarah and her sisters Hannah and Louisa at various times were teachers at the Oak Hill Female Seminary in West Haven. The death of a sister prompted Sarah's return to the Sturbridge family home.

---

5 Frances Trollope, *Domestic Manners of the Americans* (London: 1832), Chapter 26.

6 Wendy Gamber, *The Boardinghouse in Nineteenth-Century America* (Baltimore: Johns Hopkins University Press, 2007). Throughout the nineteenth century the economy of the United States was subject to twenty-year cycles of 'boom and bust': financial panics occurred in 1819, 1837, 1853, 1873 and 1893, all with subsequent depressions.

7 Helen Hunt Jackson Papers, Part 5, Ms 0351, Box 1, Folder 7, letters from Helen Hunt Jackson to her sister Ann (Mrs. E.C. Banfield), Colorado Springs, CO, 12 November 1873, available at http://www.coloradocollege.edu/library/SpecialCollections/Manuscript/HHJ5-1-7.html.

8 Plimpton–Benham Courtship Correspondence, 1853–54, Plimpton-Benham Collection, Old Sturbridge Village Research Library, Sturbridge, MA, available online as 'The Courtship Correspondence of Sarah Lovina Plimpton and Lucius Benham, 1853–1854', at http://www.osv.org/learning. Dates of letters hereafter noted parenthetically in text.

From there she carried on a courtship correspondence initiated by Lucius A. Benham (born 1824–1825), whom she had met at West Haven.[9]

Nearly a year into their courtship by correspondence, Sarah and Lucius worried about the possibility of living in his parents' house, in which he also resided. 'Should you enter into that connection of which mention has several times been made, should you all live in one family or separately in two?' queried Sarah in November 1853. '… Generally in such cases I think it more pleasant to live as two families. Your mother has things probably upon which she places considerable value and would it not be pleasanter to her to have a place which she could feel was hers, where she could retire at pleasure?' (14 November 1853). The sentiments attached to one's possessions was reason enough to set up two households, as Lucius agreed in his reply. After stating that his intention was not 'to live in the same family with parents' he observed, 'To live without the home feeling would truly be a serious drawback on one's happiness' (22 November 1853).

Lucius suggested that the house could be altered to meet each family's requirements. Along with a drawing of the ground floor plan, he introduced the question of enlarging the house. This was followed by several months of exchanging ideas and drawings about the placement of the chimney, kitchen, pantry, woodroom, bedchambers, halls, doors, cellars and stairways. In the midst of these deliberations his mother died, in late January 1854. The tone and content of letters thereafter changed. Remodelling the house would have to wait, but Lucius offered that there was enough in the house for Sarah to feel welcome should she consent to marry sooner. 'Should you conclude to enter a certain relationship earlier than seemed at first desirable,' he wrote on 1 February, 'there is a supply of common cotton sheets which may be used until there is time to make others. Almeda [Lucius's sister] thinks they had better be used than otherwise. Of comfortables, bedquilts, etc. there is not a great abundance though we have not been cold for want of them.' An added bonus, perhaps, was the 'carpet on the parlor floor which father wishes to have remain there'. Lucius did not know whether Sarah 'would think it good enough. The same may be said of the parlor chamber, hall, hall chamber, and kitchen' (1 February 1854). 'Going to housekeeping', it seems, required *new* goods.

Sarah had resisted an earlier wedding date pressed by Lucius after his mother's death. 'For the past three months I have not accomplished very much, just because I did not feel like doing much some of the time, and there is a great deal I should want to do before going to housekeeping. The duties arising from a new relation are enough without being pressed with business which ought to have been attended to before forming it' (26 January 1854). She penned two weeks later, 'my earliest

9 Lucius A. Benham is listed in the 1860, 1870 and 1880 federal censuses as 'farmer'. In the 1860 census, he owned real estate valued at \$2,000 and a personal estate valued at \$1,000. The 1870 census listed Lucius as having a personal estate valued at \$2,000. In the 1870 and 1880 censuses Sarah was listed as 'Keeping House'. United States of America, Bureau of the Census, *Eighth Census of the United States, 1860* (Washington, DC: National Archives and Records Administration, 1860), M653; United States, *Ninth Census of the United States, 1870* (Washington, DC: National Archives and Records Administration), M593, RG29; United States of America, Bureau of the Census, *Tenth Census of the United States, 1880* (Washington, DC: National Archives and Records Administration, 1880), T9.

convenience will not be before the last of May' (11 February 1854). Requiring Sarah's help to run the farm, Lucius pressed his case in person in late February. In his next letter the house plans had been redrafted, and questions about fitting the house for the engaged couple answered:

> You spoke of liking to make a carpet for the kitchen. If you wish it, it could be placed in the chamber above of the same dimensions and removed below whenever we thought best. I conversed with father last eve about the crockery and find he wishes to have it used. I think you had better not get any until you come and see what is wanted. (28 February 1854)

By 11 March, Sarah had commenced preparing for her move. 'Mrs. Belknap has been here this week sewing some for me, and today Lydia, the sister of my sister Beulah, came to visit me and put in a few stitches.' Sarah informed Lucius that she had begun asking advice about 'whether to buy what furniture I get here or in West Haven' (11 February 1854). This elicited an inventory from Lucius of household furniture that 'Father would prefer to have used':

> In the parlor is a bookcase with drawers, a table, workstand with mirror, a flagseat chair, seat painted white. In other parts of the house are eight others which were once painted, but now is nearly worn off … There are also five others of another style and some rickety ones of various descriptions, but all old companions to father. There is in the parlor chamber a dressing table with mirrors attached and a washstand, two cases of drawers in the hall chamber, and a table in the kitchen chamber and mirror so old that it don't know its age. There are mirrors in the kitchen and bedroom chambers. The rest beggars description. (15 March 1854)

Sarah hardly had time to read inventories. She was too occupied by her preparations. 'Well, for the eleven working days just passed [I] have been ripping old garments, cutting and sewing together pieces of cloth both cotton and woolen just as fast as I ever could.' Mrs Belknap was still assisting her 'all the time'. The scraps of their work were being rolled into balls, to carry 'to Aunt Thankful who will transform them into a rag carpet' (25 March 1854). Sarah directed Lucius to have her sister Louisa, then teaching in West Haven, to survey the house and make a list of necessary 'articles':

> My Dear Sister, It is rather my opinion (but I've not said it to L.) that you had better furnish the parlor with carpet, sofa, and chairs, though he said his father wished to have the parlor carpet remain where it is. You can do as you please but I think you would enjoy it better to furnish one of your own and put that in the parlor chamber where it will be used less. I mean to see L. about it. You'll need but one bed. He wants you to feel that what you do use you can use just as freely as your own. (Note included in Lucius's letter of 29 March 1854.)

Sarah agreed. 'On the whole I should rather prefer to [furnish the parlour] if it would not make your father feel unpleasantly … I have not much money, a little over $200 perhaps, but think I might furnish that room besides my other expenditures and have a little left' (29 March 1854). Those expenditures purchased 'warp blue and crimson, which is to be threaded' for the rag carpet and paid seamstresses to mend dresses and make 'two silk dresses and one summer dress'. In the week before, 'Mrs. Swift [had] fixed over my white dress, and orange delaines' (15 April 1854). Even earlier, Sarah took the opportunity provided by a travelling peddler from whom she 'purchased silver spoons to the amount of $13 and plated ones for $2' (25 March 1854). With two weeks left before her departure to West Haven, Sarah wrote to Salem and Beulah, 'All the cotton cloth I have made up to wash and iron, all my packing to do, marking and so on. Won't you come do my marking?' (15 April 1854). The last of the 'business' was to claim possession of one's labour in marking, with needle and thread, the newly made household linens. Sarah had, evidently, made up her mind not to use the 'common cotton sheets' that were probably woven by Lucius's late mother.

Sarah and Lucius negotiated before their marriage their roles in relation to their proposed household. Lucius was responsible for providing appropriate shelter, while Sarah took up the charge to provide the dwelling's interior furnishings. Though the letters do not reveal any gifts (beyond the significant donation of labour) from members of Sarah's family, the letters detail Lucius's father's beneficence. What is striking, however, are the assumptions imbedded in the discussions of various goods. What was manufactured at home? What was purchased? Why?

Industrial production of textiles had been established in New England in the 1820s, at the famed Lowell Mills, but also in the southern half of Worcester County, in which Sarah's town of Sturbridge is located.[10] Yet Sarah and Lucius both assumed that household linens would not be purchased but somehow made by Sarah and her female family members. The letters do not reveal whether Sarah wove the cotton cloth or whether she purchased the cloth to 'make up' into household linens – bedticks, sheets, pillowcases, and towels, and even tablecloths and napkins that she had to mark. As Ulrich has found, more late colonial households in Massachusetts had spinning wheels than looms; though many women may spin, they gave their work to others to weave.[11] Sarah's Aunt Thankful had a loom. Whether she purchased the cotton cloth or wove it herself or (more likely) had it woven, Sarah still needed to measure, cut, sew and mark her household linens. ('Will you please measure the length and width of that bedstead in the parlor chamber and tell me how it stands in the room …' queried Sarah in April 1854.) These goods of cloth (whether dresses or household linens) were a bride's traditional 'movables', what would become known in the nineteenth century as a trousseau.

Importantly, Sarah saved money for what could only be purchased. At some point she had purchased the silk and delaine for her dresses. Silk was imported, but delaine was a moderately priced, lightweight blend of wool or of cotton (warp) and wool

10 Donna K. Baron, 'Definition and Diaspora of Regional Style: The Worcester County Model', in Luke Beckerdite and William N. Hosley (eds), *Furniture History* (Milwaukee, WI: Chipstone Foundation, 1995), pp. 168–90.

11 Laurel Thatcher Ulrich also observes that though the practice of weaving in England and Europe was male's work, in eighteenth-century New England women were weavers, part of a strategy that recognized the rise of the market economy, incorporating market goods into household production: 'Wheels, Looms, and the Gender Division of Labor in Eighteenth-Century New England', *William and Mary Quarterly*, 3rd Series, 55/1 (January 1998): 3–38.

(weft) that was manufactured in the United States and England in this era. Delaines were everyday wear and were either plain or printed in a variety of colours. With her reference to fabric names and colour, Sarah did not correlate dress to purpose (except her 'summer dress'); that sort of distinction, related to fashionable or specialized activities such as calling, would await the further growth of market goods that served increasingly to delineate status through the goods related to social ritual. Still, Sarah's impending role as wife and mistress necessitated a wardrobe update. At the same time, Sarah's choice to 'fix over' her dresses rather than purchase new ones exemplified the 'stewardship of goods'[12] counselled by household advice writers in this period. 'The true economy of housekeeping,' Lydia Maria Child stated in the very first sentence of the popular New England housekeeping guide *The Frugal Housewife*, 'is simply the art of gathering up all the fragments, so that nothing be lost.'[13]

What goods Sarah purchased or would purchase to make a home were of course, those that could not be manufactured within the household. Silver spoons were purchased from a travelling peddler, perhaps one of the 126 listed in Worcester County in the 1850 Census.[14] Since the 1830s, silver, whether coin standard, sterling, or 'German', had been rolled in steam-powered flatting machines and made into affordable and very popular spoons by New England manufactories; the same manufacturer could also produce silver-plated brass or copper utensils.[15] Output of spoons increased and allowed for ready duplication of designs, via stamping machines, which appealed to consumers seeking matched sets of flatware.[16] Given the price, Sarah's spoons were probably manufactured by these methods. Manufacturers were also wholesalers who employed salesmen to increase trade. The itinerant merchant who sold her these wares was necessary in the decentralized system of household, mill and artisan shop production and manufacturing in the early nineteenth century. 'Peddler and consumer could both share in the self-fashioning of new identities', David Jaffee writes, 'through the exchange of goods that facilitated the democratization of gentility and the fluidity of social identity.'[17]

12 The term is Susan Strasser's: *Waste and Want: A Social History of Trash* (New York: Metropolitan Books, 1999). On 'making over' clothing to reflect fashion, see also Joan L. Severa, *My Likeness Taken: Daguerreian Portraits in America* (Kent, OH: Kent State University Press, 2005).

13 Lydia Maria Child, The *Frugal Housewife. Dedicated to Those Who Are Not Ashamed of Economy*, 2nd edn (Boston: Carter and Hendee, 1830), p. 3.

14 David Jaffee, 'Peddlers of Progress and the Transformation of the Rural North, 1790–1860', *Journal of American History* 78/2 (September 1991): 522.

15 The Scovill Manufacturing Company of Waterbury, Connecticut, now known historically for its manufacture and distribution of photography supplies, also produced German spoons: Theodore F. Marburg, 'Manufacturer's Drummer, 1852, with Comments on Western and Southern Markets', *Bulletin of the Business History Society*, 22/3 (June 1948): 106–14.

16 Deborah Dependahl Waters, 'From Pure Coin: The Manufacture of American Silver Flatware 1800–1860', *Winterthur Portfolio*, 12 (1977): 19–33.

17 Jaffee, 'Peddlers of Progress', p. 513.

Sarah lived in a place and at a time in which the Industrial Revolution flourished. Along with textile manufacturing, Worcester County was the home for rural production centres, providing shoes, braided straw, books and chairs, to be sold in urban markets such as Boston. Improved roads, the Blackstone Canal (1828) between Worcester and Providence, Rhode Island, and the railroad (1837) facilitated distribution. Furniture, if Sarah chose to make her purchases in Worcester County, was plentiful and cheap – at least when it came to chairs. Specialization in chairmaking (rather than woodworking or traditional joinery work) was complete by 1850. As Donna K. Baron has determined, over 1,200 men worked in the furniture trade in Worcester County in the years between 1790 and 1850. This number included 400 cabinetmakers, 36 furniture retailers and nearly 800 workers involved in some aspect of the chairmaking business. Chairs were being produced for markets outside the county. By 1850, six northern towns were producing over 800,000 chairs per annum. In turn, cabinetmakers in port towns such as Salem, Providence and Boston purchased these chairs wholesale for retail in their shops. Many cabinetmakers moved to Worcester County, bringing with them knowledge of fashionable styles. Water-powered tools, such as lathes and veneer saws, enhanced output but signalled the decline of shop artisanship. By 1850, inhabitants of Worcester County need not travel far to find cheap, stylish furniture in nearby warerooms.[18]

Chairs Lucius had aplenty, rickety though several of them were. Sarah and her sister lobbied for new parlour furniture: carpet, sofa and what may have been matching upholstered chairs. The purchase of a sofa in particular or a then-fashionable matched parlour suite signalled Sarah's wish to appear genteel. By the 1850s, as Katherine C. Grier has found, domestic parlours (like their commercial counterparts in hotels and at daguerreotypists' rooms) testified to their owners' respectability and of all the rooms in the middle-class house required the most expense.[19] Going to housekeeping, for the newlywed Benhams, meant entering into society at large. A new parlour suite would bow to taste and make Lucius's family dwelling their home.

From Home Production to Mass Consumption

Society itself would change after the American Civil War (1861–65). A wedding, especially in the nation's cities and large towns, became a more public event that celebrated not only marriage but the ability to portray fashionableness. More than family members feted the newlywed couple; friends, neighbours and social acquaintances offered gifts as warm wishes for the bride and groom at marriage rather than afterwards. By the 1880s 'Society' pages in the nation's newspapers, often edited by women, regaled readers with intelligence about engagement parties, brides' preparations and, of course, the ceremonies, with all the attendant descriptions of

---

18 Baron, 'Definition and Diaspora of Regional Style'.

19 Katherine C. Grier, *Culture and Comfort: People, Parlors, and Upholstery, 1850–1930* (Amherst, MA: University of Massachusetts Press, 1988). The term 'parlor' was used in the US for rooms that would have been designated drawing rooms in the homes of better off households in Britain. See also Richard L. Bushman, *The Refinement of America: People, Houses, Cities* (New York: Knopf, 1992).

gowns and flowers, decorations and decorum. Mentions of honeymoon destinations and of residences usually completed these narrative tableaux of happiness.[20]

Weddings themselves became rites celebrating status consumption. No longer did friends and family need to donate their skills and labour in aiding the bride's preparations for marriage and her eventual housekeeping. Etiquette guides by the 1880s devoted pages to wedding gift-giving, acknowledging implicitly the rise of mass consumption as the means by which 'proper' gifts were defined. Indeed, the spectre of losing the practice of preparing the bride's trousseau through the labour of family and friends raised the question of whether gifts should be considered at all. Did the very act of purchasing a gift devalue its sentiment? 'There is much to be said for and against the custom of wedding presents', Maud C. Cooke opined in 1891. 'And while the fact remains that they too often become the vehicle for an expenditure so uncalled-for as to encroach upon vulgarity in its excess, another fact still exists, that the simple remembrances of friends are very grateful to the bride, who, perhaps, is bound for a distant home where every loving token will recall a well-known face.'[21] In addition, the myriad choices available risked competitive show rather than appropriate feeling towards the bride. The abundance of selection made 'the question of the appropriate wedding present a very difficult one', one editor noted in 1885, '... oftentimes a bride will find herself possessed of three or four articles of the same kind'. The editor concluded that 'The gifts that are most truly gifts are those that we make rather than buy.'[22]

Etiquette book authors acknowledged the rising practice of purchasing gifts. They agreed that gifts were to be sent in advance of marriage and from which stores they should be purchased. The authors parted ways, however, when it came to the display of gifts on the wedding day. By 1891, Mrs. Annie R. White could assert that 'Wedding presents are no longer exhibited on the day of the wedding, ticketed and labeled with the names of their givers, like dry goods in a shop window.' Yet Mrs. White quickly celebrated those goods in the shop window of the printed page:

> There are so many beautiful articles which can be fittingly sent as wedding gifts, that it is almost impossible to particularize. Among them are pictures, albums, bric-a-brac, vases, clocks, mantel ornaments, jewelry, books, and even pieces of furniture. Formerly it was

20 Maureen E. Montgomery, *Displaying Women: Spectacles of Leisure in Edith Wharton's New York* (New York: Routledge, 1998), discusses the dilemma of newspaper reportage and women's publicity.

21 Maud C. Cooke, *Social Etiquette or Manners and Customs of Polite Society Containing Rules of Etiquette for all Occasions, Including Calls; Invitations; Parties; Weddings; Receptions; Dinners and Teas; Etiquette of the Street; Public Places, Etc., Etc. Forming a Complete Guide to Self-Culture The Art of Dressing Well; Conversation; Courtship; Etiquette for Children' Letter-Writing; Artist Home and Interior Decorations, Etc.* (1899), pp. 45–6. Vicki Howard notes that etiquette books at this time 'showed signs' that the old means of creating a trousseau was declining: 'American Weddings: Gender, Consumption, and the Business of Brides', PhD thesis, University of Texas, 2000, p. 27.

22 *The Home Instructor. Indispensable to Every Household. A Compendium of Useful Knowledge Necessary for the Practical Uses of Every-Day Life ... Compiled by Thomas W. Handford* (Chicago: Donohue & Henneberry, Publishers, 1885), p. 92.

> only thought proper to give silverware and jewelry, but common sense has come to the front in these days, and ostentatious display no longer prevails in good society.[23]

Such 'beautiful articles' adorned the home rather than furnished the tools of keeping house. Other advisors understood the dilemma of appearing showy and wishing to appear grateful by displaying wedding gifts to one's close friends and family members. 'To some it seems ostentatious and subversive of all sentiment to have possibly unsympathetic and critical eyes peering at and appraising the offerings. Others desire to share with their friends what is giving them so much pleasure, and are proud to show the evidence of the kind and generous attentions of which they have been the recipients.' The solution was a compromise: 'The happy mean between the two views of the subject seems to have been reaching in the present custom of inviting only the inner circle of one's friends to see the gifts two or three days before the wedding.'[24]

How was this accomplished? Mrs. Burton Kingsland devoted much attention to this matter in her 1901 guide on weddings. 'The bride's mother writes a line upon her visiting card, saying, possibly, "Will you come in for a cup of tea on Wednesday afternoon between four and six o'clock, to see the presents?"' The bride's mother, sisters or close friends arrange the gifts for display. 'It is customary to place the gifts on tables, covered with white-damask cloths, which are set around an up-stairs room, from which the furniture is removed to facilitate convenient passage', Mrs Kingsland continued. The room should be comfortable and 'attractively arranged to tempt one to loiter – chairs set in friendly groups, a pillow-heaped divan in one corner, a tea-table all ready for afternoon tea'.

In such a way comparison to goods on a department store counter was mooted and possible accusations of conspicuous consumption muted. The display of gifts itself was so arranged so as not to invite 'invidious comparison'. Cards were removed to prevent 'comment or criticism'. Arrangement should place each gift in its own favourable light, again to deter negative comments and to distance the display from its commercial counterpart. 'The simplest gifts should be so placed as to prove to the givers that they are appreciated. The costly ones need no advantageous setting, since they are in no danger of being overlooked.' Mrs Kingsland recognized the evils of invidious comparison, countering quickly with a laudatory example of a recent bride

23 Mrs. Annie R. White, *Polite Society at Home and Abroad; A Complete Compendium of Information upon all Topics Classified under the Head of Etiquette* (Chicago, IL, Philadephia, PA, and Stockton, CA: Monarch Book Company, Publishers, 1891), pp. 145–6. The spectacle of display in urban department stores and in trade and mail order catalogues is discussed in Simon J. Bronner (ed.), *Consuming Visions: Accumulation and Display of Goods in America, 1880–1920* (New York: Norton, 1989), and William Leach, *Land of Desire: Merchants, Power, and the Rise of a New American Culture* (New York: Pantheon, 1993).

24 Mrs Burton Kingsland, *The Book of Weddings. A Complete Manual of Good Form in All Matters Connected with the Marriage Ceremony* (New York: Doubleday, Page & Company, 1902), p. 128.

who did everything 'to avoid the appearance of a shop or fair and give the effect of a daintily furnished room'.[25]

By the end of the nineteenth century, etiquette doyennes were being joined by advertisements, by specialty and department stores, and by the thick catalogues of mail order houses. All the necessary goods, from the bride's gown to the wedding invitations to items necessary for sociability, could be purchased. Yet retailers pushed certain goods (such as silver, china, flatware and stationery) at certain times (especially June) but did not target brides as a specialized market. Bridal registries as a service of department stores (apart from general gift departments) would not be uniformly instituted until the 1920s. [26] Moreover, the sorts of goods etiquette book authors listed were those intended for status display in the parlour and the dining room. What about the pots and pans, the bed linens and the towels, the furniture, those items historically provided by the bride-to-be, her family and her friends?

'A Pretty Custom' Updated: The Twentieth-Century Bridal Shower

Authors of etiquette guides did not provide answers to the question of provisioning the household. Authors of household manuals did. The distinction is telling, in that the former genre was concerned with sociability and status and the latter in the messy details of setting up and managing a house. Women's and household magazines, their success based on spurring consumption, however, bridged the gap. Their editors began discussing a new form of afternoon tea in the first decade of the twentieth century, one in which close relatives and friends informally and humorously feted the bride-to-be: the 'pretty custom' updated was the bridal shower.[27] Significantly, these occasions were intended to provide the bride-elect with her household trousseaux: 'the matter of accumulating a bride's store of household linen is made the occasion of an event, very fashionable in some quarters', observed the editors of *Harper's Bazaar* in 1900, continuing:

> The brides are invited to tea, and every one brings a present of household linen. A 'shower' is the grand total. This is a modern invention which may be an improvement on the old fashion of the bride herself weaving and sewing everything she has. At all events, it helps the family get on without going to boarding.[28]

---

25 Kingsland, *The Book of Weddings*, pp. 129–30. 'Invidious comparison' is Kingsland's term, though the term was popularized by Thorstein Veblen in his 1899 critique, *The Theory of the Leisure Class: An Economic Study of Institutions*.

26 Howard, 'The Business of Brides', p. 53.

27 The term 'shower' refers to the practice of releasing above the bride-elect's head a bag or container full of confetti or streamers, or handkerchiefs, or some other lightweight gifts. Johan Casparis, 'The Bridal Shower: An American Rite of Passage', *Indian Journal of Social Research*, 20 (1979): 11. See also Howard, 'The Business of Brides', pp. 219–30, on early twentieth-century showers.

28 'Linen Showers', *Harper's Bazaar*, 37/7 (22 September 1900): 33. The author surveyed the following magazines: *Harper's Bazaar* (1900–12), *The Modern Priscilla* (1900–30) and *Ladies' Home Journal* (intermittently) for discussion of bridal showers. On the relationship between women's magazines and consumer culture, see Jennifer Scanlon,

A 'Kensington', on the other hand, was to be held once a young woman announced her engagement. At this 'simple sewing tea' held in early afternoon invited guests – all women – bring 'some dainty piece of lingerie, which she will fashion for the bride elect'. Other popular theme showers were 'handkerchief showers' at which attendees presented the guest of honour with (what else?) handkerchiefs, often carried by brides as they walked down the aisle. The traditional connections of women and textiles continued through these ritual activities.[29]

Woman's historical responsibility to provide household tools was also modernized:

> A bride can never have too many doilies, centerpieces, tray-cloths, bureau-covers, etc., and the housewifely instinct is gratified by kitchen furnishings that, tied with ribbons and ornamented with flowers, take on quite an artistic air. A tin funnel holding a bunch of violets, a dustpan with a spray of blossoms tied to the handle, and muffin-rings tied together with ribbon, are things of beauty

observed the *Ladies' Home Journal* in 1903.[30] A writer for the *Pictorial Review* in 1904 connected succinctly the purpose of these gatherings:

> 'Showers' are usually given by a number of the young couple's friends, each contributing something, but all of the same nature. So, we have 'Linen Showers', 'Kitchen Showers', 'Stock Showers', and any other 'Shower' where a collective present can be given, depending on the position and circumstances of the bridal couple.[31]

Informal and fun, meant for women, and focused primarily on goods little seen in the public spaces of the home, the shower did not fit the hetero-sociability of polite society and its emphasis on status consumption. Still, the gifts offered to brides-elect at such events were not casually considered. As one magazine columnist noted in an answer about kitchen showers:

> It is well to make out a list beforehand of kitchen needfuls (or get a printed list from a hardware dealer or a department store, which usually has such trade circulars on hand), and either suggest to the guests what they shall bring or ask to be notified of their choice to prevent duplication. … No expensive thing should be suggested, of course, outside the family.[32]

The shower took the place of the women-centred and –controlled activities of 'going to housekeeping'. Shower gifts were not the showy wedding gifts indicative of the rise of conspicuous consumption but rather the humble stuff, the 'inconspicuous' tools and goods that kept a household clean, warm and fed.

Inarticulate Longings: The Ladies' Home Journal, Gender and the Promises of Consumer Culture (New York: Routledge, 1995).

29 'Girls', *Harper's Bazaar*, 37/7 (July 1903): 672; 'Questions of Good Form', *Harper's Bazaar*, 33/50 (15 December 1900): 6.

30 'The Lady from Philadelphia Tells of the Etiquette of Easter Weddings', *Ladies' Home Journal* 20/5 (April 1903): 30.

31 'Social Observances about Weddings', *Pictorial Review* (February 1904): 21.

32 'Good Form and Entertainment', *Harper's Bazaar*, 39/7 (July 1905): 28.

Nevertheless, the bridal shower arose when both women's roles and the domestic environment were dramatically changing. Suffragists sought in these years, and eventually achieved, the vote in 1920 in America. In more numbers than ever before, American women attended college, sought professional careers, and volunteered and worked outside the home. They married later than their mothers had and they bore fewer children. The houses in which they lived after marriage were easier to build due to prefabrication methods that lowered costs. As the middle-class house was adapted to modern electricity and plumbing, its square footage dropped, requiring fewer pieces of furniture, but offering built-in storage and multi-use spaces. More Americans could own homes of their own. By the 1930s, American mass production had ushered in new synthetics, innovative household gadgets and equipment, and modern styling of domestic interiors and furniture. At the same time, Americans looked backwards, adopting the popular Colonial Revival style. From architecture to furnishings, Americans saw in this 'classic' style historically cherished traits of hard work and frugality, individualism and resoluteness. During the Great Depression architects and interior designers, the federal government, and popular authors and magazines popularized these values. American houses in the 1930s were a blend of old and new: traditional in living, dining and bedrooms, modern in the rooms redefined by technology: the kitchen and bathroom. Wedding and shower gifts reflected this distinction, one that also reflected the change in women's work in the domestic dwelling.[33]

May Aurora Swanson (born 1915) wed Joseph B. Fennell (1911–90) on 11 June 1938 in Brookfield, Connecticut. Like Sarah Plimpton and Lucius Benham nearly a century before, the couple had planned together their future home. Joseph, fresh from graduating at Danbury Trade School, built a small, Cape Cod-style house on land his parents had given the couple as a wedding present. House construction commenced on 13 February 1938 with the inspection of lumber delivered to the site. The site was plotted and the foundation dug in March 1938. Throughout April cement was mixed by hand and poured, and the foundations were completed. Photographs dated May 1938 document the framing, sheathing, and roofing of the house. Clapboards and interior finish work went unrecorded, but it appears that by the Christmas holidays the window curtains as well as a door wreath signal the house's occupancy. The photo-chronicle of the house's construction is found in the 45-page scrapbook in which May recorded the busy months of preparation for their marriage: the construction, decoration and furnishing of their home through shower and wedding gifts.[34]

---

33 Alan Gowans, *The Comfortable House: North American Suburban Architecture, 1890–1930* (Cambridge, MA, and London: MIT Press, 1987); Clark, *The American Family Home*, chs. 5–6; Victoria Kasuba Matranga, with Karen Kohn, *America at Home: A Celebration of Twentieth-Century Housewares* (Rosemont, IL: National Housewares Manufacturers Association, 1997); Susan Strasser, *Satisfaction Guaranteed: The Making of the American Mass Market* (Washington, DC: Smithsonian Institution Press, 1989.

34 May Swanson Fennell's scrapbook was purchased at an estate sale in 2000 and resold via the Internet auction site eBay to the author. Though Mrs Fennell is still living, at this writing the author has not been able to meet her and discuss with her the contents of the scrapbook. It is not clear whether the scrapbook was created during the period leading up to the wedding

May had graduated from Woodbury High School in Woodbury, Connecticut. Home economics were part of high school curricula in the 1930s, and certainly home economics was very much part of American popular culture. Newspaper 'women's' pages often had home economists as advice writers and home editors, for example. Manufacturers of foodstuffs, home furnishings and housewares hired home economists to test the market and convince consumers of the quality and usefulness of their goods. Radio programmes broadcast their findings and advice. Home economists preached the power of technology to relieve women of the drudgery of housework and taught the benefits of efficiency and good consumerism.[35]

May's album displays the sort of planning home economists counselled. (At least one well-wisher wrote that May 'certainly [had] things well in hand and very nicely planned'.) On the page before the black and white photographs of Joseph's housebuilding activities May recorded her colour scheme for the house and its interior. The diagram tells us that the living room would boast cream walls, white woodwork with deep wine draperies and rug. The room's furniture would include an 'autumn Brown' studio couch and chair and a 'Deep blue chair'. The kitchen was to be adorned with white woodwork, yellow and orange highlights, and a deep blue and white linoleum floor. 'Blue gadgets' (describing a paint sample entitled 'Venetian Violet') complemented this colour scheme. Light blue walls offset with white tiles and woodwork and white fixtures appeared in the bathroom. Five pastel hues were chosen for the towels. The Master bedroom was to be dressed in pale green (or 'aqua') walls with white woodwork and rust-coloured draperies. The guest room soothed with pale coral-coloured walls, white woodwork and turquoise-blue draperies. Deep maroon blinds filtered light at unspecified windows. Interestingly, the paint colours (some with captions) were cut from a contemporary Sears, Roebuck mail order catalogue, the popular 'wish book' that helped to revolutionize retailing in the late nineteenth century.[36]

Influential home economist Christine Frederick, who had introduced 'Mrs Consumer' to the American reading public in 1929, maintained that the wishes of women, as housewives, must be accounted for in housewares and house design. Frederick suggested that colour was primary in manufacturers' appeals to Mrs Consumer:

> American women have to a degree reached genuine cultural sophistication, and they are resolved to have more and more beauty in their surroundings; better homes, more artistic furnishings, more beautiful goods of every variety, even more colorful and decorative

---

or at some remove afterwards. Nevertheless, the order of the notations, photographs and other ephemera is chronological.

Stationery stores sold albums for the purpose of keeping souvenirs and notices of the wedding. May Swanson Fennell used a general large blank-page book in which to create this keepsake.

35 Stage and Vincenti (eds), *Rethinking Home Economics*.

36 The author compared the cut and pasted paint samples to 1938 Sears, Roebuck catalogues. The matches of hue and description were exact.

kitchen utensils. They have become 'style conscious' in regard to everything they use and wear.[37]

This new interest in synthetic colour (what Frederick called the 'new rapid-drying lacquer paints'[38]) corresponded to the new popular interest in the kitchen. As servants left the American middle-class household in the early decades of the twentieth century, technological advances in heating, cooking and refrigeration ('electric servants') replaced them. Concomitantly, middle-class women, for better and for worse, were entering the once-drab space formerly populated by servants. By the 1910s, the kitchen was enlivened with colour, made possible through the cleanliness of electric appliances and electric light, gas cooking ranges with thermostats, and iceboxes and refrigerators. Curtains and utilitarian textiles, purpose-built cabinets, standardized fixtures and furniture, and other amenities brought the kitchen into the main block of the house.[39] A flood of colourful kitchenwares and electric appliances entered the American market.

May Swanson was showered with gifts that reflected the modern homemaker's desire for colour, style and efficiency. (See Table 7.1)[40] May, according to local newspapers and her own notation, was 'tendered a kitchen shower' by fourteen members of the Federated Church Choir on 5 May. A short time later, May's future sister-in-law, Mrs Albert B. Lambert, hosted a 'miscellaneous shower' for the bride, at which she received from the forty-five guests 'many useful and attractive gifts'. A third shower was thrown for May by her relatives at her parents' home in Woodbury. Members of St Paul's Episcopal Church choir in Brookfield gave a party for the couple in the parish rooms, where they presented Joseph and May with an electric toaster. On 4 June 1938, members of the Federated Choir gave her a linen tablecloth during a luncheon at Mrs Leslie Turner's in Southbury.[41]

The question that cannot yet be answered is whether May chose to register her preferences at a local department store. It seems unlikely but not impossible. The Great Depression of the 1930s forced retailers to focus on brides (and their mothers) as a reliable market. By the mid 1930s jewellery stores had instituted bridal registries, while a few department stores touted 'trousseaux rooms' to serve what managers hoped would become lifelong customers. Regina Lee Blaszczyk asserts that the establishment of the bridal registry as a merchandizing devise was 'pioneered' by Lenox China and the founder of *Bride's Magazine*, Wells Drorbaugh. Though marriage rates dropped in the first half of the decade, department stores, specialty stores and even chain stores organized their marketing strategy around a constant

37 Christine Frederick, *Selling Mrs Consumer* (New York: The Business Bourse, 1929), pp. 7 and 5.

38 Frederick, *Selling Mrs Consumer*, p. 220.

39 Clifford Edward Clark. Jr, *The American Family Home, 1800–1960* (Chapel Hill and London: University of North Carolina Press, 1986), chs 5–6.

40 May did not distinguish between items given at showers and those given as wedding presents, adding to the scrapbook when she received items in a way that correlated only loosely to the delivery of wedding gifts and the dates of her showers and parties.

41 Fennell scrapbook. Newspaper clippings from the *Waterbury Republican* and *Danbury News-Times*.

(if smaller) market for wedding goods. Bridal showers by the 1930s became venues in which modern, stylish housewares were elicited, introduced and inspected.[42]

By some means, May let it be known to her friends and family her preferences, at least in colour. For example, what was probably May's wishes for blue goods (mentioned on the colour chart) were granted. Among the discernible kitchen shower gifts were blue and white linen towels, a blue linen luncheon set, a blue and white cookie jar, a nest of six blue bowls, a blue 'Mexican cookie jar' and blue-handled can opener and tea strainer, all given by women.[43] May chose what would today be called cobalt blue for her kitchen. Modern at the time, this deep, rich colour would, with white and orange, be the official colours of the New York World's Fair of 1939–40. For the bath, pastel towels in coral, yellow, green, blue, and peach and white were supplied aplenty, again in concert with May's preferred palette. The coral- and peach-coloured towels also matched the wall colours and draperies of the guest bedroom.

Familiar brand names appear next to some household linens in May's scrapbook, often in matched sets: 'Martex' bath towels and washcloths, 'Lady Pepperell' sheets and pillowcases and 'Pequot' pillowcases. These goods went straight from factory to retailer, so that the companies benefited from national marketing. The Pepperell Manufacturing Company had been established by 1850, near Saco, Maine, on the site on which Sir William Pepperell had owned a sawmill in the early eighteenth century. The company from the outset manufactured sheets. By the 1920s, the company capitalized on its name and published *The Romance of Pepperell*, linking the aristocrat with its linens in true Colonial Revival fashion.[44] By 1928, however, the company had mills in Boston and in Georgia. In 1928 Pepperell was the first company to introduce coloured sheets, in their Lady Pepperell line. The 'Pequot' pillowcases May received were produced by the Naumkeag Steam Cotton Company,

42 Howard, 'The Business of Brides', pp. 64–5; Regina Lee Blaszczyk, *Imagining Consumers: Design and Innovation From Wedgwood to Corning* (Baltimore: Johns Hopkins University Press, 2000), pp. 257–8. Certainly, an unintended function of showers, like later Tupperware parties, was to introduce attendees to new goods.

43 All the items noted as 'blue' in the scrapbook, save one, were given by women and were primarily kitchenwares, luncheon dishes and textiles. Luncheon dishes – small sets of plates, and often cups and saucers – became popular in this period and reflected women's social activities in clubs and similar voluntary organizations that met in members' homes. With her participation in the Federated Choir, May could expect to entertain its members. Frederick, *Selling Mrs Consumer*, pp. 39–41, 355–6, discusses the 'Color in the Kitchen Movement'.

44 Pepperell Manufacturing Company, *The Romance of Pepperell, Being a Brief Account of the Career of Sir William Pepperell, Soldier, Pioneer, American Merchant and Developer of New England Industry, for Whom the Pepperell Manufacturing Company was named, and the Towns of Saco and Biddeford in the State of Maine, Wherein the First Manufacturing Unit of the Pepperell Company was Established* (Boston: Pepperell Manufacturing Co., 1943; reprint of 1921 edn).

of Salem, Massachusetts, and were available in six pastel colours.[45] Again, May's colour choices were well understood.

New brands also were noted, especially in kitchenwares that were manufactured of new materials, such as Corning Glass Works' Pyrex Ovenware. Heatproof but aesthetically displeasing when introduced in 1915, the ovenware suffered from poor sales. Not until 1937, when Corning opened a new factory and cut prices, did Pyrex become a mass-market success. As Blaszczyk points out, 'a pie plate that retailed for a dollar sold for twenty-five cents in 1938; a two-dollar casserole was sixty-five cents, and so on'.[46] May's family and friends were thrifty: she received six presents of Pyrex dishes. The modern homemaker's choice of aluminum cookware is evident in a 'Wear-Ever' kettle and pan. Manufactured by Wear-Ever Aluminum, Inc., since 1901, a company of the Aluminum Company of America (Alcoa), these wares had been sold door to door by male college students during their summer vacations – some 20,000 by 1913. By 1938 Alcoa was the largest producer of kitchen utensils; Wear-Ever was sold in hardware stores as well as chain and department stores. Its advertising was pitched to the smart homemaker who understood the science behind aluminum's ability to conduct heat and its easy handling due to its light weight – surely an improvement over cast iron.[47] Also to be found in May's kitchen were a stool and a ceramic 'Dripolator' coffeepot made with 'chromium' – that is, stainless steel. Along with other electric appliances – a 'black and chromium electric alarm clock', a Universal iron and a Universal toaster (the last two items made in nearby New Britain) – May's kitchen was sophisticatedly streamline in design.[48]

However modern May was, her house would contain evidence of women's historic relationship with the needle, provided in the items made or given by female family members and close, if older female family friends. May's mother gave her two 'knitted scatter rugs'. 'Aunt Betty' Anderson presented a hooked rug (elsewhere May called this a 'crotcheted' rug). Aunt Em gave tatting (lace) for four pillowcases, and others gave embroidered and 'initialed' (monogrammed) pillowcases (though it is not clear whether the stitching was done by the donor or professionally). In all, much of the household linen May received was given by women.

Friends and family members offered the newlyweds traditional wedding gifts: sterling silver serving pieces, monogrammed linens and silver, ceramic dinnerwares and crystal glassware. The appeal to the traditional was also seen in the widespread adoption of the Colonial style. In the Fennell's traditionally Cape Cod-style house, this was reflected more in the living room than elsewhere in the house. Antiques were also received: an antique table lamp with glass base and yellow silk shade and an 'antique glass dish' were considered appropriate wedding gifts. Two pictures by

---

45 'Colored Sheets Popular', *Wall Street Journal*, 6 June 1928, p. 9. The author has yet to trace the history of the Martex brand, though its appearance in newspapers extends back into the nineteenth century.

46 Blaszczyk, *Imagining Consumers*, p. 247.

47 Matranga, *America at Home*, p. 21; Rosemary D. Hale, 'Cookware: A Study in Vertical Integration', *Journal of Law and Economics*, 10 (October 1967): 169–79; Sarah Nichols *et al.*, *Aluminum by Design* (New York: Harry N. Abrams, Inc., 2000).

48 David A. Hanks and Anne Hoy, *American Streamlined Design: The World of Tomorrow* (Paris: Flammarion, 2005).

Wallace Nutting, photographs of Colonial scenes taken in one of Nutting's historic houses or of New England landscapes, melded new technology to an 'antique' – but ever present – past. A 'Duncan Phyfe' walnut coffee table was a revival style, named after an early-nineteenth-century New York City furniture maker. 'We have carloads of machine-made replicas of all period furniture *ad nausea*, until a Bronx or a Podunk, Michigan, apartment house, so new that there are still mortar spots in the hallways, boasts of being a dim-lit replica of an ancient Tudor palace', Christine Frederick wrote in 1929.[49] Her disdain for 'aristocratic' antiques and their modern copies fell on deaf ears. Department stores such as Jordan Marsh in Boston had for several decades installed departments dedicated to antiques and their replicas. Joseph and May Swanson's Cape Cod house, itself a historic house form 'borrowed' and updated by architects, was furnished with 'something, old, something new, something borrowed, and something blue'.

Conclusion

'Going to housekeeping' and the modern bridal shower are means through which the house and the market are historically and inextricably entwined. Historians have been quick to criticize the bridal shower as a 'consumer rite' dependent on retail goods exemplifying the commodification of social experience. To a certain extent, they are correct. It is clear, however, that the bridal shower in the early twentieth century was not the product of the modern wedding industry; the shower helped to fashion the industry. It is also clear that the bridal shower provided the means through which the American home was re-imagined, updated and furnished. In the economic crisis of the 1930s retailers saw in brides and their homemaking needs a reliable strategy through which to survive the financial downturn. Manufacturers, department stores and other retailers cultivated an existing women's practice that dated back several centuries. They employed the popular Colonial Revival style to appeal to Americans' sense of a collective past in the face of an uncertain future. At one and the same time, that future entered the middle-class house through the kitchen door, in the forms of rich, vivid colours of paint and ceramics, modern materials such as aluminium and ovenproof glass, and Art Deco styles created in bakelite and chromium. The scientific imprimatur of these materials, as seen in advertisements and product manuals, was understood by the modern homemaker familiar with home economics. Tracing historically an integral aspect of American women's gift economy allows us to explore more fruitfully the meaning of home in a culture of consumption.

---

49 Frederick, *Selling Mrs Consumer*, p. 248. On the Colonial Revival and influence of Connecticut-based Wallace Nutting see Thomas Andrew Denenberg, *Wallace Nutting and the Invention of Old America* (New Haven: Yale University Press, 2003).

Table 7.1 May Swanson and Joseph Fennell wedding and shower gifts

Gift	Giver
6 Pair Ruffled Curtains	Mother & Dad
1 Garden Basket Pair of Down Pillows Satin Slip and Nightgown	Ma Fennell
White and Chromium Kitchen Stool Trowel Set	Bert Lambert
1 Scarf & Pillow Set	Abbie Cruise
1 Hooked [Crotcheted] Rug	'Aunt Betty' Anderson
Wallace Silver Platter (initialed M.S.F.)	Ingeborg Nelson
Covered Silver Vegetable Dish Quilted Blue Silk Handkerchief case, with Vanity cover to match	Miss Hinman
Sterling Silver Sugar & Creamer	Elsa Nelson
Wooden Tray Crystal Butter, Cheese, and Bread Dishes Eight Red and White Glasses 'Swedish Modern' Chest, Service for 8 – Eighty Pieces Rogers Silverware – Priscilla Pattern	Henry Fennell
Copper and White Chenille Bedspread [counterpane]	Margaret Gallagher, Abbie Cruise, and Celia MacDonnell
Peach Wool Blanket Two Linen Towels Two Knitted Scatter Rugs Pyrex Custard Cups Wearever Aluminum Pan Two Linen Towels [repeat?]	Mother
Maple Lamp and Smoking Set	Dorothy Scott
1 Antique Glass Dish	Mr. & Mrs. Thomas Rawdon Fisher (delivered from The Old House, Southbury)
Lot on which house is built Five pound box of candy to take on trip 1 Electric Waffle Iron (Double)	Ma & Pa Fennell
1 Universal Electric Toaster	St. Paul's Choir
Walnut End Table and Book Trough	Betty and Ruby Nelson
1 Silex Coffee Pot	Mr. & Mrs. W. Thompson
'Paul Revere' Cut Glass and Sliver Hors D'Oeuvre	Rev. & Mrs. Charles Blake Carpenter
1 Electric Clock	Sally and Billy McKinstry
1 French Fry Pan & Basket	Pauline Manton
1 Dripolator (Pottery and Chromium)	Emma Lambert
1 Pr Blue Glass Vases 1 Blue [illegible] Luncheon Set	Mrs. Frank (Augusta) Rounsveldt
Tatting for Four Pillowcases	Aunt Em
1 Pr Embroidered Pillowcases	Aunt Grace and Uncle Tim
Tray – Six Yellow and white Iced-Tea Glasses Six Yellow Bakelite Iced-Tea Spoons	Uncle Ed and Aunt Georgia and May Beers
1 Casserole & Stand	Aunt Sue

1 Fostoria Hors D'Oeuvre	Helen Travers
8 Goblets	Thafia [?] Anderson
Set of Eight Crystal Sherbet Glasses	Harriet Swanson
Bottle Capper	Dad
Root Beer Bottle Caps	Richard Swanson
1 Pr Initialed Pillowcases (Pequot)	Helen & Tommie Riley
1 Blue & White Luncheon Set	Herb and Kate Beers
Cake and Berry Set Six Crystal Goblets	Mrs. Louis [Chas] Anderson
Pink Dinner Plates	Mrs. J. Blanche Douglass
Green Glass Berry Set	Georgia Elwell
Salt and Pepper Shakers Bridal Wreath Bush	Mary Jane Whitney
6 Crystal Tumblers	Olga Whitney
Pyrex Dish with Pie-plate cover	Harriet Swanson
6 Blue Bowls (Nest)	Jeanette Stone
Blue Mexican Cookie Jar	Elizabeth Carlson
Blue Pitcher Ice Tea Glasses Enameled Rack (Service for Six)	Adelaide Hickock
Egg-Shell Sugar & Creamer	Ester Voytershaik [?]
Ruby Glass Buffet Set [Pair of Ruby Glassware Candlesticks and Fruit Dish]	Anson & Alberta [Mr. and Mrs. Coe]
Green and White Pottery Bowl Iron Stand	Mr. and Mrs. Oscar Olson
Chinese Luncheon Set	Betty Nelson
'Lady Pepperell' Hemstitched Sheet Pillowcases (2)	Ingeborg Nelson
Salad Bowl with fork and spoon (Blue and white)	Elsa Nelson
Pyrex Top-of-the-Stove Dish	Esther Stone
Eleven-inch Rausburg Salad Bowl, Hand Decorated	Hazel Turner
2 Bath [Cannon] Towels Blue and White Cookie Jar	Mabel Hunt
Hand-painted Bavarian China Cake Plate Pink Duster and Oilcloth Bag [Cookie Jar?]	Josephine Pinckney
$15.00	Mr. & Mrs. Edward Hinman, Jr.
Waste Basket Can of Black Pepper 3 Japanese Towels 2 Dish Clothes Tea Strainer Pie Roller 2 Pc. Knife Set Potatoe Masher Set of Gadgets (potatoe peeler, etc.) Pot Holders and Case	Jean Manley
Set of three Blue Refrigerator Dishes	Ethel Reed

6 Pyrex Custard Cups & Rack	Louise & Gladys Smith
Blue Cogswell Chair	Emma and Bert Lambert
Coral Bath Towel Set	Jun & Eva
One Hundred Dollars Bottle Capper	Dad
Four Blue and White Linen Towels	Harold and Len (Jr.) Taylor
Green Towel and washcloth Yellow Towel and washcloth	Alice L. Johnson
One Dolgo Crabapple tree Two Peach Trees Two Apple Trees (Cortland and Baldwin) – a large donation of flowers for the wedding	Jennie Hinman
Italian Cut-work Napkins	Mrs. H.B. Lane
4 Martex Washcloths	Ruth Adamson Alice Wahlstrom
$10.00	Gram Williams
2 Yellow & Dish Linen Towels	Byron and Alice Ferry
2 Green Cannon Towels & Cloths	Elsie D. Dickinson
Green Crockery Pitcher	Ethel Hall
Mirror	Harold and Anna Galpin
2 Wallace Nutting Pictures	Axel and Lisa Severson
'Lady Pepperell' Sheets (Double Sheet)	Mother
Pair of framed Japanese Prints Pair of Embroidered Guest Towels	Ulla Gorham
Pair of China (Flowered) Salt and Pepper Shakers with Stand	Kathryn Leavenworth
Ivory Soap Soil-Off-Cloth- Dish Cloths Towels Kitchen Pad and Pencil	Mrs. Maurice Jack [Lilly] Swetland
Aluminum Measuring Cup Walt Disney's Pluto, carved from soap	Tony Cruise Hinman (Abbie's Terrier)
Wooden Spoon – Carved from an Apple twig	Sarah Carlson
Bouquet of Linens	Mrs. Sundin Mrs. Swanson
Peasan[t?] [Embroidered] Apron Pair of Pot Holders	Mrs. R. Ehrhardt
Crystal and Silver Butter Dish Silver Butter Knife	Mrs. Lundin
Salad Spoon & Fork, Salad Recipes	Mrs. C.G. Swanson
Hand-Carved Wooden Plaque	Jim & Barbara Lockwood
Sterling Bon-Bon Dish	Mr. & Mrs. Edward Hinman, Jr.
Green Glass Smoking Set	Ann Hinman
Crystal and Silver Hors D'Oeuvre	Oscar Johnson's-Brookfield
Pottery Base Table Lamp	Neenie & Spence DePue
Chicken Fryer	Maude E.
Pyrex Baking Dish with Pie-Plate Cover	Ruby & Ted
Cut flowers for my wedding Porcelain Love seat with a Colonial Dame and gentleman	Lillian B. Remmey and Mrs. Albert Aston
Bed Lamp (Pale Blue)	Florence and Jean Lindbergh

Pair Pillowcases	Arthur Suidberg's
Knickknacks – jokes, etc.	Mrs. C.G. Swanson
Pair of Pequot Pillow Cases	Harriet Swanson
Set of Towels and Washcloths 1 Peach 1 Blue	Elsie D. Dickinson
Pair of Lace Scarves	Emma Bennett
Two Blue and White Linen Towels	Mrs. James Edward [Barbara] Lockwood
Pair of Blue and White Linen Dish Towels Can Opener (blue handle) Tea Strainer (blue handle)	Mrs. Harvey Stone
'Lady Pepperell' Sheets and Pillowcases	Allie
White Linen Dinner Cloth	Federated Choir: Hazel Turner, Ethel & Ruth Reed, Jeanette and Esther Stone, Jean and Felix Manley, Mabel Hunt, Gladys and Louise Smith, Mother and Harriet Swanson, Barbara Lockwood
Two Linen Towels Two Huck Towels Pot Holder	Yvonne Bliss
'Lady Pepperell' Sheets and pillowcases	Harry and Bee
Crewel-embroidered Pillow-Case and Scarf (Made by her sister, [illegible] (Mrs. Eugene McCabe)	Abbie Cruise
Pyrex Baking Dish Silver Standard	Aunt Sue Carlson
Universal Electric Iron	Mr. and Mrs. C.G. Swanson and Family
Large Green Bath Towel Large Blue Bath Towel	Mrs. Shaw
Black and Chromium Electric Alarm Clock	Florence Campbell
Peach and White Cannon Towel Set (Two Large-Two Small Towels-Four Washcloths)	June Taylor and Eva Peck
Dutch Oven	Mr. and Mrs. Howard Eyre
Wearever Aluminum Kettle	Mr. and Mrs. J. Travers
Blue and White Linen Luncheon Cloth	Helene De Pue
Walnut Coffee Table (Duncan Phyfe)	'The Gang': Emma and Bert Lambert, Betty and Ruben Nelson, Kate and Herb Beers, Helena and Spencer DePue, Eva Peck, Len Taylor, Jr., Harold Taylor, Mary and Carl Borodeulco [?]
Red-enameled on white salt and pepper Mustard jar Black Stand	Beulah ('Boo') Strasberger and Bob Reeves
Filet Table Cloth	Jenny See
Table Lamp-Antique Glass Base Yellow Silk Shade	Celia McDonnell

PART FOUR
Consumption for the Home as Cultural Practice

Chapter Eight

The Milkman always Rang Twice: The Effects of Changed Provisioning on Dutch Domestic Architecture

Irene Cieraad

It is seldom realized that retailing, and more particularly door-to-door delivery influenced not only the exterior characteristics of Dutch domestic architecture and its urban setting, but also the interior characteristics and ritual zoning of domestic space. Daily door-to-door delivery was the main provisioning system of Dutch households until the nation-wide emergence of supermarkets in the early 1960s. The predominance of apartment blocks in the new urban areas, especially of highrise housing blocks, with front doors arranged along narrow galleries proved to be a major stumbling block for home delivery of fresh food by among others the baker, the milkman and the greengrocer. In combination with the rival retail system of the supermarket, and the new societal trend of rising labour participation of young married women, the new domestic architecture was the deathblow to the traditional door-to-door delivery that had moulded Dutch domestic architecture for more than two centuries.

Like the history of domestic architecture, the history of Dutch domestic provisioning is for the most part written along class lines. Since the eighteenth century, when class distinctions were solidified in the town houses of the upper classes, suppliers were relegated to separate entrances where they dealt with servants. In that period upper-class women more and more refrained from the public eye, and left outdoor shopping and market visits to their maids. It resulted in the nineteenth century in a situation where food markets were more and more concentrated in working-class districts. While households in upper- and middle-class districts were provided by suppliers in a system of daily home delivery, households in working-class districts were not served and depended on local shopkeepers, markets, street vendors and stalls. The daily provisioning of the working classes was an outdoor affair. They carried their shopping home in buckets and baskets. The nineteenth-century working-class background of food markets may well explain why market halls, so prominent in the urban context of Southern and Eastern Europe, were rarely built in the Netherlands.[1]

1 Some seventeenth-century market spaces, like the ones for trading butter, were covered with a roof to protect the product. The trading of meat, however, was originally situated in halls. Markten, *Markten in Amsterdam* (Amsterdam: Stadsdrukkerij, 1984), pp. 7, 9.

In the 1960s when the supermarket superseded door-to-door delivery, the changed provisioning stimulated a radical restructuring of the traditional floorplan of family houses, which was characterized by a long hallway. Modern family houses, however, were designed without hallways, and in due course traditional middle-class houses were modernized by their new owner-occupiers according to this new model. The hallway had once been the main domestic traffic route for the housewife, connecting the kitchen in the back of the house to the front door. At that time the door had to be answered numerous times a day, both to suppliers and to bill collectors. The strikingly similar ways by which owner-occupiers integrated the space of the former hallway into open plan living signalled a new ritual zoning of domestic space parallel to a re-zoning of its immediate outdoor space. The urban layout of residential areas changed in response to the changed provisioning of households.

A public facility like the supermarket, however, also affected the use and zoning of domestic space, especially where the storing and the indoor distribution of purchased food is concerned. Students of architecture have collected ample material in describing the shopping and storing protocols in their parental homes.[2] If anything, they have made it painstakingly clear that modern domestic architecture has ignored the need for additional storing facilities implied in the weekly drive to the supermarket. Storing and conserving fresh and frozen food warrants considerable larder space, and implies the presence of refrigerators and freezers. Such problems of storing and conservation were unknown in the former daily provisioning system of door-to-door delivery. This explains why in the post-war years the sales figures of refrigerators were still very low in the Netherlands compared to for instance Finland, where daily home delivery did not exist.

In the following chapter the relation between Dutch domestic architecture and household provisioning will be put into a more extended historic perspective, focused on the rise and fall of door-to-door delivery. The chapter deals with the intricate relation between the public world of retail and the private world of domestic consumption as mirrored in the evolution of domestic architecture. It is about the ritual zoning of public and private space through consumption, and touches upon issues as diverse as class, gender, food conservation, household technology, transport and urban planning.

---

2 Former colleagues of the Women's Studies group at the Faculty of Architecture of Delft University initiated the project in 1996. Students analysed their parental home and in particular the use and zoning of domestic space by describing the trajectory of food. How the family managed the food shopping, storing, preparing, eating and discarding. Not only where the food was bought and the distance involved, but also where it was stored, where it was eaten, who did the shopping, by car or by bike and how often. Who did the cooking, and whether the family had breakfast, lunch or dinner together were taken into account. Similarly, not only descriptions of the type of meals and the family's food philosophy, but also the unwritten rules of eating were noted. For example, if it was allowed to eat in one's bedroom. On the floorplans of their parental homes, the students mapped the trajectories of the food and drink. These maps indicate in a very visible and straightforward manner how domestic space is used and where activities are concentrated.

The Intertwining of the Public and the Private

The Advent of Door-to-Door Delivery

Up until now, historians have ignored the relation between urban domestic architecture and provisioning.[3] Experts, both in the field of the history of domestic material culture and the history of retailing confirmed the scant information on the topic. The negligence is not only due to a lack of primary sources, but also due to a cross-over within the historic discipline where the history of the public and the private domain are still more or less separate fields of knowledge. This leads to a curious situation, for although there are numerous seventeenth-century paintings of Dutch domestic interiors, of urban streetlife and still lifes with an abundance of food, we do not know whether the daily household provisions, such as bread, butter, milk, meat, fish, fruits and vegetables, were delivered by street vendors or door-to-door suppliers, or fetched by maids.[4] The same is true of fuel, which was not wood but peat, and came like wine and beer in heavy barrels.

An additional source for late-seventeenth-century Dutch domestic architecture are a few surviving ceremonial doll's houses, which were more or less faithful replicas of the period's town houses of rich merchant families. Being precious show objects the creation of doll's houses is best described as private art projects of wealthy women, most of them merchants' wives. For example, in the case of the famous doll's house of Petronella Oortman, there is a cellar situated under the kitchen, only a small part of which is filled with barrels of beer, and wine and all kinds of vessels, bottles and pots, locked away behind a wooden fence.[5] The large cellar space in front of the fence, however, is – except for some brooms and buckets – empty.[6] If the space was used to store daily quantities of food, or for the preparation of raw fish, or meat, we do not know. We do know, however, that in affluent seventeenth-century households the housewife controlled access to the provisions and kept the keys to the cellar.[7]

A painting of Pieter de Hooch titled *Woman with a Child in a Pantry* also offers a peek into a cellar space, seemingly situated below street level. It portrays a maid or mother handing a jug with wine or beer to a little girl, and suggests that the drink was

---

3 This contrasts, however, with a number of historic studies on traditional farm architecture, notably dairy farms, in relation to home provisioning, cheese making and subsistence farming.

4 H.P. Chapman, W.Th. Kloek and A.K. Wheelock, *Jan Steen: schilder en verteller* (Zwolle: Waanders, 1996); S. Schama, *The Embarrassment of Riches: An Interpretation of Dutch Culture in the Golden Age* (New York: Knopf, 1987). Similarly, a historic account of the food products used does not refer to this type of information either. J. Jobse-Van Putten, *Eenvoudig maar voedzaam. Cultuurgeschiedenis van de dagelijkse maaltijd in Nederlan* (Nijmegen: SUN, 1995), pp. 96–107.

5 C.W. Fock, '1650–1700', in C.W. Fock (ed.), *Het Nederlandse interieur in beeld 1600–1900* (Zwolle: Waanders, 2001), p. 163.

6 Although probate inventories are considered the most informative source on material culture in the past, they seldom describe the perishable contents of the vessels, pots and baskets, with the notable exception of bottles filled with wine.

7 H. De Mare, 'Domesticity in Dispute: A Reconsideration of Sources', in I. Cieraad (ed.), *At Home: An Anthropology of Domestic Space* (New York: Syracuse University Press, 1999).

tapped from the huge barrel visible in the dark space below.[8] Although seventeenth-century paintings seem to be lifelike portrayals of domestic situations, De Mare points to the spatial inconsistencies when reconstructing the domestic architecture according to these paintings, illustrated by among others the above-mentioned painting. Still, it seems safe to suggest that these heavy barrels were home delivered. Unlike fresh food supplies, which were probably bought by maids, or the housewife herself at specialized food markets or from street vendors.[9] (Illustration 8.1). A shopping protocol is suggested by the numerous portrayal of maids carrying a kind of metal shopping 'basket', which looks like a bucket with a lid suitable for the transport of fresh fish and meat.[10] However, there is also some pictorial evidence of costermongers and street vendors, male or female, who have entered the front hall of the house offering their merchandize to the housewife, a then honourable title for the mistress of the house.[11]

In contrast to the informal portrayals of seventeenth-century housewives in the company of their maids, or when dealing with costermongers, eighteenth-century pictorial sources bear witness to social distancing.[12] Growing class differentiations are mirrored in the domestic architecture of the huge eighteenth-century town houses, for example, the patricians' houses built along the canals of Amsterdam. These houses looked more like palaces, with stairs to majestic front doors.[13] As a matter of course the habit of leaving the front door open during daytime, and giving access to visitors and suppliers alike, grew obsolete. Located on street level – below the majestic front door – there was a low service door, which gave access to the basement kitchen in the back of the house, and to pantry and cellar spaces.[14] The crucial difference between the situation in the seventeenth and the eighteenth century where the gentleman's townhouse was concerned, pertained to the social distancing of staff and suppliers on one side, and the inhabitants and their visitors on the other.[15] (Illustration 8.1.) Servants not only dealt at the basement level with suppliers, but also answered the front door on the first floor and guided visitors through the central corridor, a long hallway, to the living quarters of the family.[16]

8 De Mare, 'Domesticity in Dispute', p. 27.

9 As illustrated by Jan Steen's seventeenth-century painting of the river fish market in The Hague. Chapman, *Jan Steen*, p. 116. Steen also painted a baker in front of his shop and portrayed a milk vendor pouring milk into a maid's bucket. Chapman, *Jan Steen*, p. 124.

10 Fock, '1650–1700', pp. 118, 119, 137. In Vermeer's famous painting *The milkmaid* there is a brass 'basket' and a reed basket hanging on the wall, and in his painting *View on Delft* women are carrying these baskets. A.K. Wheelock (ed.), *Johannes Vermeer* (Zwolle: Waanders, 1995), pp. 9 and 14.

11 De Mare, 'Domesticity in Dispute', pp. 114, 118.

12 For example, an eighteenth-century view of a square in Amsterdam shows figures such as a man rolling a barrel, a street vendor and a wheelbarrow with barrels in the background. (Painting by Isaac Ouwater in a private collection.)

13 I. Cieraad, 'Dutch Windows: Female Virtue and Female Vice', in Cieraad, *At Home*, p. 35.

14 Fock, '1650–1700', p. 85.

15 Class differentiation had already begun by the second half of the seventeenth century. Fock, '1650–1700', pp. 84–5.

16 J. Pijzel-Domisse, '1700–1750'. in Fock, *Het Nederlandse interieur*, pp. 184 and 192; E.F. Koldeweij, '1750–1800', in Fock, *Het Nederlandse interieur*, pp. 267 and 316.

8.1 Growing class differentiations are mirrored in the domestic architecture of the eighteenth-century canal houses of the Amsterdam urban elite, who favoured separate entrances for suppliers and visitors. The suppliers' entrance was located on street level, below the majestic front door that welcomed visitors to the house.

Class Distinctions

Throughout the nineteenth century the class distinction between upstairs and downstairs became even more pronounced. It was a development characteristic of domestic architecture of the well-to-do in most of the western world.[17] The provisioning of the households of the respectable middle classes in the early nineteenth century, however, did not differ greatly from the situation as described for the seventeenth century. Costermongers are portrayed offering their wares to the housewife seated at the open front door, or even in the privacy of the living room, which was still in the vicinity of an open door.[18] In the late nineteenth century, however, middle-class housewives did

17 Matrix, *Making Space: Women and the Man-made Environment*, London: Pluto, 1985), pp. 64–7.

18 T.M. Eliëns, '1800–1850', in Fock, *Het Nederlandse interieur*, p. 368. The first painting is titled *A Cherry Peddler* and painted by Abraham van Strij, located in the Rijksmuseum Amsterdam and the second is titled *The Greengrocer* (1818) and painted by Adriaen de Lelie, location unknown.

not do their daily shopping at the market any more. By that time the eighteenth-century upper-class code of female decency had trickled down, and had influenced the social behaviour of middle-class women in their retreat from the public eye.[19] Decent women were not allowed to be observed in their home, let alone to be seated in front of their house, or walking unaccompanied.[20] In due course food markets became characteristic of working-class districts. A large proportion of stallholders and vendors were lower-class women, who ridiculed the upper-class code of female decency.[21]

This social development was reflected in the domestic architecture of the upper-middle classes, which adhered to a strict separation of the classes. By creating separate suppliers' windows in the basement kitchens, domestic staff could deal directly with suppliers and vendors, who were considered social peers. Ironically, though, the distinguished front door was situated next to these service windows to the kitchen below. Therefore, visitors to the house were able to observe the servants in the kitchen, while waiting for one of the maids to answer the door. The more simple middle-class town house, however, without a basement kitchen and service window remedied the absence of separate entrances by either integrating a kind of service window in the front door, or by delegating suppliers and servants to the back door which was also the entrance to the kitchen. The architecture of upper-class villas built in the late nineteenth and early twentieth century on the outskirts of Dutch towns, however, mirrored the distinct social spheres as these urban villas were provided with separate service wings. Out of sight of the family quarters, there was a service entrance for suppliers, where they dealt with servants. By that time all food supplies were home delivered, and stored in adjacent cellar spaces and pantries.[22] The very few images of nineteenth-century cellars look very similar to the situation in the seventeenth-century doll's house with the wooden fence behind which the provisions were locked away and the empty space in front, where, cupboards in stead of brooms and buckets were placed.[23]

At the turn of the century, not only American but also European upper classes were under the spell of what was called the servant problem, or servant issue, which was more correctly described as a problem for their mistresses.[24] Working-class girls did not fancy domestic service any more, and preferred the regular labour times of factory work and offices. Although upper-class mistresses of the house were not forced to do the household chores on their own, they had to be satisfied with fewer personnel. Middle-class women, however, feared the day their only servant would leave them.[25] The shortage of domestic staff propelled architectural and managerial solutions.

Architects commissioned to design fashionable country houses – the latest trend among the new upper class – were very keen on designing efficient servants' routings

19 For example, Weissenbruch's painting of the vegetable market in The Hague probably dated between 1850 and 1860, shows females in humble dress (private collection).

20 Cieraad, 'Dutch Windows'.

21 J. Schagen, 'Brutale Coba en Blonde Beckie. De "Vissteeg" in de jaren dertig', *Ons Amsterdam*, 54/3 (2002): 114–17.

22 I. Cieraad, ' "Out of my kitchen!" Architecture, Gender and Domestic Efficiency', *The Journal of Architecture*, 7/3 (Autumn, 2002): 263–79, p. 268.

23 T.M. Eliëns, '1850–1900', in Fock, *Het Nederlandse interieur*, p. 452.

24 I. Montijn, *Leven op stand, 1890–1940* (Amsterdam: Thomas Rap, 1998), pp. 212, 232.

25 Cieraad, 'Out of my kitchen!'.

and comfortable servant quarters. Some Dutch architects, however, were inspired by the revolutionary idea of apartment hotels propagated by an American feminist. A central kitchen and professional staff catered for the families living in kitchen-less apartments.[26] Although some apartment hotels were built in the Netherlands, it was considered too luxurious for the middle classes. The newly founded Dutch Association of Housewives (1912) favoured all kinds of solutions to remedy the servant problem, but became most famous for their involvement in efficient kitchen designs in the Netherlands. Efficient kitchen designs fostered the illusion that the housewife could manage the household all on her own, without the help of any servant. Kitchens, however, were in the best of Dutch middle-class traditions located in the back of the house. The efficiency of the kitchen design was annihilated when combined with the class-bound tradition of daily door-to-door delivery. Numerous times a day housewives were compelled to interrupt their work to answer the door to suppliers and bill collectors.[27]

8.2 On her doorstep the housewife dealt with a legion of male suppliers, vendors and bill collectors. In the 1960s, not only the rise of the supermarket and the incrementing labour participation of Dutch women, but also the predominance of apartment blocks without any facility for suppliers signalled the fall of a once nationwide provisioning system of door-to-door delivery.

26 Cieraad, 'Out of my kitchen!', pp. 269–70.

27 I. Cieraad, 'Rituels domestiques au xxe siècle aux Pays-Bas. Habitudes d'habiter', in B. Collignon and J.-F. Staszak (eds), *Espaces domestiques: construire, habiter, représenter* (Paris: Bréal, 2003).

Gendered Domains

The ideal of full-time housewifery spread throughout Dutch society, not only actively propagated by the upper classes to civilize the working classes, but also eagerly adopted by the lower classes for status reasons. Within the first decades of the twentieth century, a silent revolution took place, when the workers' wages were raised to realize the ideal of full-time housewifery. From that moment on breadwinners – be it workers, suppliers or street vendors – were predominantly of the male gender. It became a very visible gender split in the public domain. Males, like the milkman, the postman and the baker and butcher's boy, were the ones to dominate for the most part the empty streets of the newly built working-class housing estates. (Illustration 8.2.)

The importance of door-to-door delivery in the design of even working-class apartments of that period is best illustrated by a social housing project in Rotterdam, designed in 1919 by architect M. Brinkman. His design was unique in more than one way. Not only in constructing a four-storey apartment block for the working classes, which consisted of two layers of maisonettes, but also by including in his design a giant service elevator. (Illustration 8.3.) The elevator was constructed to lift the suppliers' carts, including the horses, onto the gallery on the second floor. Not only the elevator, but also the width of the gallery was designed to fit the dimensions of the suppliers' carts, of which the greengrocer's wagon was the biggest. Suppliers rang the doors and housewives could deal with suppliers by opening their kitchen window, which was situated next to the front door.[28] Although very efficient in its spatial organization, the architectural design mirrored the social hierarchy as expressed in the late nineteenth-century town house where servants also dealt with suppliers through the service window in the basement kitchen. However, unlike their middle-class counterparts, these working-class housewives did not need to run up and down the hallway to answer the door. As such, the architectural design of a kitchen situated next to the front door was also revolutionary, because it preceded the 'reversed' floorplans of apartments and family houses common in the latter half of the twentieth century.

In the first decades of the twentieth century, architects in cooperation with the Dutch Association of Housewives came up with different solutions to tackle the servant problem. Apartment hotels and especially efficient kitchen designs were among the most adopted solutions. Both parties involved realized, however, that more efficiency could be attained when circumventing the time-consuming dealings with suppliers, who also demanded the housewife's presence and availability during all hours of the day. In 1924, the Dutch architect Wegerif suggested kitchens designed at the side of the house with a delivery box in its outer wall.[29] With lists in the delivery

---

28 I. Cieraad, 'Droomhuizen en luchtkastelen. Visioenen van het wonen', in J. Huisman, I. Cieraad *et al.*, *Honderd jaar wonen in Nederland 1900–2000* (Rotterdam: Uitgeverij, 2000), pp. 206–7.

29 A.H. Wegerif, *Van bouwen en wonen* (Rotterdam: Nijgh & Van Ditmars Uitgevers-Mij, 1924), pp. 125, 131; Cieraad, 'Droomhuizen en luchtkastelen', p. 220. Gerrit Rietveld, considered the most modern Dutch architect, in his design of the famous Rietveld-Schröder house was as revolutionary as Wegerif. Rietveld created a traditional separate suppliers'

box, the housewife was supposed to communicate with suppliers, who then left the goods there. When the housewife arrived home, she would find the deliveries, for she only needed to open the delivery box from the inside.[30]

8.3 In a social housing project in Rotterdam, designed in 1919 by architect M. Brinkman, door-to-door delivery was revolutionized by installing a giant service elevator to lift the suppliers' carts onto the gallery on the second floor. Housewives could deal with suppliers by opening their kitchen window, situated next to the front door.

In 1932, however, one-way delivery boxes were installed in the hall of a nine-storey apartment building in Rotterdam. The delivery boxes had to compensate for its narrow galleries, which were unsuitable for suppliers' carts. Although not for carts, it was the first social housing project in the Netherlands with elevators for residents. The architects W. van Tijen, J. Brinkman jr and L. C. van der Vlugt envisioned a modern lifestyle, and the end of fulltime housewifery. They linked this highrise building to a row of shops for daily provisions.[31] By this means they implied another way of domestic provisioning, which heralded the end of door-to-door delivery. Although the residents had to comply to the new order, most Dutch housewives at that time were very reluctant to change their way of provisioning, favouring the

---

entrance connected to the kitchen on the ground floor. A big sign directed suppliers to the side of the house and stipulated that they should ring and in case no one answered to use the speaking tube that allowed communication with the residential quarters on the first floor. However, the kitchen windowsill could also be used as delivery box. P. Overij, L. Büller, F. den Oudsten and B. Mulder, *Het Rietveld Schröder Huis* (Houten: De Haan, 1988), pp. 111, 31.

30 D. Oppenheimer-Belinfante, 'Radiolezing gehouden voor de A.V.R.O. op 12 April '34', *De 8 en de Opbouw*, 6/9 (1935): 98–101, p. 100.

31 Cieraad, 'Droomhuizen en luchtkastelen', pp. 204, 207–10.

more prestigious home delivery service, irrespective of its questionable efficiency. One-way boxes proved to be a rare phenomenon in Dutch domestic architecture.[32]

From the late 1920s small service elevators – often hand-operated – were frequently installed in the stairwells of three-storey apartment buildings in upper- and middle-class neighbourhoods.[33] Service elevators in upper-class apartments, however, were closed constructions with an opening in each kitchen, and in this way, the service elevator connected all floors. The communication with suppliers was by means of a speaking tube. Because cooking smells and noises spread easily through its shaft, this type of service elevator was not popular, in contrast to the open service elevators in stairwells of middle-class apartments. Unlike delivery boxes, service elevators required the presence of the housewife or a domestic servant. In middle-class apartment blocks, the housewife had to leave her apartment when the supplier had rung, and standing on the landing she had to shout her orders downstairs. Subsequently she had to lift the filled basket or case to the floor of her apartment and take the goods out of the elevator. Once a week, traditionally on Saturdays, she went downstairs to pay the supplier.[34]

These small service elevators spared housewives and suppliers numerous walks up and down the stairs, and as such enabled door-to-door delivery within the urban context of apartment blocks till the 1970s. Besides, it would have been too exhausting for suppliers to walk up and down the stairs carrying deliveries and too risky to leave their carts unattended for long. Especially in 1960, the presence of service elevators was warranted, because municipal governments regulated the milk delivery and allowed only one milkman to deliver in a neighbourhood. Previously a number of milkmen had served their clients in the same apartment block, which made it less exhausting for each of them. One milkman for one neighbourhood, however, implied serving all of the residents of apartment blocks in the district. Without the help of a service elevator, it was considered too exhausting.[35]

Milk delivery in apartment blocks brought about a major shift in milk preference. Traditionally, Dutch housewives had their special milk jars filled with fresh, or so-called raw milk, because it was considered to be not only of better taste and quality, but also cheaper than milk in bottles.[36] The quality aspect was irrespective of the housewife's daily anxiety to boil the fresh milk, in order to make it safe for consumption. The transport of open milk jars in service elevators, or when climbing the stairs, however, was a hazardous undertaking and milk was easily spilt. Residents of apartment blocks were more or less compelled to switch to bottled milk, much to their dismay. Other

32 Unlike former days, however, delivery boxes are now installed in the halls of luxurious apartment buildings to facilitate the deliveries of the dry cleaners' and not those of the greengrocers'.

33 P.R.D. Stokvis, *Terugblikken op het huiselijk leven in de twintigste eeuw. Een verzameling getuigenissen over veranderingen in levensstijl sinds 1920* (Voorburg: Die Haghe, n.d.), p. 55.

34 D.C. Van der Poel and J.G.F. Terwindt, 'Boodschappenliftjes. Dikwijls dankbaar gebruikt, maar nog niet volmaakt', *Bouw*, 15/10 (1960): 287–9, p. 287.

35 Van der Poel and Terwindt, 'Boodschappenliftjes'.

36 A.H. Van Otterloo, 'Prelude op de consumptiemaatschappij in voor- en tegenspoed 1920–1960', in A.H. van Otterloo (ed.), *Techniek in Nederland in de twintigste eeuw. Vol. 3: Landbouw en Voeding* (Zutphen: Walburg Pers, 2000).

bottled milk products, like ready-made porridge, custard, yoghurt or buttermilk, were far more readily accepted. Milkmen were burdened not only with heavier loads, for bottles were heavier to carry, but also with a complex return system of deposit bottles. Before the advent of the supermarket, however, there were hardly any milk shops, only door-to-door delivery.[37] In poor neighbourhoods, the milkman did not ring the doorbell, but instead pealed a hand bell to let people know he was there.

Although the two-way delivery box was a very efficient solution, it was seldom constructed. Mainly because kitchens were predominantly situated at the back of middle-class houses, out of reach of suppliers. In addition, written communication was unsatisfactory for the suppliers because the housewife could not be persuaded to buy products she had not put on her shopping list. Also for the housewives' written communication was considered exceptional and not advisable. In the absence of a delivery box, suppliers had to leave the goods on the doorstep in view of the neighbours and thereby damage her respectability, as the ideal of full-time housewifery required her presence during the day.

In American futuristic scenarios of the 1950s, the two-way delivery box still played a major role in attaining household efficiency. In the updated American version, however, the delivery box in the kitchen's outer wall was a swivel refrigerator, implying a future for home delivery. Communication with suppliers was envisioned by means of a monitor on the kitchen's control panel. With a kind of fictional webcam, the housewife made video visits to the shops, where she could screen the products on sale and communicate with suppliers on her choice of products.[38] In 1960, when the system of door-to-door delivery came under pressure, architects once more suggested not only one-way or two-way delivery boxes, but also service elevators, although without any reference to cooling.[39]

Symbolic Border

The 1930s architecture of middle-class terraced houses with its typical bay window was similar all over the Netherlands and aimed at the rising class of owner-occupiers. A parlour at the front was separated by sliding doors from the dining room in the back. A narrow kitchen was situated next to the dining room in the back of the house, and a long hallway connected the kitchen in the back with the front door situated in the facade next to the parlour's bay window.[40] In the hallway, under the stairs to the upper floor, there was a small cellar space where the housewife stored the daily quantities of fresh food delivered on her doorstep by male suppliers. Daily she dealt with the baker's boy, the milkman, the greengrocer and the butcher's boy, and on a weekly basis with the grocery

37 L. Van der Horst, 'De Melkquaestie. Melkvoorziening van Amsterdam (deel 1)', *Ons Amsterdam*, 55/12 (2003): 204–8; A.P. De Knecht-van Eekelen and A. Albert de la Bruhèze, 'De witte motor', in van Otterloo, *Techniek in Nederland.*

38 Cieraad, forthcoming.

39 Van der Poel and Terwindt, 'Boodschappenliftjes; H.O. Eckardt, 'Boodschappenkastjes. Omschrijving, doel en functie', *Bouw*, 15/35 (1960): 1028–9.

40 The 1930s architecture and floorplan of terraced and semi-detached houses in Britain looks rather similar, although hallways seem less pronounced. Matrix, *Making Space*, p. 73; G. Stevenson, *The 1930s Home* (Princes Risborough: Shire Publications, 2002).

man, the cheese and egg farmer, the oil man, the laundry man and the greengrocer.[41] On her doorstep she also paid bill collectors: weekly bills for rent, electricity and gas, and monthly contributions to funeral and health insurance, to name but a few. In the afternoons, canvassers rang the door to ask for a contribution for all kinds of charity funds. Also vendors and craftsmen offered their products and services too, like the blanket salesman, the rag-and-bone man, the scissors-grinder, the chimney-sweep and the green garbage collector.[42] Answering the door constantly interfered with the housewife's other domestic duties. It kept housewives busy six days a week. On Sundays, however, suppliers and bill collectors stayed away, and only visitors were allowed to ring the door.[43] In Jewish quarters in Amsterdam, however, it was Saturdays that were free from trading.

The doorstep was not only a physical border between the public domain and the private domain of the house, but also a symbolic border between separate economic spheres. On the one hand, the non-profit domestic services of a mother and housewife, and on the other the commercial services of suppliers.[44] Therefore, money, the currency of the public domain, was paid on the doorstep. Money transfers were banned from the domestic domain of the house.[45] Love and dedication were considered to be the legitimate domestic currencies. Moreover, door-to-door delivery marked a gender divide, between the female domain of the housewife and the public domain of male suppliers. From the symbolist perspective of a social anthropologist, however, the doorstep symbolized another important divide between two major symbolic opposites: the raw and the cooked, for in her kitchen the housewife transformed the raw supplies into cooked meals. As such, the importance of the doorstep as a ritual boundary was expressed within the retail system of door-to-door delivery.[46]

Storing and Conserving

Traditionally nineteenth-century town houses had cellars or pantries, connecting with the kitchen, to store food supplies. Potatoes, for example, were bought in large

---

41 Stokvis, *Terugblikken*, p. 73.

42 A. Van Hulzen, *Utrechters. Het dagelijks leven in de Domstad tijdens de laatste twee eeuwen* (Utrecht: Bijleveld, 1997), pp. 99–114; M. Groffen and S. Hoitsma, *Het geluk van de huisvrouw* (Amsterdam: SUN, 2004), p. 186.

43 In 1996 when a new retail law enabled extended opening hours into the evening and even on Sundays, it triggered a public debate on social values and the societal importance of Sunday as a day of rest without the buzz of commerce. H. de Jonge and A. Blok, 'Open of dicht. Winkeltijden en de Nederlandse cultuur in de twintigste eeuw', in H. de Jonge (ed.), *Ons soort mensen. Levensstijlen in Nederland* (Nijmegen: SUN, 1997).

44 Households were in disarray when large quantities were delivered. Men carrying bags of, for example, coal or potatoes had to cross the doorstep to transport the dirty bags through the hallway to the kitchen, the cellar or the backyard. Housewives not only covered the trajectory of the porters through the house with old newspapers to protect the domestic domain from pollution, but also removed decoration.

45 The only possible exception to this protocol was the delivery of the weekly groceries, which were heavy and carried into the kitchen. Grocery bills therefore were more often paid at the kitchen table, where the shopping list for next week was written in the client's booklet.

46 Cieraad, 'Rituels domestiques'.

quantities for the winter season, and stored in a giant crate in the dark cellar. Coal, the dominant fuel of the nineteenth century, was sometimes stored in cellars, but more often in annexes to kitchens.[47] Attics, however, were generally not used to store food supplies, except for the conservation of fresh apples or nuts. During World War I and the concomitant period of food scarcity, the authorities stimulated housewives to invest in the creation of larger food supplies. The technique of bottling was introduced to replace the former conservation methods of drying or salting, and which enabled housewives to create vast supplies of bottled summer vegetables, meat and preserves.[48] However, if housewives could spare the investment of bottling equipment they also needed storing space for their bottles, which put working-class households in a doubly disadvantaged position, for they lacked both.

The main characteristic of Dutch domestic architecture built in the 1920s and 1930s was a small, so-called efficient kitchen. In particular, the newly built social housing for the working classes had small kitchens to prevent any other use than cooking. The Housing Act of 1901 prohibited the traditional one-room apartments and ordained separate rooms for cooking, eating and sleeping. Designed as efficient workspaces for full-time housewives without servants, the kitchens were small-sized and lacked storage space for provisions for more than one day.[49] As apartments did not have cellar spaces, architects designed an outdoor larder or a so-called 'fly's cupboard' on the kitchen balcony. Although the outdoor larder offered some extra space, it was not cooled. Likewise, the preservation of not only fresh food, but also dairy products for more than two days was a tricky affair in summertime. As such daily door-to-door delivery, or at least daily provisioning, was implied in the urban domestic architecture of the twentieth century.

Groceries, however, were the first food products to be sold in shops and not on markets, because these items required dry storage. Since the beginning of the twentieth century grocery shops were among the first to revolutionize retail, in particular food retail. A powerful structure of competitive chains dominated the Dutch grocery market and created artistic flagship stores, really true consumption palaces.[50] A woman's visit to one of these shops to buy an ounce of freshly roasted coffee beans, or dry tea was comparable to a fun-shopping session in a department store. It had nothing to do with the exhausting chore of today's food shopping, for the store delivered the more mundane bulk groceries at home. Shopping in grocery stores was by tradition less class-related than door-to-door delivery, but like all Dutch commercial and social affairs, it was religiously segregated.[51]

---

47 Wegerif, *Van bouwen en wonen*, pp. 131–7.

48 J. Jobse-Van Putten, *Eenvoudig maar voedzaam. Cultuurgeschiedenis van de dagelijkse maaltijd in Nederlan* (Nijmegen: SUN, 1995), pp. 397–9; A.H. van Otterloo, 'Prelude op de consumptiemaatschappij in voor- en tegenspoed 1920–1960', in van Otterloo, *Techniek in Nederland*, p. 278.

49 Cieraad, 'Out of my kitchen!'.

50 Ph. Hondelink, 'Grutters worden grootgrutters. Levensmiddelenhandel in Amsterdam (I)', *Ons Amsterdam*, 49/11 (1997): 282–6; Ph. Hondelink, 'Opkomst van de supermarkt. Levensmiddelenhandel in Amsterdam (II)', *Ons Amsterdam*, 50/1 (1997): 12–16.

51 G. Blessing, 'Koopt roomsch! Coöperatie Assumptio viert eeuwfeest, *Ons Amsterdam*, 53/9 (2001): 250–4. The retail chains reflected the so-called pillarization of Dutch society

Restructuring of Domestic and Public Space

Retail Revolution

In the late 1960s the supermarket definitely superseded door-to-door delivery in food retailing. The impact of the supermarket, however, reached beyond retailing. It revolutionized not only the domestic space, but also the urban planning of residential areas as such.[52] Suppliers and their carts gradually disappeared from the streetscapes of residential areas, and in due course, the doorstep lost its symbolic meaning of being the most significant borderline. Within the setting of the supermarket the traditional gender divide dissolved, for most cashiers at the checkout desks were of the female gender like most of the customers. Of course, the process was a gradual one, for in the mid 1950s `the American way of shopping', meaning self-service and a checkout desk, was first introduced in only one grocery shop.[53] Even in 1964, when the Philips company conducted a national survey of Dutch households, door-to-door delivery was still nation-wide, the predominant system where bread, milk and vegetables were concerned.[54]

Self-service and finally the supermarket concept were integrated in the existing chain stores in the grocery retail business, in which pre-packaging of dry products had already been developed. As packaging of fixed quantities was considered the backbone of self-service, the pre-packaging of wet products like milk, dairy products and frozen vegetables soon followed.[55] Supermarket stores of the traditional Dutch grocery chains did not only eradicate the former provisioning system of door-to-door delivery and small shopkeepers, but also completely transformed or spoilt the facades of local main streets.[56] Ironically, however, today's sale of non pre-packaged products like fresh vegetables, meat and bread have become an important part of the latest success of the supermarket formula, replicating within its walls the traditional shop-like structure.[57]

In response to the more expensive pre-packaged foodstuffs in the supermarket, weekly open-air food markets offering fresh products have become increasingly popular in the Netherlands since the 1970s. Markets are nowadays not only appreciated for their low price

---

where all aspects of daily, social and political life were organized according to several religious denominations in opposition to the profane 'socialists'. J. Goudsblom, *Dutch Society* (New York: Random House, 1968). Catholics were encouraged to buy from Catholic suppliers, just as Protestants would buy from co-religionists, and socialists would buy from their cooperative stores and from political affiliates. Secularization in Dutch society started by breaking the religious ties on the commercial level.

52 T. Van der Meulen, *Anders nog iets? De teloorgang van de middenstan* (Amsterdam: L.J. Veen, 2001).

53 A.H. Van Otterloo and B. Sluyter, 'Naar variatie en gemak 1960–1999', in van Otterloo, *Techniek in Nederland*, pp. 281–95.

54 De Nederlandse, *De Nederlandse huisvrouw* (Eindhoven: Philips NV, 1966), pp. 29–30.

55 A.P. Den Hartog and A. Albert de la Bruhèze, 'Verpakking', in van Otterloo, *Techniek in Nederland.*

56 Van der Meulen, *Anders nog iets?*

57 G. Rutte and J. Koning, *De supermarkt. 50 jaar geschiedeni* (Baarn: Uitgeverji De Prom, 1988).

levels, but also for the 'exotic' farmers' or working-class background of its stall holders, the vendors' knowledge of their products, and the typical straightforward communication with clients.[58] Market visits have become relaxed outings and occasions for a friendly chat, in contrast to the stressed visits to the supermarket. Pre-packaging and deep freezing, however, characterize the crucial differences between markets and supermarkets.

The Breaking of Boundaries

The advent of the supermarket paralleled the rising labour participation of young married women in the Netherlands, and the dissolving ideal of full-time housewifery. Working women, unlike their mothers, left their houses unattended. With nobody home, there was no one to answer the door to suppliers any more. Besides, new apartment buildings lacked facilities like delivery boxes. Moreover, working women considered their weekly shop in the supermarket more time-efficient and cheaper than door-to-door delivery. In due course, not only suppliers but also bill collectors stayed away, for by the late 1960s every household managed its financial affairs by banking orders. As such hallways represented an outdated domestic protocol, for the passage had lost its primary function of linking the female domain of the house, in particular the domain of the kitchen, to the public domain of male suppliers.

In addition, the doorstep lost its symbolic meaning as a trading zone, for the money transfers has been shifted to the check-out desks of supermarkets. The weekly bulk shopping in the supermarket has become a weekend job for husband and wife, for his strength is needed to carry the heavy bags and boxes to the car and on arrival into the house. Fresh vegetables, meat and bread, however, are often fetched by bike on a more daily basis. Nowadays not only cars, but also bikes – especially in the cities – have become the main means of transporting shopping. Whereas once suppliers' carts, like the butcher boy's bike with its large basket, or the bakery boy's even larger three-wheel bike had dominated the streetscape of towns and cities.[59]

The traditionally strong ties between suppliers and their middle-class customers have produced a strange identification in the Dutch language. Since the 1960s local retailers with small businesses are referred to as 'the middle classes', while the term's former reference to a particular social layer in between the upper and the lower classes seems to have been forgotten.[60] Also, the devastating effects of the supermarket on shop holders is often described as 'the fall of the middle classes'.[61] It is as if the fall of the middle classes is mirrored in the way traditional middle-class houses have been renovated all over the Netherlands. Within two decades, roughly between the late 1960s to the 1980s, their new owner-occupiers modernized most traditional middle-class houses.

---

58 Stallholders of Amsterdam's most popular daily food market situated in a recently gentrified working-class neighbourhood have become national celebrities, because of a popular docu-soap on Dutch television portraying their 'exotic' working-class wheeling and dealings.

59 M. Van Bemmel, *Aan de deur wordt veel gekocht* (Rotterdam: Duo/Duo, 2001).

60 J.H. Pompe, *De kleine middenstand in Nederland. Een vergelijkende studie tussen de oude en de nieuwe middenstan* (Deventer: Van Loghum Slaterus, 1980), pp. 45–86.

61 Van der Meulen, *Anders nog iets?*

The new owners – the first DIY-generation – renovated the old middle-class houses with the reigning modern ideal of open-plan living in mind.[62] By breaking down most separating walls on the ground floor, such as the wall between dining room and kitchen, and between the hallway and the parlour, they created a large through-lounge in which the space of the kitchen was integrated. A situation nowadays described as a living room with an 'open' kitchen. The complete absorption of the hallway into the living space left the inhabitants with only a tiny hall and resulted in most cases in the blocking of the straight passage between kitchen and front door. Since the cellar space under the staircase to the upper floor was now connected to the heated living room, it had lost its cooling capacity and was transformed into a walk-in closet.[63]

Sacrificing the hallway, however, once the household's main traffic road signals major changes, not only on the home front, but also in society at large. Especially, since the restructured living space in traditional middle-class houses was more or less a faithful copy of the through-lounges in newly built family houses, just as the restructured streets and sidewalks in these old middle-class neighbourhoods resembled the layout on the new suburban housing estates. The striking similarity of the prevalent floorplan of most family houses in the Netherlands, in combination with a desire for a child-friendly and suburban environment in the urban context of old neighbourhoods, illustrates the intertwining of these changes in the public and the private realm.

The Shopping Car

As commerce was held at bay, not only the rigid outlook of front doors and name plates changed, but also the low garden wall – the former boundary marker between public and private – was eliminated. Although residential areas as a whole changed into a friendlier environment suited to playing children, pre-war housing estates were strongly affected by the narrowing of streets and sidewalks due to the need for more parking spaces. However, the increasing number of parked cars on the street signalled the car's new intermediary role of linking the home to the world of commerce. Hence, garages and carports were integrated into the domestic architecture on the new housing estates.

Not only the suburban housing designs, but also the estates' circulation plans defied the former rigidity of the grid structure. On entering or leaving the new housing estates by car, one had to follow a trajectory of winding narrow streets full of

---

62 This information resulted from an ethnographic research project in five Dutch households in 1990–91. The project on Dutch cultural identity was initiated by a French/Swiss marketing firm RISC in co-operation with student ethnographers from the University of Amsterdam, and synthesized by me in two unpublished research reports. Andrea Semprini, the firm's anthropologist, published an article on the reports. A. Semprini, 'Espaces privés, espaces publics. Privé et public comme catégories pratiques', *Espaces et sociétés*, 73 (1994): 137–64.

63 In 1964, 60% of Dutch households still had a cellar or a cool space, and only 40% had a refrigerator. De Nederlandse, *De Nederlandse huisvrouw*, p. 72, n 23. In 1972, more than 88% had a refrigerator, and at present, every household has at least one and sometimes two. Groffen and Hoitsma, *Het geluk van de huisvrouw*, p. 130.

traffic calming 'sleeping policemen'. A popular layout was a keyhole structure with houses arranged around green courts, with limited access for cars of non-residents. Each house was provided with a private parking space, like a carport or a garage, which was situated at the back of the house, where often the 'front' door was situated too. From an efficiency perspective, however, these suburban layouts were deemed unsuitable for any commercial door-to-door delivery.[64]

In response to the changes in domestic architecture and suburban layout, and to fight the monopoly of the supermarket, the organization of milk retailers, traditionally a stronghold in Dutch society, developed a system of mobile self-service shops. These so-called 'SRV' mobile shops reflected in its abbreviation their collective goal 'together selling rationally'. In suburban and rural areas, mobile shops have survived, run, by not only milkmen, but also bakers and greengrocers. At present, however, their viability is in jeopardy, because they mainly serve the elderly, who depend on rendered services, like carrying the shopping to the doorstep: a service reminiscent of the traditional provisioning by home delivery.

Supermarket shopping, whether brought in by car or by bike, is not carried into the house by the front door, but instead follows a different course. The shopping bags are taken out of the boot of the car, or from the bike and carried through the garage, or the bike shed through the scullery or backyard straight into the kitchen/living room. The information gathered by the students[65] indicated that the back entrance via garage or garden has become the main domestic route. Even when the front door provides a shortcut to the kitchen area, it is often ignored. In suburban areas, the former upper-class situation of separate entrances seems to have been re-invented. Front doors have become the only access point for visitors unknown to the household, and who therefore need to announce their presence. Following the English tradition, doorknockers instead of doorbells have become the latest trend in the Netherlands.

Storing and Freezing

The first electrical refrigerators in the 1920s were sold to upper-class households who had cellars and pantries in their houses.[66] The ad slogan 'It will bring your cellar into the kitchen' appealed more to the cherished efficiency than to improved conservation.[67] Those who needed the refrigerator most could neither afford it nor had room for it. When door-to-door delivery waned, apartment kitchens had to be re-arranged to fit in a refrigerator.[68] In most cases a simple cooking range replaced the former oven combination and was placed on the tabletop of the refrigerator. Tight kitchen arrangements are still very common in these old rental apartments, because taking down walls to create larger spaces was not allowed.

---

64 Newspapers, advertising magazines and the mail, however, are still delivered door-to-door on these estates.

65 See n. 3 above.

66 Stokvis, *Terugblikken*, p. 74.

67 A. Van Hulzen, *Utrechters. Het dagelijks leven in de Domstad tijdens de laatste twee eeuwen* (Utrecht: Bijleveld, 1997), p. 136.

68 Stokvis, *Terugblikke*, pp. 77–8.

In 1962 one of the main supermarket chains became famous for offering their clients a very low-priced refrigerator 'to make life easier'. In conserving perishable products, the refrigerator allowed for fewer shopping trips and encouraged housewives to buy more than necessary.[69] Most apartment kitchens could not easily accommodate a refrigerator let alone an additional freezer. In renovated family houses, extra larder space was created in former cellars, sculleries and sheds, and by installing built-in refrigerators and freezers in kitchens or by putting an extra freezer or refrigerator in the scullery, shed or garage. Although the construction of carports and garages was meant to put cars out of sight, it did not work out that way. Nowadays garages are turned into warehouses, where not only bags with potatoes, onions, vegetables and oranges are stored, but also bottles with soft drinks, fruit juices and beer cans are stocked. Often a large freezer is situated in the garage too, to store the bags and boxes with frozen food. However, if a garage or pantry is not available, the weekly supplies have to be distributed in cupboards and corners all over the place. In describing the shopping and storing protocols in their parental homes, students illustrated the time-consuming character of storing. A problem unknown when suppliers delivered only daily quantities.

8.4 The title of this cartoon 'Darling, the supermarket is on your way home, isn't it?' refers to the labour participation of most Dutch wives, which has forced their husbands to engage in daily domestic duties, like shopping and cooking. Buying fresh ingredients on a daily basis has initiated a new shopping protocol. It was propelled by not only a lack of storage space in modern housing, but also changed ideas on food qualities

69 Groffen and Hoitsma, *Het geluk van de huisvrouw*, p. 130.

Due to a general lack of storing space in most modern housing, a new pattern has emerged. The students described their parents' tendency to buy fresh ingredients on a daily basis. On their way home from work father or mother drops by the supermarket to buy fresh meat and vegetables for the evening meal. It seems a heavy burden for today's parents, when coming from work they rush into the nearest supermarket and hurry home again to prepare the family's dinner. Although a bit exaggerated, it is true that the labour participation of Dutch wives has forced husbands to participate in domestic chores, like shopping and cooking. (Illustration 8.4) Research on time-management in family households indicated that it is more time-efficient to live and work in urban surroundings, because of the vicinity of shops and supermarkets for daily shopping, than in suburban areas. Hence, freezers are far more common in suburban households.

The presence of freezers is in most cases complemented by two electrical appliances to prepare the frozen food: a microwave and a deep fryer. From a symbolic perspective, therefore, the new way of household provisioning and food preparation marks another important opposition in the household between the hot and the cold, instead of the raw and the cooked as expressed in provisioning by door-to-door delivery. As the raw and the cooked were spatially related to the doorstep and the kitchen, the hot and the cold are related to the place of the microwave or deep fryer in opposition to the place of the freezer. The preparation trajectory reflects the routing of shopping when carried into the house: from garage into the kitchen, or from the shed into the kitchen. Because of the smell, deep fryers are often operated not in the kitchen, but in the garage or shed. Just as the supermarket dissolved the gender divide, so too food preparation has lost its rigid gender connotation.[70]

70 Cieraad, 'Out of my kitchen!'.

Chapter Nine

From *Ground Force* to Garden-Making: How Ordinary Gardeners Consume Television Lifestyle Aesthetics

Lisa Taylor

> **Phoebe**: (about Diarmund Gavin, *Homefront in the Garden*) I like his ideas very much. I wouldn't steal them, but some of the … like painting the walls that Marrakesh blue, that was lovely. That was a nice idea but we wouldn't necessarily do it in paint. It might be in plants instead.

Introduction

Garden lifestyle television, with its formal ability to hook into the rhythms, practices and sites of everyday life, invites the viewer to realize their aesthetic garden dreams via retail consumption. It does so using strategies of 'ordinari-ization': experts have been levelled down, lifestyle programmes include a diverse range of ordinary people and lifestyle projects are presented in accessible and achievable ways.[1] Such strategies must be set within the more popular tone of public service broadcasting.[2] Yet the question of how lifestyle is consumed by viewers has barely been addressed. How do ordinary viewers interact with and consume lifestyle programmes such as *Ground Force*[3] or *Homefront: Inside Out?*[4] Drawing on an ethnographic study conducted in a small semi-industrial town in the North of England,[5] this chapter explores the relationship between lifestyle television, garden retailing and gardeners.

---

1 Lisa Taylor, 'From Ways of Life to Lifestyle: The "Ordinari-ization" of British Gardening Lifestyle Television', *European Journal of Communication*, 17/4 (2002): 479–93.

2 Ib Bondebjerg, 'Public Discourse/Private Fascination: Hybridisation in the "True-Life-Story" Genres', *Media, Culture and Society*, 18 (1996): 2–45; John Ellis, 'Scheduling: The Last Creative Act in Television?', *Media, Culture and Society*, 22/1 (2000): 25–38.

3 Bazal for the BBC, 1997 to the present.

4 BBC2, 1997 to the present.

5 A note on method. I couch my work within the tradition of ethnography in cultural studies. The aim of such work is to uncover local and subjugated knowledges generated 'from below'. In this way, my work draws on the work of early culturalist writers, for example, Richard Hoggart, *Uses of Literacy* (London: Chatto and Windus, 1957) and Raymond Williams, *Resources of Hope* (London: Verso, 1989) who theorized ordinary people as active agents, responsible for generating their own sense of world-being. Here culture is conceived

The continued popularity and growth of lifestyle television is the result of a wider cultural shift: the rise of lifestyle must be understood as part of the transition from civic to consumer culture.[6] At the local level, this shift is experienced through the fall of traditional, communal 'ways of life' to the rise in the construction of consumer lifestyles.[7] This chapter examines the lived consequences for ordinary subjects of these recent shifts in promotional lifestyle culture and the ethos of public service broadcasting. It investigates how these changes concretely interact with the sites that gardening viewers both experience and imbue with meaning. In these ways, it aims to contribute to an understanding of how such macro changes are experienced at the micro level by people at the point of media and retail consumption. How viewers interact with and consume lifestyle programming and how they subsequently consume their own domestic garden is a key focus. It asks: how do viewers respond to the garden make-over and to 'personality-interpreters'? What do people think of the aesthetics promulgated by lifestyle programmes? How do people conceive of the notion of garden media 'lifestyle' as both citizens and consumers? And do viewers draw on the resources offered by lifestyle or do they garden in ways which draw on more traditional, local garden competencies?

Reading Garden Lifestyle Texts

According to recent social theory, contemporary culture is still in the process of social and cultural transition: mass societies are moving from 'ways of life' to 'lifestyle'.

---

as a lived, historically and locally generated entity, which must be explored according to its own terms of expression.

In order to garner the data in this chapter I drew on a family of ethnographic research methods. I lived, for an eight-month period, in the same small town community as the gardeners on which this study is based. I engaged in participant observation: that is I conducted semi-structured and informal conversational interviews in the living rooms and gardens of the people of the study. I became familiar with their gardens and helped them garden. On an invitation from my chief informant Maud, I joined the Spen Valley Flower Club, which arranged lunches, garden visits and flower arranging events at the local church and secondary school. In these ways, I used ethnographic techniques as a means of gathering data, which would build a 'picture' of gardening as an ordinary aspect of everyday familial life, as an activity that generated interaction between the participants and as a cultural entity in a typical small town community.

The ethnographic data for this chapter was gathered between 1998 and 1999 in a semi-industrial town in West Yorkshire. I interviewed, observed and gardened with twenty-one gardeners: twelve were women and nine were men. All the respondents were white and heterosexual and their ages ranged from 27 to 96. I locate my respondents between two class groups: working class and middle class. I use pseudonyms to protect the identity of my subjects.

6 Zygmunt Bauman, *Legislators and Interpreters: On Modernity, Postmodernity and Intellectuals* (Cambridge: Polity Press, 1987).

7 David Chaney, *Lifestyles* (London: Routledge, 1996); David Chaney, 'From Ways of Life to Lifestyle: Rethinking Culture as Ideology and Sensibility', in James Lull (ed.), *Culture in the Communication Age* (London: Routledge, 2001), pp. 75–88.

The idea of culture as a whole way of life, based on shared traditions and communal identity has lost its capacity to define social existence as a totality. Chaney argues that traditional conceptions of culture have virtually given way to new social forms. One of the most significant examples of a new social form that typifies social change is the growth of lifestyles. Lifestyles draw on the symbolic repertoires on offer in contemporary culture. Indeed, the lifestyle, in contrast to the traditional conception of the 'way of life', is utterly dependent on the leisure and culture industries and consumer patterns. Playfully and reflexively constructed by those who invest in them, lifestyles are performed improvisations in which authenticity is conceived as an entity that one can manufacture.

The cultural and social shift from ways of life to lifestyle has important consequences for subjectivity. Traditional cultural forms offer a high degree of social stability to their subjects; whereas those in the process of building lifestyles out of the free play of cultural symbolism lack firm social grounding and are relatively insecure. In this way, the lifestyle project as a new social form becomes a primary identity marker. People, according to critics like Chaney, make serious investments in using cultural forms as a means to actively express their identity and differentiate themselves from others.

More importantly, for individuals and groups who are relatively destabilized by the lack of permanence offered by more traditional ways of life, the practice of lifestyle construction can serve an important function as a means of coping with social change. For David Chaney, lifestyles are reactive modes of behaviour or, 'functional responses to modernity'.[8] Changes in employment; conceptions of the family and gender relations; the development of mass society; increased secularization; and new urban landscapes in the form of suburbia, have meant that lifestyles, 'offer a set of expectations which act as a form of ordered control' in the face of changes wrought by modernity.[9] Seen in this way, lifestyles can serve an invaluable role for people in post-industrial societies: they act as resources of stability or coping mechanisms, which help people to manage their own relationship to social change.

Chaney is careful to point out, however, that the move from 'ways of life' to 'lifestyle' is *currently in transition*; in this way his work offers an interpretation of 'social change as it is happening – a form of contemporary history'.[10] It is not simply the case that ways of life have been wholly replaced by lifestyles, as he argues: 'Ways of life and lifestyles are not mutually exclusive, as they clearly to some extent co-exist in contemporary experience.'[11] In what follows, I ask whether ways of life are currently in the process of being replaced by lifestyle in the small semi-industrial town of this study, in the manner Chaney describes. As a means to do this I ask: what do ordinary people think about the make-over, the personality-interpreter and the social uses of garden lifestyle practices?

8 Chaney, *Lifestyles*, p. 11.

9 Chaney, *Lifestyles*, p. 11.

10 Chaney, 'From Ways of Life to Lifestyle', p. 86.

11 Chaney, 'From Ways of Life to Lifestyle', p. 83.

Approaches to the Make-Over

As Chaney argues, a central feature of the changes wrought by modernity is the breakdown of old established communities.[12] Lifestyle media programmes recognize the inherent instability of contemporary social life – indeed lifestyle producers recognize that the wane of civil society has produced stand-alone subjects capable of producing their own present and future identities. Yet my empirical data revealed that there are enclaves in British culture, beyond the urban anonymity of the city or the suburb, where subjects still retain strong community ties and roots. All my respondents had been born, brought up, and had lived to middle- or old-age in the small town where they were interviewed. Even in cases where respondents had studied for qualifications at universities located outside the region, they had returned 'home'. Consequently, the majority of my interviewees lacked the need to utilize lifestyle as a coping mechanism and tended to reject the idea of gardening as a consumer activity. Indeed, several of them interpreted lifestyle garden ideas as undesirable and symbolic of a wider, lamentable decline in traditional, authentic garden practices.

Some respondents reacted quite violently to the mention of the garden make-over genre. As David remarked:

> **David**: It's since this blooming *Force* came on.
> **Lisa T**: *Ground Force*?
> **David**: I think it's blooming awful.

Moreover, John told me, 'I've seen two or three programmes and I think "garbage".' However, beyond simply excoriating the make-over, respondents had a critical approach to the garden media. There is by now a long-standing tradition in media and cultural studies, which credits the powers of the discriminating, critical and 'active' media audience.[13] In line with this work, the people of this study had a thought-out rationale on which to base their criticisms of garden lifestyle. For many of them 'real' gardening was a pursuit that required the investment of time. The make-over was therefore seen as 'instant' and had very little to do with gardening in the true sense. Authentic gardening was a pursuit that took many years of perseverance and those who gardened 'instantly' simply had not earned the right to be called 'gardeners'. As David told me:

> **David**: I don't like instant gardening. It's taken sixty years to do that and for these people to say they're gardeners and then you can get a lorry to take all the muck away and get

---

12 Chaney, 'From Ways of Life to Lifestyle'.

13 David Gauntlett and Annette Hill, *TV Living: Television, Culture and Everyday Life* (London: Routledge, 1999); Marie Gillespie, *Television, Ethnicity and Cultural Change* (London: Routledge, 1995); Henry Jenkins, *Textual Poachers* (London: Routledge, 1992); Mica Nava and Orson Nava, 'Discriminating or Duped? Young People as Consumers of Advertising /Art', in Mica Nava, *Changing Cultures* (London: Sage, 1992); Paul Willis, *Common Culture* (Milton Keynes: Open University Press), 1990).

another lorry with £100.00's worth of plants all at one go. So you've got so much new stuff to look at in one go …
Lisa T: It goes against …
David: Anybody who's done that can't call themselves gardeners really.
Lisa T: No.
David: It shows that they want a nice garden and they want to spend a week at the seaside don't it?

Similarly, Rosemary told me that make-over programmes were a 'good idea for people who are not gardeners,' adding, 'a garden grows over years'. For others, 'real' gardening was about executing garden labour properly and methodically. For John and Stephanie, instant gardening was the antithesis of authentic garden construction; it meant superficial, slip-shod work that simply did not warrant the title 'gardening':

Stephanie: Cuttings and things like that, that's how gardens are built up I think over't years. Cuttings from each other's things.
John: All these programmes seem to do is change stuff that look different. They don't actually do any gardening. They just dig an 'ole, put a water feature in, stick some trellis in.
Stephanie: Yeah, but they've only two days 'aven't they? Takes time.
John: They just throw a bit o' bark over rough ground instead o' diggin' it out or riddling it and putting plants in how yer should. It's just quickness, it's just hype.

While Chaney argues that those who embrace lifestyles accept the production of authenticity using resources from the consumer and leisure industries, the gardeners I spoke to decried manufactured gardening consumption and bemoaned the fall of authentic methods of garden-making.[14] Take for example, the following points made by David about his soil and compost making:

David: I have a feeling that a lot of these blokes on gardening programmes have some lovely soil there. They've made it look so easy for people to garden. But you see I don't go off into a – say garden centre – and see all these lovely green and yellow coloured bags. I never buy any. I have things out there that have been there years and years. The soil's improved. Dug over and composted, year after year.

For these gardeners, manufactured, media make-over gardening was linked to what they saw as the unnecessary expense of the garden centre. Rosemary described make-over programmes as quite simply, 'expensive', remarking that some of her garden features, for example her retaining wall, would be far too expensive for such programmes to create using 'original' materials. Others noted that the problems with make-over recommendations were that they were based, as Keith remarked, on 'spending all that money in one go'. Going to the garden centre, for John, quite simply 'wastes brass'. These gardeners were not interested in improvising new lifestyle ideas from the symbolic repertoires on offer in consumer culture. Gardening for them was about working with the authentic, and sometimes challenging, natural

14 Chaney, 'From Ways of Life to Lifestyle'.

materials offered by the garden itself – and if that required time, respect for the seasons, authentic garden knowledge and methodical labour – then so be it.

For Chaney, the lifestyle is a new social form, redolent of the wider social shift away from traditional, civic ways of life.[15] I would argue that the gardeners I interviewed were at least partially sentient of that shift. Experientially, they regarded the move to lifestyle as a decline in traditional local methods and aesthetics. David, for example, suggested that lifestyle media ideas, with their preference for convenience gardening, were serving to render traditional garden features obsolete: 'they're doing away with lawns 'cos they're too difficult'. For him this has had an impact on the aesthetic look of gardens – he added, 'but you're loosing the green, aren't you?' Similarly, for Rosemary the outdoor spaces subject to make-over on programmes such as *Ground Force* were 'shapes' which even when finished lacked any sense of three-dimensional garden space. 'Well,' she told me, 'they're usually very flat aren't they, an absolute flat square. There's plenty of spare earth, but no garden.'

Approaches to Personality-Interpreters

Media garden legislators,[16] who addressed audiences up until the late 1960s using an instructional mode of address, have largely been replaced by what I have termed 'personality-interpreters'.[17] As part of the discourse of achievability which pervades the lifestyle media, presenters such as Anne McKevitt and Diarmund Gavin carry only scant measures of gardening expertise. In line with the argument that society is undergoing a transitional shift from civic to consumer culture, personality-interpreters have become friendly well-researched consumers, interpreting the latest shopping ideas for the would-be lifestyle gardener. Personality-interpreters might well prove popular amongst those who seek to manufacture lifestyle ideas out of the symbolic repertoires available in garden consumer culture. But those who interpret lifestyle as an erosion of traditional garden aesthetics and knowledges, tended to be unreceptive to the friendly advice of media garden presenters. My group of gardeners, with their roots in a relatively stable semi-industrial community had investments in the continuation of traditional gardening as a way of life. As a result, most of them tended to bemoan the demise of the instructional, public service gardener.

Several of the gardeners I spoke to had a wistful nostalgia for late 1960s gardeners such as Percy Thrower and Peter Smith. When I asked Geoff, for example, if he had ever been influenced by the contemporary gardening media, he told me that he still refers back to his 'Percy Thrower books upstairs' for help with how to

---

15 Chaney, *Lifestyles*; Chaney, 'From Ways of Life to Lifestyle'.

16 In *Legislators and Interpreters* Bauman argues that authority figures or 'legislators' have fallen in the shift from civic to consumer culture. In the post-modern period, legislators are no longer consulted for their opinions; rather (p. 124), 'it is the market which now takes it upon itself the role of judge, the opinion maker, the verifier of values'. Here I coin Bauman's term 'legislator' to refer to garden 'experts' in the late 1960s, such as Percy Thrower, whose address to television viewers was more instructional than the contemporary lifestyle interpreter.

17 Taylor, 'From Ways of Life to Lifestyle'.

garden. As Keith told me, 'Percy Thrower and Peter Smith … they showed actual gardening techniques and they were showing people as we were taught when we were kids'. And many of my respondents were deeply sentimental about the late Geoff Hamilton. Many of them spoke of their 'admiration' for what Millie called, 'a marvellous man'. Interestingly, as Geoff reveals below, Geoff Hamilton straddled instructional gardening advice and lifestyle ideas:

> **Geoff**: I tell you who we used to like, we used to watch that one, that Geoff Hamilton, that died. He was sort of in-between, sort of serious and games really.

However, perhaps the most vociferous critic of the gardening personality-interpreter was James, who, at the end of his lifelong career as a professional gardener and florist, had a great personal investment in arguing for the preservation of traditional methods of gardening that had been his stock-in-trade. For James, contemporary television programmes such as *Gardeners' World* [18] and *Ground Force* only serve to remind him of the severed link between the gardener and traditional gardening tools. Neglect for how garden tools work with the soil has led to a decline in techniques for the care and preservation of tools:

> **James**: Today, I mean these people paddle about, you never see them come out with a clean spade. It's always a dirty, grubby spade and it's ten times harder to use. Titchmarsh is as bad as them all. It's ten times harder because it doesn't slide in the soil and it's like a drag, it's like a parachute, it's simply slowing you up as you're going in.

The problem with these kinds of programmes for James is that they simply lack instruction. From his point of view, audiences need to be shown what he termed 'the basics':

> **James**: They don't teach it now and they're going more gimmicky than they were. I say they're not showing enough of the basic potting and growing. And it's time they taught people how to garden and how to use the tools. I mean for newcomers and people new to it, it's what they want to see.

Lifestyle Gardening for the Social Good

The 'ordinari-ization' of lifestyle television must be read as part of the wider cultural move to help people to make the social and cultural transition from ways of life to consumer lifestyles.[19] Yet to malign lifestyle as a signifier of consumer culture alone is to choose to ignore the attributes in factual entertainment that might promote citizenship. Rachel Moseley[20] for example, argues that to read the primetime shift as, 'a move from hard to soft, from documentary to make-over, from address to citizen to consumer, from public to private and from "quality" to "dumbed-down"

18 BBC, 1956 to the present.

19 Chaney, 'From Ways of Life to Lifestyle'.

20 Rachel Moseley, 'Makeover Takeover on British Television', *Screen*, 41/3 (2000): 299–314.

television is to ignore the complex issues made by that shift'.[21] For her, lifestyle address straddles these dualisms: viewers are 'citizen-consumers' who can, 'on a small scale, learn to make changes, make a difference, improve the personal for the national good'.[22] Analysis of lifestyle programming undoubtedly reveals that lifestyle ideas hold a measure of educational value for citizens, and while most of my respondents were too firmly bound to their stable communities to be motivated to activate the possibilities of consumer gardening lifestyle, many of them recognised the benevolent role of lifestyle gardening in promoting the social good.

Of all my respondents, university-educated mother and daughter Anne and Phoebe had the most positive response to the make-over genre, personality-interpreters and the idea of lifestyle garden transformation. Marked out as the only respondents to have studied higher qualifications outside of their hometown, they were people who had experienced a sense of temporary uprootedness. In this way, they serve to support the efficacy of Chaney's argument, that subjects open to lifestyle improvisation are relatively destabilized. Garden lifestyle programming was positive for these women because they could act as catalysts of creativity:

> **Lisa T**: And what do you think of them when they're finished after a couple of days? They've used things like stapling and decking?
> **Anne**: I'm all for it. I think a garden helps people. I know I used to go out if I'd had a row with Richard. I'd go outside and I'd dig. That's creating something and a lot of people have difficulty being creative, whereas if you stick a plant in and it goes there's a great deal of satisfaction in it.

Anne and Phoebe recognize that while creativity holds therapeutic value and can be used as a coping mechanism for the travails of everyday life, ordinary people need some kind of reassurance for its release. Lifestyle programming can help to get people started:

> **Anne**: Most people, if they had a completely blank canvas it would be like a clean sheet of paper, they wouldn't know where to start, they'd be frightened. So in a way them talking about, you know, just draw your garden and measure around it, just outlining ways of doing, it is sort of increasing their confidence.
> **Phoebe**: I think that they help people to see what's possible as far as their gardens go.

And even those who bemoan the 'gimmicky' feel of the lifestyle make-over programme tended to concede that the aims of the lifestyle garden media were positively laudable. Despite James' reservations, for example, he told me that garden lifestyle programmes were serving to democratize gardening as an activity: 'I like some of the developments they're making', he said, 'They're opening up avenues for anybody.'

Moreover, the wider 'social good' of garden lifestyle was linked, for some of my respondents, to the idea of urging people to keep their gardens from falling into

---

21 Charlotte Brunsdon, Catherine Johnson, Rachel Moseley and Helen Wheatley, 'Factual Entertainment on British Television: The Midlands TV research Group's "8–9 project"', *European Journal of Cultural Studies*, 4/1 (2001): 29–62, p. 33.

22 Brunsdon *et al.*, 'Factual Entertainment', p. 34.

dilapidation. Working-class gardeners have historically been urged, either by the council estate regulatory handbook, council competitions or through an invidious self-regulation, to monitor their gardens in a bid to maintain respectability.[23] For some of the working-class gardeners I spoke to, the garden lifestyle media served a function in continuing the project of local councils by urging other working-class people to take 'responsibility' for the space outside their homes:

> **Keith**: These programmes help get people interested in gardening again basically. Because I think people will ignore gardening for as long as they can, but if they have a responsibility to look after something, then they tend to go and look after it ... and then they start looking at garden centres. I suppose at end at t'day, I just want 'em to realise what they've got.

For others, the media is already playing a central role in promoting gardening as citizenship into the working-class societal enclaves that need it most. Stephanie and John believe that garden lifestyle television already makes some gardeners sufficiently self-conscious to keep their gardens tidy. 'If it wasn't for telly,' Stephanie told me, 'people wouldn't do owt with their gardens.' Her husband John backed her up – demonstrating even less trust in his working-class counterparts:

> **John**: Yeah telly's doing some folk good 'cos whereas some might 'ave a shit 'ole for a garden, they've actually got some flowers and they're taking a bit more pride in it.

In these ways, my data demonstrate that some of my respondents do recognize that lifestyle programming is socially beneficial for the nation, for generating creativity amongst ordinary people and for democratizing gardening knowledge. However, for some of those located as working-class, the importance of lifestyle programming lies in its efficacy to address *others* as 'citizen-consumers' in a bid to help the working-class to 'improve'.[24] In this way, the 'national good' is effected by communicating values of respectability to those likely to neglect their untidy (front) gardens in ways that 'let the side down' in areas where working-class people live.

The experience of my respondents testified to the continued existence of 'ways of life' in relation to gardening as opposed to the import of garden lifestyle practices. No doubt in other sections of contemporary British social life, garden lifestyling is replacing traditional ways of life in relation to gardening in the ways Chaney describes. However, in the small semi-industrial town where my data was gathered, my respondents enjoy the security offered by shared communal garden practices where authentic, local gardening traditions are still valued. Indeed, it was through

23 For a historical account of the ways in which gardening has been used as a civilizing agent for the working class since the late nineteenth century, see S. Constantine, ' Amateur Gardening and Popular Recreation in the 19th and 20th Centuries', *Journal of Social History*, 4/1 (1981): 151–74. See also Joanna Bourke's exploration of working-class autobiography. She documents the pride working-class men took in gardening and DIY during the interwar years in Britain. Joanna Bourke, *Working-Class Culture in Britain 1890–1960: Gender, Class and Ethnicity* (London: Routledge, 1994).

24 Beverley Skeggs, *Formations of Class and Gender: Becoming Respectable* (London: Sage, 1997).

my respondents' approach to garden lifestyle media consumption that I discovered gardening is still regarded as a traditional 'way of life'.

From Lifestyle Ideas to Garden Practice

The Uses of Media Lifestyle Ideas

Thus far, this chapter argues that my group of ordinary gardeners were too firmly rooted to their traditional 'way of life' to be interested in the pursuit of new, consumer-driven lifestyle garden projects. However, the garden lifestyle media were by no means superfluous for these gardeners; indeed, while they were more traditional in their approach to the garden, they still used garden media products in specific ways.

For several respondents, television lifestyle gardening, in particular the make-over, offered an important source of 'entertainment'. As Philip told me, 'they're for entertainment now as much as teaching'. Similarly, Kate told me that it is, 'the entertainment rather than anything' that motivates her to watch *Ground Force*. Another use for the garden make-over, and this was especially the case among female respondents, was that it allowed one to be a voyeur of other peoples' gardens. 'I think I'm quite nosey about other peoples' gardens', Phoebe told me. And Catherine said, 'it's entertainment, it's peeking into somebody's private life'.

Others approached the garden media as 'consumer-citizens'; for them it served an educational role by providing information, tips and advice. As Millie told me, 'You get ideas, but you also get good advice. I mean I've learnt quite a lot from them. How to take cuttings, what to do and what not to do and what to put them in.' One of the most popular educational television features amongst my sample of gardeners, however, is the *Gardeners' World* slot where, as Thomas describes, 'they take you to an established garden and show you around it'. What was of primary interest to several of my gardeners was the fact that these features provided valuable information, as Alan continued, about, 'what grows in those conditions, the colour combinations, the height'. Millie and Jack also use these features for their information about plants:

> **Lisa T**: What features interest you most?
> **Millie**: I like to see the country ones, the bigger ones, where they go 'round and they're all … and they're saying well you could grow this, but we've tried now and you know.
> **Jack**: And they give you various plants that you grow in a certain situation, you know, like shade, or they like dry … this will grow in acid soil and this will grow in a clay soil …

These responses give weight to Moseley's[25] argument: that the 'citizen-consumer' address of lifestyle can, at the micro level, help people make a small personal difference and thereby contribute to the national good.

Others recognized that the role of these programmes is to address audiences as consumers and some respondents were grateful to the media for showcasing new

25 Moseley, 'Makeover Takeover'.

products and for proffering product advice. Anne and Phoebe, for example, used the media to find out about products for pest control and mulching. But perhaps even more significantly, some of my respondents did recognize the part presenters play as adjudicators whose role is to *interpret* new ideas for the would-be gardener. As Kate describes:

> **Kate**: They show you what you can do. They show you what is available and, you know, whereas you just have these set ideas and they come up with different variations of it. Like flagging, you know, we don't just want square flags everywhere, we want it nice.

Preparation, plans and ideas: gardening and modern imaginative hedonism

What is perhaps most interesting about Kate's response above, is that her remarks testify to a willingness to *apply* media interpreters' ideas to her own garden. While most of my respondents were too 'rooted' to traditional garden ideas as a way of life to be hooked in to what the lifestyle media had to offer, I found that not all of them were immune to lifestyle ideas. For some, lifestyle captured the gardening imagination; the new ideas of lifestyle tapped into their dreams and aspirations. For Kate and Geoff, for example, the lifestyle media had captured their fantasies of making a Mediterranean garden. Notice the imaginative possibilities sparked by the lifestyle media in the following exchange:

> **Geoff**: I was going to create our own bit of the Mediterranean, aren't we?
> **Kate**: Yeah. Terracotta, definitely, I love the terracotta. We love Greece. You see things out there and these television things show you … blue … to tell the truth and the brilliant colours. It's just lovely.

In addition, Anne and Phoebe showed enthused engagement with lifestyle images, particularly in relation to the ways in which personality-interpreters used design in the garden. As fine art and textile graduates, they were able to use their cultural capital[26] as a means to both understand and imaginatively appropriate the post-modern eclecticism of how design is used in the make-over genre:

> **Phoebe**: (about Diarmund Gavin) … some of the ideas he's come up with are really nice. I like his way of thinking. To me he's a designer and it wouldn't matter what he was designing … He has a vision of what is good design and he could be designing cars and he'd still be a good designer. And it's that imagination that he's taken into the garden and it's appreciated.
> **Anne**: We appreciate that …
> **Phoebe**: 'Cos he's asking people to make a leap of faith in essence.

What is important about these comments is that Anne and Phoebe are prepared to use 'experts' as interpreters. According to Chaney,[27] lifestyles, as a new social form are fashioned out of two distinctive components: sites and strategies. Sites are the

26 Pierre Bourdieu, *Distinction: A Social Critique of the Judgement of Taste* (London: Routledge, 1986).

27 Chaney, 'From Ways of Life to Lifestyle'.

physical spaces where people can appropriate their own agency; they are places, which become meaningful because they afford people a measure of control. Strategies are the projects in which people invest; they become manifest as implanted metaphors which articulate identity.[28] The 'leap of faith' Anne describes is a recognition that lifestyle interpreters suggest lifestyle strategies for audiences to appropriate and order in the context of their own garden sites. In what follows, Phoebe and Anne discuss how they have selected interpreters' ideas that they plan to go on to translate through their own creativity:

> **Phoebe**: (about Diarmund Gavin) I like his ideas very much. I wouldn't steal them, but some of the … like painting walls that Marrakech colour blue, that was lovely. That was a nice idea but we wouldn't necessarily use it in paint. It might be in plants instead.
> **Lisa T**: So you wouldn't, alright, so you'd actually be quite uncomfortable with just nicking an idea?
> **Anne**: Oh no!
> **Phoebe**: Oh no!
> **Anne**: You'd never … I mean our space is our space and therefore it's quite unique to us. So no matter what idea you've chosen, it wouldn't be exactly the same because it would have to fit.

Making it 'fit', using plants rather than paint shows their own aesthetic use of lifestyle programming in order to adapt their own strategies into the physical environment of the garden site. Yet even though, as these comments show, lifestyle ideas were powerfully attractive to some respondents, I saw no evidence of practised engagement with transformative gardening as action. Rather, I found that lifestyle ideas captured the head rather than the hand or arm; the idea of transformation tended to exist in the imagination and at the level of conversation rather than in practice. Why, I wondered, was it the case that even those imaginatively fired up by the notion of lifestyle gardening showed no evidence of putting those ideas in to action?

In his book *The Romantic Ethic and the Spirit of Modern Consumerism*,[29] Colin Campbell argues that consumption must be understood in relation to the modern self's unique ability to generate pleasurable thoughts through fantasy. Modern consumerism, which Campbell dates from the eighteenth-century English consumer revolution, is characterized by 'an outgrowth of modern, autonomous, imaginative hedonism … the widespread adoption of the covert habit of daydreaming'.[30] For Campbell, the distinctive faculty of being able to generate illusions and fantasies that are 'known to be false but felt to be true' distinguishes modern hedonism.[31] In this way, fantasizing and daydreaming become so pleasurable that it is wanting, as opposed to having, which becomes the key element in the pursuit of pleasure. Indeed, consummating the desire to have things by actual acts of consumption can be relatively 'disillusioning' for people. Campbell goes on:

---

28 Chaney, 'From Ways of Life to Lifestyle', p. 86.

29 Colin Campbell, *The Romantic Ethic and the Spirit of Modern Consumerism* (Oxford: Basil Blackwell, 1995).

30 Campbell, *The Romantic Ethic*, pp. 88–9.

31 Campbell, *The Romantic Ethic*, p. 78.

> individuals do not so much seek satisfaction from products, as pleasure from the self-illusory experiences which they construct from their associated meanings. The essential activity of consumption is thus not the actual selection, purchase or use of products, but the imaginative pleasure to which the actual product lends itself, 'real' consumption being largely a resultant of this 'mentalistic hedonism'.[32]

The credence of Campbell's concept of 'modern, autonomous, imaginative hedonism' is directly relevant to the responses some of my ordinary gardeners have to the actual consumption of garden lifestyle ideas. Kate and Geoff testified to their dream of a Mediterranean garden, but I know through my continued contact with this community of gardeners that their plans remain plans. Stimulated by the Mediterranean 'looks' they have gleaned from viewing the garden make-over genre and from their holidays in Greece, they continue to defer the gratification of fantasy rather than to actually execute the work. Similarly, Anne and Phoebe were full of new ideas to transform their back garden using the inspiration of garden designers such as Diarmund Gavin, but they have never moved beyond excited sketches (see Illustration 9.1) and animated talk. Acts of mixing cement or laying bricks are not yet in evidence.

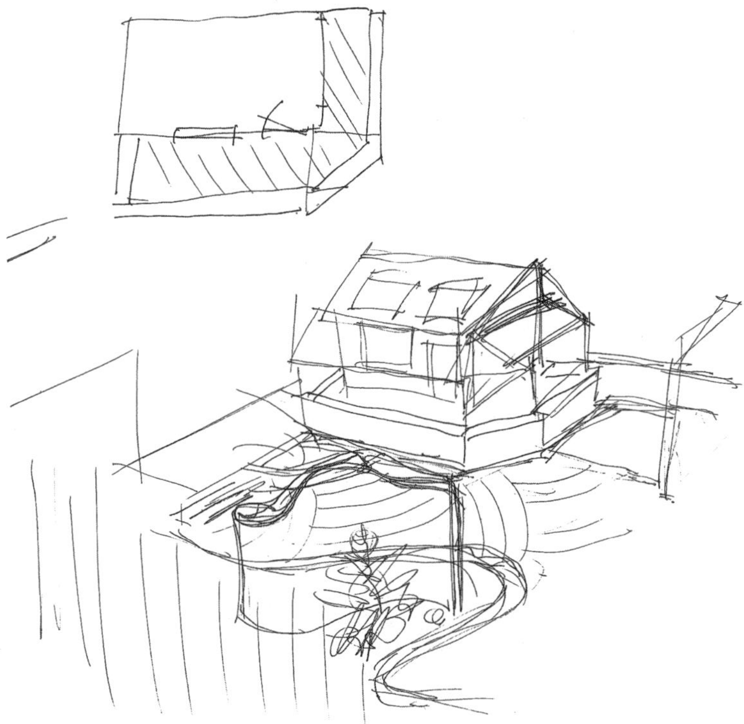

9.1 Anne's sketch of her future plans for the garden 'mezzanine', Spring 1999

32 Campbell, *The Romantic Ethic*, p. 89.

Integral to Campbell's argument about the nature of modern consumption is the idea that a whole swathe of cultural artefacts that represent goods, for example, calendars, posters, works of art – and texts, which advertise goods in the media and communications industries – work to *facilitate* imaginative hedonism. Indeed, 'window-shopping' that is performed without purchasing goods is itself a pleasurable experience. In this way, Campbell provides a useful way of conceptualizing why my respondents use lifestyle ideas to dream and fantasize about how their gardens might be, without ever feeling the need to actually purchase or actively garden. Pleasure, he argues, 'comes from the imaginative use of the objects seen; that is from mentally "trying on" the clothes examined, or "seeing" the furniture arranged within one's room'.[33] Lifestyle interpreters have captured the imagination of some ordinary gardeners, but rather than inciting people to manufacture garden lifestyles, they often provide material for garden day-dreams. Wanting, longing, fantasizing and daydreaming were more desirous activities than the messy, flawed, imperfect realities of actually executing the plans.

Conclusion

The macro changes identified by contemporary social theory – such as the transition from 'ways of life' to lifestyle – are not yet in evidence in the micro context of the small British semi-industrial town. For the bulk of my respondents, gardening remains a traditional enthusiasm, fastened to a relatively stable sense of a 'way of life'.

Significantly, the lifestyle programme was lauded by working-class respondents because of its potential to improve *other* working-class people. Class was significant for how people regarded the social value of the garden lifestyle programme; working-class viewers regarded their uses as both educational and productive. Aware that there were members of their class who refused to 'improve' in ways which fuelled representations of the working-class as lazy and worthless, this chapter shows that these gardeners saw the lifestyle programme as an educational aid which might urge the lazy working-class contingent to get motivated about gardening. In this way, these gardeners recognized and valued the civic aims of lifestyle because of their class location.[34]

However, in terms of how viewers regarded lifestyle in relation to the consumption of their own gardens, their responses were on the whole pejorative. The trappings of lifestyle which find their expression in the garden make-over and the personality-interpreter were largely rejected as superficial and expensive products of popular entertainment. For the people of this study, 'lifestyle' – regardless of their locations

33 Campbell, *The Romantic Ethic*, p. 92.

34 This does not mean, however, that working-class garden aesthetics are necessarily embraced by national lifestyle television. For an analysis of the differences between national and local mediated lifestyle aesthetics see Lisa Taylor, 'It was beautiful before you changed it all: class, taste and the transformative aesthetics of the garden lifestyle media', in David Bell and Joanne Hollows (eds), *Ordinary Lifestyles*: *Popular Media, Consumption and Taste* (Maidenhead: Open University Press), pp. 113–27.

of class and gender – remains a media construction rather than a lived experience. This does not mean that they were entirely untouched by lifestyle ideas, indeed some people made innovative interpretations of the ideas they encountered. However, in these exceptional cases where imaginations were captured by fresh lifestyle ideas, people tended to allow their interpretations to remain at dream or fantasy level.[35] Gratifying their dreams through actual consumption held small priority for these ordinary gardeners.

35 Campbell, *The Romantic Ethic.*

Chapter Ten

Taking a Look at the Wild Side of DIY Home Décor

Judy Attfield

Repositioning DIY

> Exclusion – excluding the nonbeautiful from the realm of objects worth contemplating – is the primary function of aesthetics and the rhetoric of beauty as these have conventionally been wielded.[1]

This essay seeks to position the amateur practice of 'Do-It-Yourself' (DIY), here referring specifically to domestic interior décor and recognized within the field of Design History as a legitimate, though relatively unexplored area of the history of design, within a more secure frame of analysis that does not confine it to a high/low binary opposition.[2] One of the main aims of such a study is the pursuance of an understanding beyond the somewhat contradictory concept of the aesthetics of popular taste. Contradictory because, strictly speaking, aesthetics by its discriminatory nature does not readily embrace middle-of the-road or popular taste within its remit.[3]

---

1 A. Jones, '"Every man knows where and how beauty gives him pleasure": Beauty Discourse and the Logic of Aesthetics', in E. Elliot *et al.* (eds), *Aesthetics in a Multicultural Age* (Oxford: Oxford University Press, 2002), p. 218.

2 Hi/Low has a become a shorthand identified in popular culture discourse with debates concerning the value of popular forms relative to high or, the more critical term: elitist, culture. It seems to be a rule that popular forms cannot be accommodated on an equal footing within the conventional frame of reference that assumes fine art to have a more prestigious position within the hierarchy. Even though reams have been written about 'mass art' and schools of critical discourses have debated these issues for years, nevertheless there is still difficulty in accommodating popular taste without setting it up as an easy target for criticism. See, for example, N. Carroll, *A Philosophy of Mass Art* (Oxford: Clarendon Press, 1998); D. Strinati, *An Introduction to Theories of Popular Culture* (London and New York: Routledge, 1995); K. Varnedoe and A. Gopink, *High and Low: Modern Art and Popular Culture* (New York: The Museum of Modern Art, 1991).

3 The definition of the term 'aesthetics' meaning the philosophy of the fine arts, automatically assumes an established standard of higher so-called 'good' taste based on a certain type of contemplation nourished by an educated intellect and a sensibility that can recognize beauty. It implies a critical understanding, or at least an awareness of what is beautiful and therefore good in terms of taste. Whereas 'popular taste' when placed in contradistinction to 'good taste' suggests a dumbing down, a degraded version of beauty that makes it easily assimilable and, by implication, admired by those who know no better – with

Therefore, it is proposed to *reposition* DIY as a material manifestation of an aspect of everyday life and social production by situating this type of non-professional domestic décor and furnishing practice within a critical discourse associated to three recognized fields of study. These comprise the history of domestic interiors, consumption studies and contemporary craft theory – all fields of academic enquiry acknowledged as central in the discipline of Design History. A main objective for the enquiry is to locate the practice of DIY within some kind of aesthetic context in order to develop a space for the discussion of it as a visual manifestation of popular taste that acknowledges the place of DIY as design, and as such, that can contribute to studies on the material culture of the everyday.

One alternative for recontextualising DIY would be to define it as contemporary craft practice; but doing so would strip it of the wild status that links it to that catalogue of made objects and making practices that lie outside the model that predominates in the History of Design. Rooted in Ruskinian principles of the Arts and Crafts movement, the study of craft within the discipline of Design History has by and large insisted that its duty is only to consider so-called *Good* design.[4] In making a case for calling DIY a craft, the purpose would be to contest the parameters of a History of Design that does not include the kind of ordinary aesthetic that arises out of non-professional un-designed domestic decorating and furnishing practices.

Every Man His Own Mechanic

Amateur building and decorating was a necessity ever since the suburban 'poorer middleclass', as represented by Mr. Pooter in *The Diary of a Nobody*,[5] became householders who could not always afford to employ tradesmen and needed to do some of their own repairs and decorating to keep up a respectable standard of home maintenance.[6] As Charles Pooter wrote in his opening entry (c. 1881) shortly after moving in to his London town house, 'The Laurels' in Holloway, 'There is always something to be done: a tin-tack here, a Venetian blind to put straight, a fan to nail up, or part of carpet to nail down.'[7] He identified with 'homely people … superior

no taste in other words. In *Distinction*, Bourdieu demystifies the ineffable characteristic that makes beauty unexplainable by attributing it to education, which thus makes the acquisition of good taste quantifiably contingent upon wealth and power. P. Bourdieu, *Distinction: A Social Critique of the Judgement of Taste* (London: Routledge, 1984). Also see, for example, L. Buck and P. Dodd, *Relative Values or What's Art Worth?* (London: BBC Books, 1991).

4 Apart from the odd exception usually associated with women's, non-professional and third world practice, e.g. P. Kirkham, 'Women and Inter-war Craft Revival', in J. Attfield and P. Kirkham (eds), *A View from the Interior: Women and Design* (London: The Women's Press, 1995), pp. 174–83; P. Dalton, 'Housewives, leisure crafts and ideology' in G. Elinor *et al.*, *Women and Craft* (London: Virago, 1987), pp. 31–6; J. Turney, 'Here's One I Made Earlier: Making and Living with Home Craft in Contemporary Britain', *Journal of Design History*, 17/3 (2004): 267–93.

5 George and Weedon Grossmith, *The Diary of a Nobody* (London: Pan Books, 1946).

6 C. Brooks, 'The Amateur Mechanic', in Design Council, *Leisure and Design in the Twentieth Century* (London: Design Council, 1976), pp. 24–31.

7 Grossmith, *The Diary*, p. 16.

to the follies of fashion' who 'preferred to lead a simple and wholesome life to gadding about to two-penny-halfpenny tea-drinking afternoons, and living above their incomes'.[8] This would explain his keen though inept dabbling with 'the new Pickford's enamel paint', much to the consternation of his wife who accused him of always falling for 'some new fangled-craze', which he had enthusiastically applied to some flower pots, the coal scuttle, the worn-out backs of his Shakespeare bindings, and the washstand, towel rail and chest of drawers in the servant's bedroom as well as the bath. The latter application proved particularly unsuitable. Alarmingly it turned Pooter 'red all over' after having a hot bath that melted the paint, after which he decided to call in Farmeson, the local ironmonger to repaint it white.

Prior to the widespread usage of the term 'do-it-yourself', the consumer attending to his own painting and decorating, characteristically masculine, was referred to as 'the amateur mechanic'. The *Amateur Mechanic, Illustrated* was a magazine launched in 1881 as a supplement to *Every Man His Own Mechanic*, by Ward Lock with the intention to 'fill up the hiatus in the literature of self-help' by providing instructions for 'practical work' and jobs around the house in carpentry, gardening and 'the various constructive and decorative arts'.[9] It must be remembered that boys were taught woodwork and metalwork at school as a matter of course and therefore had some basic training in those crafts. Innumerable manuals and magazines available for the do-it-yourself enthusiast were particularly prolific in the interwar period.

Practical Householder was the name adopted by a magazine launched in 1955 that heralded the post-war II DIY boom, closely followed in 1957 by the launch of the *Do-It-Yourself* magazine.[10] (See Illustration 10.1.) Just one example of the plethora of manuals produced for amateur do-it-yourselfers was The *Ideal Home: Householders Guide*[11] in four volumes first published in 1966 and sponsored by the makers of Fablon, the ultimate DIY product – a self-stick vinyl sheet material that came in a variety of 'contemporary' colours and patterns. It was aimed at the unskilled consumer and advertised for its ability to transform instantly any flat surface with a simple application.

The commoditization of DIY since the post-World War II era has seen the rise of fashionable styling in DIY products for the general public widely disseminated by publications, TV programmes like the Barry Bucknell's[12] 'Do It Yourself' programme and through chain stores like B&Q, whose first store opened in 1969. Before then consumers had to make do with products and tools aimed at skilled tradesmen only obtainable from builders' merchants. By the late 1960s DIY started to be marketed by a new type of retail outlet for which a whole new range of products were created – from magazines, to tools, workbenches and decorating materials, like Formica, specifically dedicated to the amateur decorator. These products, aimed

8 Grossmith, *The Diary*, p. 31.

9 Brooks, 'The Amateur Mechanic', p. 24.

10 D. Johnson, 'The History and Development of Do-It-Yourself', in Design Council, *Leisure and Design in the Twentieth Century* (London: Design Council, 1976), pp. 68–71.

11 *Ideal Home Householders' Guide* [3 volumes] (London: Odhams Books, 1966).

12 D. Barker, 'Barry Bucknell: DIY Hero to Post-War Women', *The Guardian* (27 February 2003).

at an unskilled consumer, enabled the so-called 'practical householder' to repair, refurbish, decorate and refashion their domestic interiors without intervention from the skilled craftsmen.

10.1 Cover of *Practical Householder*, June 1959

DIY still flourishes today, but in much more sophisticated forms – in glossy magazines, radio and TV programmes supported by celebrity experts. The popularity of nostalgic retro styling has even managed to aestheticize what is now ironically looked down upon as cute kitsch mid-twentieth century style. So that we see experts like Laurence Llewelyn-Bowen putting on a radio show based entirely on the *Practical Householder* called 'Dream On' at peak-time mid-morning Saturday on Radio Four described by the *Radio Times* as 'this slightly camp look' at DIY.[13] In this instance, 'camp' would appear to be inter-changeable with kitsch.

13 'Dream On', *Radio Times* (31 January 2004), p. 116.

The One Wild Place

However not only has the romanticization and aestheticization of past styles, however tacky, entered the popular imagination today via the media; it has become more accessible through DIY products and practices. With the increasing awareness that popular taste defies conventional standards of good taste my aim is to offer an interpretation of DIY as 'wild'[14] and representative of the kind of domestic design paraphernalia that clutters the homes of most people and has until now tended to escape academic notice. The underlying objective in putting DIY into the frame of objects and practices that constitute the 'design' of Design History is to expand the limits of functional productionist approaches to Design History and to examine consumption as a creative practice. Taking a look at the wilder side of design practice, exemplified by DIY, spotlights the amateur case where the consumer is also the producer. Two examples of recent studies of this phenomenon are Jo Turney's study of amateur home crafts[15] and Roni Brown's thesis on Self-Build.[16]

The rise of studies in Material Culture and the emergent theory of 'Everyday Life' as specific fields offer a framework for the investigation of the history and theory of craft that refuses to privilege it, as it is customarily classified, as a special type of skill or artefact, but allows the exploration of the wilder side beyond the more respectable margins of Design History. Ben Highmore defines 'everyday life theory' as 'an arena of life that manages for the most part, to avoid scrutiny'.[17] Social anthropologists researching modern material culture have readily adapted to investigations into the personal tastes invested in the private spaces of domestic interiors with increasing enthusiasm, regardless of whether in good taste or otherwise. Daniel Miller, the editor of one of the more recent publications of this type – *Home Possessions* – explains the rise in interest in the home when he writes – 'In industrialized societies, most of what matters to people is happening behind the closed doors of the private sphere … people are paying increased attention to their relationship to their own home, to its structure, its decoration, its furnishing and the array of objects that fill its spaces'.[18]

Except for a paper given at an early Design History Society conference in 1976 by David Johnson, the founder of *Do-It-Yourself* magazine,[19] some of the few references that are made to it are by economic historians and sociologists from a 'critique of consumerism' point of view. Economic history classifies DIY as a leisure activity, a hobby, and at the same time, an aspect of the so-called 'hidden economy' of self-provisioning insisted upon by the conventional refusal to define the home as a place of work. The economic historian R.E. Pahl in *Divisions of Labour* has acknowledged the reality that 'work' did go on in the home long after the industrial

---

14 J. Attfield, *Wild Things: The Material Culture of Everyday Life* (London and New York: Berg, 2000).

15 Turney, 'Here's One I Made Earlier'.

16 R. Brown, 'Making Home: A Study of Recent Self-Build Projects in the UK', unpublished PhD thesis (De Montfort University, 2004).

17 B. Highmore, *Everyday Life and Cultural Theory* (London: Routledge, 2002).

18 D. Miller (ed.), *Home Possessions* (Oxford and New York: Berg, 2001).

19 Johnson, 'The History and Development of Do-It-Yourself'.

revolution, but notes that we 'have little idea of how widespread self-provisioning was',[20] tracking some of it via the growth of the DIY industry.

The commoditization of DIY from the mid twentieth century culminated in the early 1980s with more than half the adult population engaging in some form of it.[21] This flourishing, commonly attributed to the sale of local authority houses and the encouragement of owner-occupation by the Conservative government under Thatcher's regime in particular,[22] is also to do with the reappropriation of a sense of self in the face of mounting alienation induced by mass consumption. One has only to watch any of the many popular TV programmes on interior décor to see how much importance is given to catering for individual taste and individuality – that is, producing a totally unique original result albeit within a recognizable popular lifestyle genre.

The importance of home-centred culture has been characterized negatively by critics of privatization like Alan Tomlinson, as 'the embodiment of the triumph of privatisation with home-based consumption representing the retreat from the public realm'.[23] These social symptoms were seen as analogous to the erosion of old class barriers with everyone becoming more middle class by buying into the 'ideal home' lifestyle, with DIY enabling the transformation of the domestic interior into an expression of individuality and personal taste. Increasingly home-centred so-called leisure activities, seen as a symptom of social alienation, prompted Alan Tomlinson's biting attack – 'Do it yourself, then. Build your own cultural environment. Thematize all your spare time activity. Express your familiarity with ... *consumer culture* by the choices you make in this sphere: and also, with DIY make some canny investment decisions'.[24]

His dismissal is not unlike the crude critical analysis of the production of home by means of 'personal style' mounted by Rosalind Coward who denied the possibility of individual expression, stating simplistically – 'Personal style is, in reality, nothing other than the individual expression of general class taste and the particular ideals promoted by that class.'[25] Without wishing to deny Bourdieu's brilliant class analysis of French taste in *Distinction*,[26] more recent studies of material culture have demonstrated that the exercise of taste in such practices as home improvement is a much more complex dynamic process with the capacity to objectify social relations.[27]

---

20 R.E. Pahl, *Divisions of Labour* (Oxford: Blackwell, 1984), p. 100.

21 Euromonitor Publications published in *Report on DIY/Home Improvement* (London: Earnshaw, Hayes and Sons [privately printed] 1980), p. 6.

22 T. Chapman and J. Hockey, *Ideal Homes? Social Change and Domestic Life* (London and New York: Routledge, 1999).

23 A. Tomlinson (ed.), *Consumption, Identity and Style: Marketing, Meanings and the Packaging Of Pleasure* (London: Routledge, 1990), p. 58.

24 A.J. Clarke, 'The Aesthetics of Social Aspiration,' in Miller, *Home Possessions*, p. 23.

25 R. Coward, *Female Desire* (London: Paladin, 1984), p. 65.

26 Bourdieu, *Distinction*.

27 D. Miller (ed.), *Material Cultures: Why Some Things Matter* (London: UCL Press, 1998).

Furthermore, I would suggest DIY and the popular aesthetic of home décor can be posited as an example of autonomy – of making material the sense of self through home arrangement. G.K. Chesterton's version of the home as 'the one wild place',[28] illustrates the way in which the domestic interior is the space where individuals can be free to express themselves:

> Of all modern notions,
> The *worst* is this: that domesticity is dull.
> Inside the home, they say, is dead decorum and routine;
> Outside is adventure and variety.
> But the truth is the home is the only place of liberty,
> The only spot on earth where a man can alter arrangements suddenly,
> Make an experiment or indulge in a whim.
> The home is not the one tame place in a world of adventure,
> It is the one wild place in a world of rules and set tasks

Curating the Self

DIY can be seen as a form of curating the self, of putting identity on display through the changing disposition of furnishing arrangements. Whether of each individual or the group of occupiers, the domestic interior manages to accommodate a form of material culture of the household, *because* as a space it is particularly adept in embodying extraordinary strategies in redemptive everyday practices that pass as ordinary. The ordinary remains hidden, but once spotted can be seen to represent interpersonal relations materialized within the spatial organization of the home interior through interior décor tastes, furnishing arrangements or disarrangements, as the case may be.

The current increasing interest in clearing clutter is particularly significant in this connection, evidenced by such TV programmes as *The Life Laundry* that case studied disorganized households demonstrating how to put them in order. These programmes always contain a design element. A recent article by Saulo Cwerner and Alan Metcalfe – 'Storage and Clutter: Discourses and Practices of Order in the Domestic World'[29] – suggests that domestic storage needs to be analysed in terms of both space and time 'as objects are subject to various practices of dispersal, divestment and displacement in the gaps between consumption as acquisition, use and their eventual disposal. Therefore, in considering DIY as a practice of home arrangement and consumption it is just as important to take into consideration the processes of divestment as it is the *investment and additions* of new decorations, furnishings and layouts.

---

28 Quoted in P. Garvey, 'Organised Disorder: Moving Furniture in Norwegian Homes', in Miller, *Home Possessions*, pp. 47–68.

29 S.B. Cwerner and A. Metcalfe, 'Storage and Clutter: Discourses and Practices of Order in the Domestic World', *Journal of Design History*, 16/3 (2003): 229–39.

But before presenting a more nuanced framework for the analysis of DIY as an act of agency as in Miller,[30] Clarke[31] and Attfield,[32] rather than an effect of ideology as in Coward,[33] it is helpful to consider the history of the rise and commoditization of DIY since the mid 1950s. Reyner Banham[34] attributed the introduction of the electrically powered pistol drill with all its attachments as one of the innovations that enabled amateurs to tackle basic woodwork and home repairs. Another important DIY product development was water-based paints in ready-mixed colours that could be applied effectively by the non-specialist. The earlier oil-based paint required skill and knowledge both to mix in the pigments and judge the final paint finish effect and to apply it smoothly in several coats without leaving unsightly brush marks.[35] Finally, the introduction of retail outlets for the sale of decorating products to the general public, where previously they could only be obtained from wholesale builders' merchants, made DIY much more accessible to the general public.

Product developments like easy-to-use 'Contact' sticky-backed plastic-coated sheeting, and Polycel for 'making good', that is, smoothing out the holes and blemishes on plaster walls prior to decoration, went hand in hand with publications to instruct the layman. There already existed a range of manuals and journals for the male homemaker but the term 'DIY' first appeared in 1951 as an added section to *Popular Handicrafts*, a craft magazine aimed at women. The supplement called 'Do-It-Yourself' added a section to deal with simple home repairs and home maintenance. This was followed by *Do-It-Yourself* magazine launched in 1957 amalgamating with the already existing monthly – *Handyman.*[36] The thesis that DIY rose to prominence with the privatization of housing during the Thatcher regime can and has been disputed within the field of material culture studies which looked at the interrelation between people and things. My study of Harlow New Town houses[37] – 'Pram town', Daniel Miller's ethnographic study of kitchens in *Household Choices*[38] and Alison Clarke's more recent project on aesthetic practice in the home,[39] have shown that people can and do appropriate their domestic space even when they do not own it.

30 Miller, *Home Possessions*.

31 Clarke, 'The Aesthetics of Social Aspiration'.

32 Judy Attfield, 'Inside Pram Town: A Case Study of Harlow House Interiors, 1951–61', in Attfield and Kirkham, *A View From the Interior*, pp. 215–35.

33 Coward, *Female Desire*.

34 R.Banham, 'Detroit Tin Re-visited', in T. Faulkner (ed.), *Design 1900–1960: Studies in Design and Popular Culture of the 20th Century* (Newcastle upon Tyne: Newcastle Polytechnic, 1975), pp. 120–40.

35 The information on the difficulties of using traditional decorating materials derives from my own experience having undergone training in the City and Guilds decorating course (which I failed) as part of the course in Interior Design at the Northern Polytechnic that I attended between 1955 and 1959, and from using the new amateur-friendly materials decorating my own house in the mid-1960s.

36 Johnson, 'The History and Development of Do-It-Yourself'.

37 Attfield, 'Inside Pram Town'.

38 D. Miller, 'Appropriating the State on the Council Estate', in T. Putnam and C. Newton (eds), *Household Choices* (London: Futures, 1990).

39 Clarke, 'The Aesthetics of Social Aspiration'.

A case can certainly be made for a long-standing practice of DIY in rented housing. The critique of consumerism which runs alongside the notion that DIY only flourished in the privatized arena is quickly dismantled by looking for example at the illegitimate DIY practices of corporation house tenants in the 1950s New Towns. In my study of Harlow,[40] I quoted what one of the architects involved from its inception told me, referring in particular to the tenants' dislike of open plan. He said:

> Every architect thought that after his house had been built … it should be furnished as he thought it should … Of course, that didn't happen. At one time we used to be very conscious of the interior decoration. We'd pick the wall colours, the ceiling colours, the colour of the doors … fairly early on we came to the realisation that we were utterly wasting our time because no matter what we put on the walls … no sooner had people moved in, they couldn't even wait for a year to pass ... they'd paper them direct with some of the most awful wallpapers. And you'd throw your hands up in horror. Then you'd get the house where there was the do-it-yourself handyman who'd put up all these sort of shelves and divisioning walls and change doors … despite the fact that they were renting housing … Right from the beginning people did things themselves … they weren't allowed to change fireplaces and things like that but a lot of them did it surreptitiously … Architects, especially if you're working in mass housing, have got to try and design a basic framework in which people can do their own thing, because they're going to do it anyhow.

Similarly, Miller's study of a London Council[41] estate in the late 1980s, which penetrated the intimate area of the domestic interior behind front doors, found that home ownership had nothing or little to do with the act of appropriation. It showed that it was more a matter of feeling 'at home' that was manifested in how people furnished. And taking that further I would suggest that feeling 'at home' is not just to do with being comfortably ensconced or accommodated within a physical location – that it is just as much, if not more to do with a strong sense of self in relation to others and the world at large.

An Overlooked Craft Activity?

An alternative to the frame of reference that would otherwise relegate DIY and the popular domestic interior to problems of taste, mere subjectivity, kitsch, or dated post-modern sneering, is to discuss it as an overlooked craft activity carried out within the home as a practice of everyday life. Since Bourdieu in *An Outline of a Theory of Practice*, first published in 1972,[42] and later material culture studies have acknowledged: the domestic field presents a microcosm of society. And in recent years the home seems to have become the paradigmatic site for the analysis of material culture, with publications proliferating on the topic of home decoration

40 Attfield, 'Inside Pram Town'.

41 Miller, 'Appropriating the State'.

42 P. Bourdieu, *Outline of a Theory of Practice* (Cambridge: Cambridge University Press, 1982 [1972]).

such as those cited above and Colin Painter's *Contemporary Art in the Home*.[43] There is even a new interdisciplinary journal recently launched under the title of *Home Cultures* recognizing that 'the domestic sphere is a highly fluid and contested site of human existence as well as one of the most primordial aspects of human experience'.

The term 'DIY' is used rather broadly here to include not only the usual home improvement activities promoted by the development of commercial decorating products and tools as sold by stores like Homebase and B&Q, but a more general activity of homemaking which includes the self-conscious act of appropriating the domestic space by arrangement and what Daniel Miller refers to as 'accommodating'. He explains that 'By considering our relationship to the home through the term 'accommodating' we face the home not as a thing but as a process.'[44] What distinguishes DIY is that particular propensity it has for the appropriation of space through individual acts of renewal and transformation, that is to say – the production of the home by its inhabitants themselves.

In his exposition of Agnes Heller's theory of everyday life, Patrick Wright points out that

> the experience of *'home'* plays such a prominent part in everyday life because [it] has a subjective resonance, expressing the coherence of a person's self-understanding and what Heller has called the 'emotional household'. Her point is that the subject of everyday life is constantly re-evaluating and rearranging itself – a process which is centrally concerned with the relationship of inner and outer, with the problem of the unity of the inner life and the feeling of finding a 'home' in the 'world'. 'Home' is therefore not just evocative of the familiar ... disposition of personalities in which so much everyday life is experienced; it is also the interior space in which some recognition can be given to endowments and potentials which have no opportunity for realisation in the world as it is outside.[45]

Thus the act of 'doing it yourself' in the interior space of the home as a personal process of curating or displaying the self, can be investigated as one facet of the material culture of everyday life. The home is one of the most ubiquitous physical manifestations of sociality and one of the few geographical areas over which individuals have some measure of control, however circumscribed. It is also relevant in this context that in psychoanalysis the house represents the self. In containing the self, the domestic interior represents a particular kind of eccentric order or ecology of personal possessions[46] – the objectification of the contradictory nature of modernity, the impulse to reintegrate the increasingly fragmentary tangled texture of contemporary postmodern culture.

There is much to be gained from considering the dwelling as the materialization of space and part of a network of associated practices such as the craft of DIY in terms

---

43 C. Painter (ed.), *Contemporary Art in the Home* (Oxford and New York: Berg, 2002).

44 Miller, *Material Cultures*, p. 10.

45 P. Wright, *On Living in an Old Country* (London: Verso, 1985), pp. 10–11.

46 Attfield, *Wild Things*, pp. 149–72.

of material effects.[47] In locating the private abode as a personal space, it is possible to consider the material contextualization of the individual within the home as the repository or objectification of social relations. What is meant by objectification here, based on Miller's definition,[48] is the material resolution – the making of the idea into a reality, whether of the temporal kind as in ephemeral, the seemingly eternal type as in authentic, or more often than not a combination of both in which some sort of mediation takes place at the point of materialization and forms an internal logic of sorts which can be characterized as an ecology of personal possessions. And where the appropriation has been carried out through the actual physical making process of DIY, the act takes on a particular flavour of original individuality even if the effect is similar in style to another household down the road.

Household arrangements and associated furnishing DIY practices play a dynamic part in the process of self-creation. Although located within the household as furnishing arrangements, effects also take place beyond the physical container that can only be perceived by contextualizing the household on the broader canvass of the cultural field that encompasses public as well as private life. In his study of social production of space, referring to the dwelling, Henri Lefebvre has acknowledged that 'Private space is distinct from, but always connected with, public space. In the best circumstances, the outside space of the community is dominated, while the indoor space of family life is appropriated.'[49] He elaborates this private 'indoor' life as 'a spatial practice which, though still immediate, is close, in concrete terms to the work of art' referring to the creativity of the practice of homemaking and notes that 'appropriation is not effected by an immobile group, be it a family, a village or a town' acknowledging that 'time plays a part in the process, and ... cannot be understood apart from the rhythms of time and life'.[50]

In detailing the materiality of the dwelling as context and process with effects beyond the geographical boundaries, the notion of identity is also conceptualized beyond the sociological groups that tend to stereotype gender, class, age and ethnicity. When the ecology of personal possessions is embodied by the household as both a social unit and a material accumulation of things contained in time and space, a feasible framework is formed to investigate how people form their identities through processes like DIY.

Consumption studies have encouraged the contradictory twin concepts of 'choice' and 'lifestyle', suggesting that either people choose what they buy according to what they consider their own sense of in-built individuality, or that what they buy is dictated by manipulative market forces that target consumer groups and entice them with products that promise entry into particular ready-made lifestyles. This caricatured interpretation of choice as entirely inwardly generated and lifestyle as

47 For example G. Bachelard, *The Poetics of Space* (Boston: Beacon, 1964 [1958]); H. Lefebvre, *The Production of Space*, trans. Donald Nicholson-Smith (Oxford: Blackwell, 1996); A. Rapaport, *House, Form and Culture* (Englewood Cliffs, NJ: Prentice Hall, 1969).

48 Miller, *Material Culture and Mass Consumption.*

49 Lefebvre, *The Production of Space*, p. 166.

50 Lefebvre, *The Production of Space*, p. 166.

totally imposed by external forces is intended to dispel the notion of a unidirectional process.

The concept of choice represents the consumer's point of view as an individual with the right and freedom to buy into a fashion or choose to desist and thus make a statement, in contradiction to the critique of consumerism along the lines of Veblen's 'conspicuous consumption'[51] which implied a much more manipulated consumer. But rather than exhibiting extravagant profligacy most everyday consumption practice represents a degree of control and self-conscious decision-making which has been amply justified in research on consumption. Susan Benson-Porter provides a good example of choices made in spite of budget control by thrifty housewives in the United States between 1919 and 1941 as a form of strategic survival[52] and is reiterated in Daniel Miller's account of shopping in *A Theory of Shopping*.[53] Although represented by some critics as a false way of life imposed upon duped consumers by greedy commercialism, 'lifestyle' does nevertheless refer to a possible, even if unattainable, real way of life in the first place. Pierre Bourdieu's theory of 'habitus' that explains the way individuals form their identity through their relationship to a group or class by means of sets of shared attitudes and tastes, and the French sociologist Maurice Halbwach who devised the theory of 'genre de vie' based on an earlier study of the working-class, are just two examples of the way in which 'lifestyle' has been used to study a way of relating individual identity to the world through consumption practices. However, as a number of critics have observed, they do not account for social mobility nor for any kind of social difference other than class.[54]

Another way of casting the DIY phenomenon is to see it as an aspect of the aesthetics of popular taste. Clarke's analysis of low income households in terms of an aesthetics of social aspiration concludes, 'the proliferation of home decoration and the popularization of design has become a key, contemporary component of a relationship that was never simply between an internal private sphere and an external public sphere, but a more complex process of projection and interiorization that continues to evolve'.[55]

In order to recontextualize the practice of DIY home improvements beyond the consumption phase as part of the 'ecology of personal possessions' I propose appropriating two terms used in cultural analysis – 'Bricolage' and 'Culture Club'.[56] I see this as an appropriate use of terms originally adopted to describe urban youth subcultures that had not previously been subjected to academic analysis because they

51 T. Veblen, *The Theory of the Leisure Class* (New York: The Modern Library, 1934 [1899]), ch. IV.

52 S. Benson-Porter, 'Living on the Margin: Working-Class Marriages and Family Survival Strategies in the United States, 1919–1941', in V. de Grazia (ed.), *The Sex of Things: Gender and Consumption in Historical Perspective* (Berkeley and Los Angeles: University of California Press, 1996), pp. 212–43,

53 For example see D. Miller, *A Theory of Shopping* (Cambridge: Polity, 1998).

54 For example de Grazia, *The Sex of Things*, p. 153.

55 Clarke, 'The Aesthetics of Social Aspiration', p. 25.

56 P. York, *Modern Time* (London: Futura, 1984).

were not seen as worthy of serious scrutiny except as the butt of elitist criticism.[57] 'Bricolage' is culled from Dick Hebdige's adaptation of it from anthropology to describe 'how subcultural styles are constructed'.[58] 'Culture Club' is loosely lifted from Peter York's reportage on London youth styles. It is not just that *bricolage* is the term used in French for DIY, that makes it so apt, but because Hebdige's interpretation of it describes the genre as a category of subculture where it can exist in its own right rather than as a poor copy or 'reproduction' of the real thing. The aesthetics of popular taste as characterized by DIY once personalized, can become highly stylish and 'wild' in a similar way to that which Hebdige applies bricolage to punk and other spectacular youth sub-cultures. *Bricolage* is used by anthropologists to describe the process used by particular groups to 'think' their world in a material logic of their own by means of improvisation and appropriating commodities inappropriately. Hebdige gives the example of the 'teddy boy' stealing the Savile Row suit. An example of incorrect appropriation in DIY would be the 'Georgian' door with integral fanlight, incorporating the curved top glass panel that customarily would have been situated over the doorway into the top panel of the door itself.

Peter York's use of 'the Culture Club' serves to describe a *de rigeur style* which must be adopted in order to belong to a particular subcultural group but has nothing to do with conforming to a fashion set from above. In the cases of both Bricolage and Culture Club, style depends on the hybridization of 'proper' styles through a process of amateur re- or rather dis-organization, using disparate elements that would not necessarily be considered to 'go together', or adapted to make up a personal style of self-expression which at the same time announces membership of a particular 'Culture Club'. The idea of Peter York's 'Culture Club' adapts very well to the personalization of standard housing like, for example spec builders' vernacular because, like all the various clubs' styles it allows infinite variation while still belonging to a particular over-arching home-centred suburban lifestyle. The possibilities of nuances between up-to-date home improvers and graduates from improvers to owners are endless.

J.M. Richards – an architect, author of *Modern Architecture* (1940)[59] and editor of *Architectural Review* – was the one exception to advocates of modern architecture of the first half of the twentieth century, who invariably condemned suburbia. In 1946, he wrote a sensitive appreciation of suburbia[60] that he described as 'an enchanted jungle' recognizing the wildness of its total disregard of 'good design'. He had been careful to specify that he was not trying to represent or perpetuate suburbia as 'some phoney "Merrie England" that has no part in the mainstream of cultural development' but to rescue the ability of the ordinary individual to use their own creativity, the quality that modernism quashed, insisting that architects know best.

57 Along the lines of the critique of the commodification of culture mounted by adherents to the Frankfurt School, see, for example, J. Storey, *An Introduction to Cultural Theory and Popular Culture* (London and New York: Prentice Hall / Harvester Wheatsheaf, 1997, 2nd edn [1993]), pp. 104–14.

58 D. Hebdige, *Subculture: The Meaning of Style* (London and New York: Methuen, 1979), pp. 102–6.

59 J.M. Richards, *Modern Architecture* (Harmondsworth, Middlesex: Penguin, 1940).

60 J.M. Richards, *The Castles On the Ground: The Anatomy of Suburbia* (London: Architectural Press, 1973 [1946]).

In the introduction of the 1973 edition, Richards' intention was to take the lessons of suburbia to create the space to allow individuality to flourish incorporating the new idea of encouraging 'user-participation', unlike the project of Scott-Brown and Venturi or even Oliver *et al.* for architects to learn from suburbia. In spite of Richards' slightly condescending tone in referring to the 'amateur', taking the period in which he was writing into consideration he displayed an unusual respect for the creative home improver, of whom he wrote

> the picturesque tradition represented by the English suburban scene is preserved by the enthusiastic if somewhat inexpert efforts of the amateur. Owing to the expense of building as a hobby, the amateur architect is rare, although at one time he had a good deal to do with the founding of the villa tradition which the suburban style has adopted as its own ... But if not with amateur architects, the present day suburb is peopled with amateur gardeners, amateur landscapists, amateur decorators, with contrivers of all sorts of effects, with handymen and with the individualists from whom the suburban jungle draws much of its vitality and for whose creative instincts it dates in a way that nothing else can ...[61]

There are several degrees of separation between the house and the home; between the acquisition, whether by purchase or tenancy, of a piece of space for dwelling when it is still a raw commodity, and the process of transformation it undergoes in becoming a home. And within the home itself, the space is also divided up into personal and communal shared spaces and assimilated into everyday life. The acquisition and installation processes which territorialize and transform the commodity into an individualized domestic space requires a pliable neutral background space as that Harlow architect so insightfully concluded. It also requires an engaged producing-consumer rather than a highly designed finished product with a ready-made consumer in mind. Therefore to return to the question of why such standard forms as the suburban semi have managed to retain their popularity – perhaps one of the reasons that it has remained such a desirable place is that it caters for the individual even though it was a form of mass product designed for an unidentified 'average family'. The secret of its success undoubtedly lies in its ambiguity – neither ancient nor modern, urban nor rural – a quality that has made it adaptable to a limitless range of tastes that offered its occupants infinite possibilities for self-individuation through such processes of production as creative DIY.

61 Richards, *The Castles On the Ground*, pp. 66–7.

Index